BEYOND THE
CITY LIMITS

Conflicts in Urban and
Regional Development,
a series edited by
John R. Logan and Todd Swanstrom

Edited by
John R. Logan and
Todd Swanstrom

Urban Policy and

BEYOND THE

Economic Restructuring in

CITY LIMITS

Comparative Perspective

 Temple University Press

PHILADELPHIA

Temple University Press, Philadelphia 19122
Copyright © 1990 by Temple University. All rights reserved
Published 1990
Printed in the United States of America

The paper used in this publication meets the minimum
requirements of American National Standard for Information
Sciences—Permanence of Paper for Printed Library Materials,
ANSI Z39.48-1984

Library of Congress Cataloging-in-Publication Data
Beyond the city limits : urban policy and economic restructuring in
comparative perspective / edited by John R. Logan and Todd
Swanstrom.
    p. cm. — (Conflicts in urban and regional development)
    Includes bibliographical references.
    ISBN 0-87722-733-0 (alk. paper)
    1. Urban economics—Congresses. 2. Urban policy—Congresses.
3. Urban renewal—Congresses. I. Logan, John R., 1946–
II. Swanstrom, Todd. III. Series.
  HT321.B49 1990
  307.76—dc20   90-10862
                                          CIP

Dedicated to the memory of
LEWIS MUMFORD (*1895–1990*)

Think globally, act locally

CONTENTS

PREFACE

This book has a complex history, and that history
clarifies its central theme. In the spring of 1987 the editors had the
idea for a conference on local growth politics in the United States.
After a long period of deindustrialization and economic stagnation, cities in the Northeast were at that point enjoying an economic boom that raised new issues of growth control—housing
inflation, gentrification, traffic congestion, and urban sprawl. California and some Sunbelt cities had struggled with similar issues
for years. At the same time, other Sunbelt cities, those based on oil
economies, were facing painful issues of decline that older industrial cities of the Northeast had long experience with. We believed
that a conference of urban scholars from different regions would
present a chance to learn new policy responses without having to
reinvent the wheel.

At the time, we thought an explicitly comparative book on
American urban political economy would be on the cutting edge of
scholarship. We soon realized, however, that *Restructuring the
City*, edited by Susan Fainstein and colleagues, had already paved
the way in this area, followed by other books edited by Clarence
Stone and Woody Sanders, Scott Cummings, and Bob Beauregard.

After conversations with a number of contributors to this volume, we decided to broaden the comparisons to cities in different
countries. Not surprisingly, we again found that others had already
beaten us to the punch: Michael Smith and Joe Feagin's book, *The*

Capitalist City, was just out, as well as a comparison of local state responses in the United States and Great Britain by Ted Gurr and Desmond King.

Undaunted, we decided to proceed with the conference, comforting ourselves with the thought that if we did not create the wave at least we were riding the crest. Moreover, we increasingly sensed that the central question we wanted to focus on was whether cities could make a significant difference in their restructuring. The greater variation encompassed in comparing cities across nations, we reasoned, would help us evaluate the degree of policy freedom open to cities facing powerful international economic forces.

To sharpen the focus for a conference on comparative urban development, we invited seven scholars to a workshop in Albany in the fall of 1988: Susan Fainstein, Richard Hill, Michael Parkinson, Harvey Molotch, Edmond Preteceille, Bryan Jones, and Joe Feagin. We titled the workshop "A Tiger by the Tail: Local Responses to Economic Restructuring in Comparative Perspective." Early in the workshop it became clear that we could not simply focus on local responses to economic restructuring; cities are embedded in national political contexts, the workshop participants reminded us, with varied state structures and national urban policies. While city policies vary within nations, policy options varied more *across* nations than *within* them. Or, to put the matter differently, it is the national political economy and political structure that set the limits within which city governments must operate. At the end of the workshop, Harvey Molotch put into words the goal of the conference we were planning for the spring of 1989: To use the comparative method to determine to what extent the social and distributional implications of urban development are built in to economic restructuring or to what extent they are subject to choice.

The conference was held on April 7 and 8, 1989, cosponsored by the Department of Sociology and the Lewis Mumford Center for Comparative Urban and Regional Research at the State University of New York, Albany. At the conference, John Logan and Todd Swanstrom, editors of this volume, plus the seven workshop participants, presented papers. Hank Savitch, John Mollenkopf, David Perry, Dennis Judd, Nancy Kleniewski, Peter Marcuse, and

Saskia Sassen served as discussants. About eighty scholars and practitioners from around the United States and several foreign countries attended. The dominant impression was of variety and diversity. It also became clear that the field of urban political economy was not static but was groping to keep up with its changing object of study. If we were wont to follow the prevailing intellectual fashion of the day, we might even say that the conference had a distinctly postmodern feel.

By the end of the conference, we, the editors, became aware of our dissatisfaction with the dominant metaphor for the project: A Tiger by the Tail. Implying that cities are buffeted about by economic forces over which they have little control, the tiger metaphor suggested that the best that cities can do is hang on and be taken for a ride. The subtitle of the workshop, Local Responses to Economic Restructuring, suggested, likewise, that the economic forces come first and are followed by political responses. We believe it is ultimately impossible to separate economic forces from their particular political and social contexts, and misleading to focus on the local level.

For these reasons, we decided to give the book a different title from the workshop and conference: *Beyond the City Limits: Urban Policy and Economic Restructuring in Comparative Perspective.* The title is a takeoff, of course, on Paul Peterson's influential book, *City Limits,* which argued that cities are strictly limited in their policy options by the need to attract mobile wealth. This book goes "beyond the city limits" in three distinct senses. First, we propose to go beyond individual cities to look at the ways cities are embedded in institutional contexts, such as intergovernmental relations, and are shaped by the policies of the central government. Second, the chapters in this volume stress the need to go beyond city limits to look at the international context and how it shapes urban development. Finally, and most important, this book challenges the idea of a separate economic imperative that severely limits what cities can do; in place of a global logic of economic restructuring, we see relations of political economy, shaped by particular political contexts and cultural values. For this reason, we believe *Beyond the City Limits* is more optimistic than most recent work in urban political economy.

Besides intellectual nurturance, the project required material sustenance as well. The following organizations provided generous support that made the workshop, conference, and book possible: the American Sociological Association, the Rockefeller Institute of Government, and the following institutions of SUNY, Albany: the Office for Research, the Graduate School of Public Affairs, the Public Policy Program, and University Center for Policy Research.

Finally, we wish to recognize Louise Tornatore, whose competence and organizing ability made possible the successful conference on which this book is based. We cannot thank her enough.

PART I

Introduction

CHAPTER I

Urban Restructuring:
A Critical View

John R. Logan and Todd Swanstrom

The failure of the centrally planned economies of China, Eastern Europe, and the Soviet Union has captured the world's attention. As market-oriented reforms have spread in those countries, accompanied by political changes, the reaction in the West has been one of smug self-congratulations. Imitation, after all, is the highest form of flattery. We knew all along that communist leaders could not indefinitely prop up inefficient industries or subsidize selected consumer goods without causing gross misallocations and inefficiencies. If they are not to fall even further behind the West technologically, communist nations must dismantle the bureaucratic hierarchies that are stifling their economies. The free market triumphs.

Our view is that this "triumph" is mostly a rhetorical and ideological device. No Western economy today operates under a "free market"; all experience the interventions of monopolistic producers, interlocked financial institutions, confederated labor unions, and the state. The real question is, what form should these interventions take? In the East, *market reform* is a synonym for raising prices, reducing some types of consumption, and accepting structural unemployment. It is also increasingly the precondition for foreign investment and financing through Western institutions. Seen in this light, the failure of communist central planning is as much a political as an economic event, and the "triumph of markets" is more a convenient rhetoric than empirical support for an economic principle.

This ideological interpretation of events in the communist world should be interesting to urban theorists because it parallels a case that is closer to home. Conservative policy elites and scholars have applied the same rhetoric of flexible markets to issues of urban development within Western nations. They argue that economies are being restructured, and that urban restructuring inevitably follows. Advances in transportation and communication technology have freed production and consumption from a dependence on the accessibility advantages of dense urban agglomerations. Correspondingly, cities have changed from centers of manufacturing to centers of advanced services, from metal benders to paper pushers. The increased mobility of capital further heightens the competition between cities for economic growth. Forced to adapt to the imperatives of economic restructuring, cities must participate in the market for mobile capital or face economic decline and fiscal crisis. Competition forces even nation-states to adapt (as also seen in the socialist bloc), cutting back on social welfare expenditures and thus leaving city governments even more sensitive to market forces.

The market, it is said, dictates policy. This is the message of political scientist Paul Peterson, whose book, *City Limits* (1981), legitimizes developmental (growth-oriented) policies over redistributive (social welfare) municipal policies. Peterson argues that cities are limited in their choices for two reasons. One is political: local politics is dominated by a mobilized elite primarily interested in growth. The second and more fundamental reason is that too great a concern for social welfare would doom a locality to stagnation and decline. In Peterson's view, concerns with welfare issues of urban growth are more realistically handled at the national level than by city governments. The market determines the local agenda.

Others, however, use similar logic to argue for a policy of benign neglect at the national level as well. Declining cities cannot be saved, they assert, because the market forces that have undermined them are unstoppable. Attempts to slow down urban decline or compensate cities for the costs of economic restructuring may be compassionate in the short run, but inevitably they slow down economic growth, harming everyone in the long run. "Federal efforts to revitalize urban areas through a national urban policy concerned principally with the health of specific places will inevitably conflict with efforts to revitalize the larger economy" (Hicks 1983, 3).

In *Beyond the City Limits* we wish to challenge the notion that there is a market logic of capitalism to which urban policy at all levels must submit. We intend this volume as a contribution to the literature on economic restructuring as it applies to the futures of cities. All too often this literature has represented markets as natural forces, separable from public policies, and portrayed economic restructuring as a unified global process. The chapters that follow argue that markets are always embedded in particular social and political relations; economic restructuring is not a single, global process. Formerly, American capitalism was regarded as the mold from which all other capitalist systems, regardless of cultural or political background, would be cast. No longer. The stunning success of the Japanese model, with its corporatist organization clearly reflecting Japanese historical experience, destroys any unitary theory of capitalism. As Rick Hill observes in this volume, there is not one capitalism; there are many "species of capitalism." And so, we believe, are there many species of restructuring. Whatever the common trends, the decline of manufacturing and expansion of services affect Detroit differently from Aichi Prefecture (the Japanese region described in the chapter by Hill) because these urban regions have different regimes of governance and labor relations, they are tied to different sorts of multinational firms, and they have different relations to national governments whose principal institutions are dissimilar.

The implication of our argument is that a great deal more

discretion exists to shape economic and urban restructuring than is commonly believed. Many cities have more options to forge their own future development and to allocate costs and benefits among social groups than they have been willing to consider. Specific examples of these options, and the conditions under which they can be realized, are described in chapters by Molotch, Savitch, and Clavel and Kleniewski.

A central theme of the chapters that follow, however, is that cities cannot be abstracted from their national context. The comparative method is most effective not when one city is compared with another but when a city in one national context is compared to a city in another national context. As Saskia Sassen stresses in her commentary, national policies have a powerful effect on urban restructuring. In particular, we argue, the limits of local policy depend to a large degree on relationships between local and national governments, which vary greatly among countries and which are themselves subject to bitter contest. The confrontation of "market forces" with urban policy in New York, for example, is considered in juxtaposition with the case of London, or Paris, or Milan. And our contributors have paid attention both to the local dynamics of policy formation and to the national political economy that is the context for municipal action.

We believe that a careful application of the comparative method to the study of urbanization and urban policy around the Western world will force researchers to refine the theory of economic restructuring, and especially to revise its implications for urban policy. There has been a revival of interest in comparative urban political economy in the past few years (Smith and Feagin 1987; Peet 1987; Gurr and King 1987; Dogan and Kasarda 1988; Savitch 1988; Parkinson, Foley, and Judd 1989). As we noted above, the decline of American hegemony has increased interest in different, sometimes highly successful, production systems in other countries. Similarly, with regard to urban development, the expectation that the American pattern is the model that other nations will necessarily follow has been shattered.

The comparative method is an excellent tool for looking behind the "economic logic" of global economic restructuring to examine more closely the variety of urban political economies. Thus our main theme is variety—variety in urban policy, in urban form, and in urban outcomes. We explore this variety through comparative case studies. By highlighting differences, the comparative method makes contingent the conditions that appeared necessary and inevitable in a single case; it reawakens our sense of surprise.

In his commentary on the volume, John Walton takes us to task for failing to deal explicitly with the "logic of comparison." In fact, we self-consciously avoided discussing the logic of comparison for fear that it would bog us down in endless discussions of method; in any case, we doubted whether the contributors to this volume could ever agree on a unified approach. Indeed, they apply the comparative method in individualized ways, making comparisons at many different levels and for many different purposes. They must be judged on the basis of their overall argumentation and evidence. Nevertheless, we think that Walton's criticism is telling. The challenge of future work in comparative urban political economy is to be more self-conscious about method and to set out a common agenda so that future work in the field can be cumulative. Walton's observations are a good start.

Urban Restructuring and the Economic Imperative

Theories of economic restructuring are relatively new, originating in the 1970s. We cannot fairly characterize the points of view of all contributors to this literature, but we can draw out some common themes. These theories rest on the notion that a fundamental crisis struck the world capitalist economy about 1973 (the date of the first OPEC oil cartel). Restructuring is the system's attempt to resolve the crisis. Part of that restructuring involves shifts in the geographical location of production, consumption, and residence that have profound implications for cities.

According to this view, city economies have reflected a global change from a goods-producing to a service-producing economy. While there has been relatively little shift in final product from goods to services, there has been a major shift in employment from goods production to service provision. Faster increases in labor productivity in the goods-producing sector have meant that progressively higher portions of total employment are in services.

Not only is manufacturing employment falling overall as a portion of total employment, but breakthroughs in transportation and communications have made industrial capital much more mobile. The result is intense competition for industry, with much routine manufacturing moving from developed to less developed regions, principally in search of lower wages. The globalization of production has rendered older, compact, industrial cities obsolete. In the United States, formerly prosperous industrial cities lost jobs to sprawled-out Sunbelt cities and to foreign countries (Bluestone and Harrison 1982). Over a ten-year period Western Europe lost 20 percent of its manufacturing jobs, principally to newly industrializing countries like Brazil, South Korea, and Taiwan (Peet 1987, 21). As the geography of industrial production changes, previously agricultural countries, such as some countries of the Pacific Rim, have become centers of manufacturing. In addition, certain areas in developed countries have become centers of high-tech manufacturing, such as Silicon Valley in California or along the M4 motorway from London to Bristol.

Far-reaching trends are also evident in the service sector. Besides the three basic sectors of the economy—primary (agriculture and mining), secondary (goods production), and tertiary (services)—Jean Gottman (1983) argues we need a fourth category, the "quaternary sector." Whereas traditional services are generally tied to the population they serve, the quaternary functions (closely associated with producer services) are freer to move about geographically. Routine, low-wage service employment tends to decentralize in search of low-cost sites of production. On the other hand, what Cohen (1979) called advanced corporate services tend to centralize in large cities (Manners 1974; Stanback et al. 1981; Daniels 1982; Noyelle 1986).

All these trends tend to reshape the interurban hierarchy. At the top sit so-called world cities, which become centers of international finance and headquarters of multinational corporations (Hymer 1971; Friedmann 1986; Beauregard 1989b). Other cities take on different functions within the changing international division of labor, from regional headquarters cities to centers of low-wage manufacturing. Within many cities, economic restructuring leads to increasing class polarization as the growth of high-wage jobs is accompanied by rapid expansion of low-wage jobs and the so-called informal sector, in which work remains undocumented and unprotected (Sassen 1988).

Economic restructuring is an elusive concept with multiple meanings. Nevertheless, it is possible to identify three core themes that are common to most, if not all, of the literature.[1]

1. *Historical rupture:* First is the idea that the world economy is undergoing a radical break with the past.

Restructuring denotes a transition from an old economic structure to a new one.[2] Scholars such as Bluestone and Harrison (1982), Castells (1985), and Harvey (1989) identify a crisis in the old regime of industrial capital that peaked about 1973. Since then, according to the economic restructuring literature, the world economy has been going through a complex transition into a new postindustrial economic order. Part of the solution of the crisis of the old structure is a "territorial fix," a rearranging of production across space.

2. *Priority of economic forces:* By calling the process economic restructuring (not political or social restructuring), theorists stress that it originates in the economy, in the processes of private exchange and wealth generation. Implicitly, the term views economic relations as more basic or deterministic than other relations.

3. *Structure over agency:* Finally, the core term *structure,* contrasted with its theoretical antonym *agency,* suggests a process that is independent of human will. The movement from one structure to another is viewed as something that takes place according to an economic logic, essentially the logic of capitalist competition and factor cost reduction. This logic is, perforce, the same no matter where it takes place, no matter what the religion practiced or the language spoken by the capitalists and the workers.

While agreeing on how to describe the broad trends of economic restructuring, scholars on the left and right disagree on how to evaluate the effects of these trends. Market-oriented analysts focus on the benefits of economic restructuring: job creation, urban revitalization, greater efficiency, and enhanced national competitiveness. Scholars on the left focus on its costs: unemployed blue-collar workers left behind by capital flight, the "missing middle" in the wage structure, displacement caused by gentrification, and the fiscal crises of local governments. Both sides generally agree, however, that the process of economic restructuring has a powerful logic and that efforts to resist it will be largely futile and may only hinder capital accumulation and growth.

In the hands of market theorists, economic restructuring has conservative implications for public policy. These are evident in the work of John Kasarda and John Hicks, both of whom influenced the report of the McGill Commission, *Urban America in the Eighties*, a seminal document in the evolution of American urban policy (President's Commission for a National Agenda 1980). These theorists view restructuring as the result of private economic forces; simultaneous deindustrialization and reindustrialization occur as capital migrates to more efficient sites for production. This process follows a logic of its own that transcends national boundaries; public policy does not play a determinative role (President's Commission 1980, 105; Kasarda 1980, 389; Hicks 1982, 5). Efforts to counteract this logic "are as unrealistic as they are nostalgic" (Kasarda 1988, 79). In the commission's words,

> The nation can no longer assume that cities will perform the full range of their traditional functions for the larger society. They are no longer the most desirable setting for living, working, or producing. They should be allowed to transform into more specialized service and consumption centers within larger urban economic systems. The Panel believes that this nation should reconcile itself to these redistribution patterns (p. 4).

Those who lobby for older cities are another "special interest" trying to get public handouts in opposition to the public interest in economic growth (McGill 1983, xiv). Urban policies should aid the process of economic restructuring. Efforts to help those who cannot take care of themselves may be needed. Redistributive policies, however, should be people-specific, not place-specific. Place-specific policies anchor people and production in places that the market has signaled are not efficient locations for production. People-specific redistributive policies, on the other hand, can facilitate labor mobility instead of hindering it. In short, social policy must adapt to the imperatives of economic restructuring. After all, "we must be able to produce wealth before we can redistribute it" (Hicks 1982, 575).

The neo-Marxist literature on economic restructuring rejects the conservative policy implications of market theorists. Instead of seeing the glass of economic restructuring as half full, scholars on the left tend to see it as half empty. If left to itself, the process of restructuring will leave many victims in its wake, exacerbating class inequalities. However, like market theory, neo-Marxist analysts do not stress the discretionary power of public policy but focus on the power of economic and technological change that manifests itself in a global process of restructuring. In a 1985 essay, for example, Manuel Castells stresses that "economic restructuring and technological change" are a "major underlying cause" of the changing spatial structure of American cities (p. 32). Specifically, he argues, new communication technologies will render most dense urban agglomerations anachronistic, while anointing a few places as centers of elite decision making, thus reinforcing the interurban hierarchy.

The global logic of economic restructuring can be seen most clearly in the theory of capitalist regulation and its reflections on the transition from a Fordist to a flexible regime of accumulation (Gramsci 1971; Aglietta 1976; Lipietz 1986). Again we stress that a brief treatment of this literature risks falling into caricature, but some main themes are clear. The concept of Fordism combines the extreme development of the technical division of labor, of Taylorization, with highly mechanized assembly-line production. The resulting massive gains in productivity required new forms of mass consumption to stave off crises of overproduction. The Fordist "regime of accumulation" required a corresponding "mode of regulation," or set of norms, laws, habits, and institutions that uphold the system of production. Under Fordism, the centerpiece of the mode of regulation was mass consumption, upheld by Keynesian economics, the welfare state, and other policies, such as those promoting suburbanization (Florida and Feldman 1988).

Scholars argue that a crisis of the Fordist regime of accumulation occurred in the 1970s; fundamentally, it was a crisis of profitability, with heightened international competition placing new pressures on the organization of production. The new regime of flexible accumulation is an attempt to resolve the crisis (Piore and Sabel 1984; Scott and Storper 1986; Harvey 1989). The new system requires less specialized and more flexible labor (usually accompanied by low rates of unionization), short production runs, and high-quality production for specialized market niches. The old Fordist cities with concentrations of industrial mass production give way to decentralized urban agglomerations with flexible specialization tied into networks of suppliers and consumers.

The new regime also brings into being a new mode of regulation, which addresses the crisis of profitability by heightening competition at all levels, depressing both private wages and the social wage. The Keynesian welfare state, which helped legitimate redistributive policies for declining urban areas, is dismantled in favor of a more decentralized entrepreneurial state deemphasizing social welfare and emphasizing developmental policies in public-private partnerships with business. The entire edifice of the mode of regulation based on mass consumption gives way to more differentiated and specialized consumption. Urban space becomes more differentiated as cities break down into playgrounds for the urban gentry and wastelands for the legions of low-paid service workers or denizens of the underground economy. Even broad cultural trends are determined by economic restructuring. "There is strong evidence that post-modernity is nothing more than the cultural clothing of flexible accumulation" (Harvey 1989, 274).

In sum, whether viewed through the lens of market theory or neo-Marxism, theories of economic (and urban) restructuring have argued that restructuring follows a global economic logic that carries other social and political institutions in its wake. Understood in these general terms, economic restructuring, we believe, is an abstraction that obscures the facts as much as it illuminates them. The economic restructuring literature imparts an unwarranted global uniformity to urban development.[3] And it implies, for better or for worse, a paralysis of urban policy.

In his commentary, John Walton takes us to task for putting neo-Marxist political economy in the same category as market theory. He asserts that market theory has always "talked past the issue of political determination," whereas the political economy approach has "privileged the study of social movements"—even if often viewing them through "refracted structural light." Many contributors to this volume would probably agree with Walton's criticism of our analysis.

We do not intend, however, to let market theorists off the hook, for they have always believed in a mythical "free market" and have never developed an adequate theory of state action. In the political economy literature, on the other hand, what we see is theoretical formulations in which political forces are acknowledged in principle but relegated to a subordinate role—despite their importance in empirical studies. It is time for theory to catch up with the variety of empirical findings. Also, in our reading of this literature, we are surprised to find little concern with the practical implications of neo-Marxist theory. Certainly the left has been heavily engaged in the politics of deindustrialization at the local level, as illustrated by the experiments in municipal socialism in Britain during the 1970s. But the burden of much theoretical writing is that urban policy is a secondary aspect of a much larger package of economic transformation.

From Global Logic to National Variation

We do not intend to ignore the effects of economic relations, especially systems of production, in shaping urban development. But as Edmond Preteceille argues in this volume, it is necessary to link the organization of work to broader social and political processes. The term *capital* is an abstraction that needs to be broken down, because different sectors of capital behave differently. By focusing on industry, Preteceille argues, the theorists of the transition from Fordist to flexible production have ignored major sectors of the economy that never adopted Fordist production methods, including large parts of the service sector (including finance capital), military production, public infrastructure, and housing. Even within industry, large sectors, including producer goods such as the tool and die industry, were never characterized by Fordist mass-production methods.

Clearly, the massive military buildup in the United States, which has had a profound effect on cities (Markusen 1987, 106–

14; Warsh 1988), was not mandated by economic restructuring. In areas such as the military or public infrastructure, the role of the political system in establishing systems of production is evident. Even in private industrial production, as Richard Hill shows in his analysis of systems of production in Japan and the United States, government plays a decisive role. Toyotaism was created not through natural market forces, Hill argues, but through a close collaboration between the Toyota Motor Corporation, Toyota City, and Aichi Prefecture. The state of Michigan has attempted to copy the developmental policies of Japan. Hill's analysis makes it clear that production systems are not easily transported across national boundaries because of the complex institutional arrangements that must be built up over time to make them work.

The role of political institutions, especially the relationship between the central government and local governments, is a central theme of this volume. In the past, theorists have argued that state structures must adapt to the imperatives of capital accumulation. In 1973, for example, James O'Connor argued that economic restructuring required the centralization of state power. In order to resolve the fiscal crisis of the state, power needed to be removed from local governments, which represented small business, into powerful regional planning bodies that would better represent the interests of monopoly capital. Today many argue just the opposite: that the restructuring of capital requires the decentralization of state power. Giving more policymaking authority to local governments can be seen as helping to privatize governmental functions, to cut social welfare spending (compared to national welfare entitlements), and to shift priorities toward business as local governments become locked in a cutthroat competition for the new mobile investment. As the comparative studies in this volume demonstrate, however, economic restructuring does not mandate any particular organization of state power. The restructuring of state power, particularly the changing national-local relationships, has been quite varied.

The comparison between Britain and the United States demonstrates the variety of national-local relations, which in turn affects the variety of urban outcomes. Both countries have moved decisively to dismantle urban and regional planning policies and to substitute market-oriented policies. After World War II Britain developed an extensive regional policy designed to bolster industry in declining areas and restrain the growth of London. By the mid-1980s, British regional policy was "in ruins" (Hall 1985, 49). The much smaller U.S. regional policies, which basically began in the 1960s, were also cut back severely in the 1980s. Urban policies directed toward declining inner cities were also cut during the Reagan years and what remained was oriented more toward aiding the private sector (Wolman 1986). While always small compared to American standards, British programs oriented toward inner cities have grown under the Thatcher government, but cuts in central government support for local authorities have meant that overall support for cities has declined (Gurr and King 1987, 161). The convergence of policy in the two countries is enough that Dennis Judd and Michael Parkinson refer to "the Americanization of urban policy in Britain" (1989, 4).

These similarities in the market-oriented shift of urban policy in Britain and the United States, however, hide important political differences. In Britain, the central government has always focused more on investment and productivity, while local governments were more oriented toward social consumption. Traditionally, municipalities in Great Britain controlled a wide range of social welfare expenditures, including social services, higher education (the polytechnics), and a massive—by American standards— public housing sector. (By 1976, 30 percent of British households lived in public housing; in the United States the figure is less than 2 percent [Headey 1978].) In the United States, the division of labor was just the opposite: "If the federal government has earned the label 'warfare-welfare state,' local and state governments deserve the name 'productivity state'" (O'Connor 1973, 99). City governments in the United States have always been directly concerned with promoting growth, especially through infrastructural investments.

As Michael Parkinson argues in his chapter, the Thatcher government saw municipalities as a threat to its goal of reducing state expenditures and promoting entrepreneurism. Many municipal governments were controlled by Labour and had pursued experiments in local socialism in the 1970s. As a result, the Thatcher government acted to remove decision-making power from local governments through such actions as abolishing regional authorities (including the Greater London Council), rate capping (limiting the local tax rate), selling off public housing, and privatizing municipal services. Control over urban economic development has been placed in the hands of development corporations that are free from local democratic control. In short, the shift to market-oriented urban policy in Britain has led to a radical centralization of power, enough that one scholarly study concluded that Britain now "stands within sight of a form of government which is more highly centralised than anything this side of East Germany" (Newton and Karran 1985, 129, quoted in Hambleton 1989, 369).

In the United States, by contrast, market-oriented urban policy has not led to a dramatic centralization of power. Under Reagan, federal grants to cities were cut but they were also deregulated, giving local governments more freedom of choice on how to spend the money. A case in point is the Community Development Block Grant: after deregulation, local governments shifted block-grant funds from the poor to economic development (Wong and Peterson 1986). Reagan, it seems, could rely on American cities' traditional preoccupation with growth to keep them in line. Indeed, most American cities are dominated by what Harvey Molotch first called "growth machines": coalitions centered around landowners whose goal is to maximize economic development, and therefore land rents, within the city (Molotch 1976; Logan and Molotch 1987). As the chapters by Molotch and Pierre Clavel and Nancy Kleniewski show, it is possible to have alternative local policies in the United States in those cities where economic conditions are strong and where political alternatives to the growth machine coalesce. While calling the system of exactions "very imperfect," Molotch nevertheless documents the real choices made by some southern California municipalities, reflecting their values and political alignments, in implementing growth controls. In the British unitary state, on the other hand, experiments in local socialism have been frustrated by a powerful and hostile central government.

Historically, France has had one of the most centralized governments in the West. Here, more than in other countries, discretionary power over urban policy was placed in the hands of governmental technocrats, relatively autonomous of immediate political pressures. Under the Gaullists, France developed some of the most powerful regional planning policies in any capitalist country. A wide array of regulations and incentives were used to disperse both population and jobs away from Paris to "growth poles" in surrounding suburbs and other regions. The policies were successful in "dedensifying" Paris; without these controls, the low-rise skyline in Paris would have come more to resemble New York's (Savitch 1988). Opposition to the unchecked power of government technocrats, however, developed out of the participatory movements of the 1960s and 1970s. By 1977, Paris had its own elected mayor and a measure of autonomy. When the socialists came to power, as Edmond Preteceille discusses in his chapter, they enacted a series of decentralizing measures to promote a "new citizenship." Local governments were given more power over their budgets and were allowed to issue construction permits and make loans to businesses. As Preteceille argues, the results have been mixed. Like in Britain, Italy, Spain, and the United States, an "economic mobilization of local governments" has occurred in France. No local politician in France can hope to stay in power without claiming, at least, to address the growing problem of unemployment. On the other hand, Preteceille points out, only about 2 percent of municipal expenditures are directly applied to economic development. Unlike the American case, he notes, "French municipalities have not, as a whole, entered a wild competition promising all sorts of deductions, abatements, helps and advantages to attract business." Primarily due to political traditions and the power of left-wing parties, decentralization has had a different result in France.

In summary, a review of state restructuring in Britain, France, and the United States reveals that economic restructuring did not dictate a uniform process of political restructuring. In the context of economic restructuring, state power centralized in Britain and decentralized in France and the United States. These comparisons are drawn out in detail in the chapter by Hank Savitch. The organization of state power was a reflection of the conflicts between different classes and groups over state policy. Rather than a result of economic restructuring, state power was more a tool used by dominant political interests to advance their economic agenda.

While the contributors to this volume agree that economic and political restructuring cannot be understood apart from each other, they are far from agreement on the specific relationship between economic and political sources of urban restructuring. Michael Parkinson's review of British urban policy under Thatcher exposes the decisive role played by ideology and politics. According to Parkinson, Thatcher's urban policy was motivated by deeply held ideological beliefs, not by any sort of "rational" response to economic imperatives. Indeed, Thatcher's commitment to an ideological vision of economic restructuring, centering on privatization and urban entrepreneurialism, was so strong she was willing to sacrifice her original stated commitment to decentralizing state power. Realizing that such decentralization would allow for continued experiments in local socialism by Labour-dominated municipalities, Thatcher acted to drain municipalities of significant policymaking authority.

In her comparison of London and New York, Susan Fainstein is less willing to grant politics such autonomy. The convergence of public policy in New York and London would suggest, she argues, that both are responding to the global imperatives of economic restructuring. Like Parkinson, Fainstein argues that urban policy is not an automatic response to economic forces: "The direct cause of state policy, therefore, is political-ideological: the electoral triumph of conservative regimes." Adopting a "synthesizing viewpoint," however, Fainstein brings economic forces in through the back door, arguing that economic restructuring has altered the composition of class forces in such a way as to weaken the ability of the left to offer a coherent alternative. Specifically, the decline of the unionized blue-collar work force has decimated what was historically a pillar of socialist and social democratic coalitions locally in New York City and nationally in Britain.

Image and Agenda in Urban Restructuring

How people view economic restructuring may be as important as the facts of economic restructuring themselves. Between the stimulus of economic restructuring and the response of urban policy lies the "image" that politically relevant actors have of economic change and what problems need to be addressed by public policies. As Bryan Jones and Frank Baumgartner show (1989) using survey data, in the United States the public's image of the primary problems facing the country has shifted between economic growth and social issues. Partly this is due to the underlying objective conditions of the country, but it is also due to changing public perceptions of similar facts. The prevailing growth rhetoric in recent times has defined the problems of the United States in terms of lagging economic expansion, not in terms of fairness or the distribution of wealth. This has the effect of narrowing the political agenda in ways favorable to conservative political interests.

In urban policy, the dominant image of economic change has, likewise, legitimated conservative policies in the present period. (While less sophisticated, the prevailing image closely resembles the abstract formulations of economic restructuring found in the academic literature discussed earlier.) The dominant metaphor is the image of mobile capital spanning the globe in search of the lowest-cost production sites. The implications are far-reaching: economic development is a matter of attracting more of this thing called capital, which is increasingly demanding of its potential suitors.

At the national level in Great Britain and the United States the capital-mobility model has dominated thinking about economic development. The goal of national policy under Thatcher and Reagan/Bush has been to free up capital, reducing its social and financial obligations. At the local level, this leads to what Clavel and Kleniewski, following Markusen (1988), call bidding down (against other cities to attract manufacturing jobs) and bailing out (of manufacturing to attract mobile service employment).

At best, this image of how cities grow is incomplete; at worst it is grossly misleading. Of course some kinds of capital, such as routinized manufacturing, are highly mobile. But relying upon that type of capital can lead to what has in a Third World context been called "dependent development" (Evans 1979). In dependent development, capital investment is based on how the investment fits into the firm's international holdings rather than how it fits into the local economy. The local multiplier effects of the investment are minimal, and the firm exacts important concessions on labor control and financing or taxation. The jobs created are often low value-added, low-skilled, and low-wage. Such economic growth depends on maintaining a low wage structure, including a low social wage.

An alternative image of economic development would recognize that the most valuable forms of capital investment are deeply embedded in particular social and geographical contexts.[4] This is an old-fashioned concept, but in this respect perhaps the insights of agglomeration theory have been jettisoned prematurely in an effort to keep up with economic restructuring. While the physical barriers to capital mobility have increasingly been overcome by technology, many sectors of capital remain dependent on what could be called a social ecology of skilled labor that ties them to particular geographical contexts. The concentration of white-collar decision-making functions in the central business districts of cities is a good case in point. Another example is the revival of mature industrial regions, like northern Italy and western Massachusetts, based on the flexible specialization of small machine shops using skilled labor (Doeringer, Terkla, and Topakian 1988). Such embedded industries are more attractive than hyper-mobile capital, because they will not move at the drop of a hat when asked to contribute to the commonwealth.

Basing their argument partly on the embeddedness of certain kinds of capital investment, Clavel and Kleniewski argue that "local governments have more room to maneuver than is commonly assumed." Cities with strong service economies, for example, recognizing that capital will not take flight when required to contribute to the commonweal, have enacted linkage policies designed to redistribute some of the benefits of growth. In both Britain and the United States, as Clavel and Kleniewski describe, there have been numerous attempts at the local level to go beyond such redistributive measures to actually shape economic restructuring before it occurs. Experiments in alternative local economic development have been based on an image of economic development that does not revolve around attracting mobile capital but focuses, instead, on nurturing community relations—between labor and capital, between networks of small businesses, between the political system and firms.

An alternative image of economic development, then, would shift from the masculine metaphor of cutthroat competition for mobile capital to a more feminine image of nurturing the strengths of the local context. The alternative image of economic development based on embeddedness shifts attention from cutting the costs of capital to upgrading the skills of labor and nurturing the context of self-generating economic development. Educational expenditures have the potential of transcending the supposedly iron-clad tradeoff of equality and growth. Research has shown that local economies can buck national and international trends.[5] By upgrading skills, innovating new businesses, or finding specialized niches within flexible systems of production, it is possible for mature economies to nurture development with higher wages and broader benefits for the population. This requires, however, that we move beyond a simplistic concept of economic growth mesmerized by the mobility of capital.

The variety of experiences documented in this volume, we believe, establishes that alternative images of economic restructuring are possible. Our hope is that this will help to legitimate alternative public policies. Instead of adapting cities to economic restructuring, let us adapt economic restructuring to the needs of cities and the people who live in them.

NOTES

1. In what follows we draw freely from Robert Beauregard, "Space, Time, and Economic Restructuring" (1989a).

2. Susan and Norman Fainstein (1989) argue convincingly that there was no historical break in the evolution of capitalism in the 1970s.

3. Beauregard (1989a) accounts for the variety of urban outcomes by arguing that economic restructuring takes place in a highly uneven and fragmented manner across time and space. But he still argues that underlying this variety is a global process of economic restructuring. We take a different approach, arguing, on the basis of outcomes, that there is no such unified global process.

4. For a related argument, see Granovetter (1985).

5. For citations on this point, see Doeringer, Terkla, and Topakian (1988, 8).

REFERENCES

Aglietta, Michel. 1976. *A Theory of Capitalist Regulation: The U.S. Experience*. London: New Left Books.

Beauregard, Robert A. 1989a. *Economic Restructuring and Political Response*. Newbury Park, Calif.: Sage.

———. 1989b. *Atop the Urban Hierarchy*. Totowa, N.J.: Rowman and Littlefield.

Bluestone, Barry, and Bennett Harrison. 1982. *The Deindustrialization of America*. New York: Basic Books.

Castells, Manuel. 1985. "High Technology, Economic Restructuring, and the Urban-Regional Process in the United States." In *High Technology, Space and Society*, ed. Manuel Castells. Beverly Hills, Calif.: Sage.

Cohen, Robert. 1979. "The Changing Transactions Economy and Its Spatial Implications." *Ekistics* 274:7–15.

Daniels, Peter. 1982. *Service Industries: Growth and Location*. Cambridge: Oxford University Press.

Doeringer, Peter B., David G. Terkla, and Gregory C. Topakian. 1988. *Invisible Factors in Local Economic Development*. New York: Oxford University Press.

Dogan, Mattei, and John D. Kasarda. 1988. *The Metropolis Era*, vol. 1. Beverly Hills, Calif.: Sage.

Evans, Peter. 1979. *Dependent Development: The Alliance of Multinational, State, and Local Capital in Brazil*. Princeton, N.J.: Princeton University Press.

Fainstein, Susan S., and Norman I. Fainstein. 1989. "Technology, the New International Division of Labor, and Location: Continuities and Discontinuities." In *Economic Restructuring and Political Response*, ed. Robert A. Beauregard. Beverly Hills, Calif.: Sage.

Florida, Richard L., and Marshall M. A. Feldman. 1988. "Housing in U.S. Fordism." *International Journal of Urban and Regional Research* 12(2):187–209.

Friedmann, John. 1986. "The World City Hypothesis." *Development and Change* 17(1):69–83.

Gottman, Jean. 1983. *The Coming of the Transactional City*. College Park: University of Maryland, Institute for Urban Studies.

Gramsci, Antonio. 1971. *Selections from the Prison Notebooks*, ed. and trans. by Q. Hoare and G. N. Smith. London: Lawrence and Wishart.

Granovetter, Mark. 1985. "Economic Action and Social Structure: The Problem of Embeddedness." *American Journal of Sociology* 91(3):481–510.

Gurr, Ted Robert, and Desmond S. King. 1987. *The State and the City*. Chicago: University of Chicago Press.

Hall, Peter. 1985. "Technology, Space, and Society in Contemporary Britain." In *High Technology, Space, and Society*, ed. Manuel Castells. Beverly Hills, Calif.: Sage.

Hambleton, Robin. 1989. "Urban Government under Thatcher and Reagan." *Urban Affairs Quarterly* 24(3):359–88.

Harvey, David. 1989. *The Urban Experience*. Baltimore: Johns Hopkins University Press.

Headey, Bruce. 1978. *Housing Policy in the Developed Economy*. New York: St. Martin's.

Hicks, Donald A. 1982. "Urban and Economic Adjustment to the Post-Industrial Era." *Hearings Before the Joint Economic Committee, Congress of the United States, Ninety-Seventh Congress, Part 2*. Washington, D.C.: U.S. Government Printing Office.

Hymer, Stephen. 1971. "The Multinational Corporation and the Law of Uneven Development." In *Economics and the World Order*, ed. J. N. Bhagwati. London: Macmillan.

Jones, Bryan D., and Frank Baumgartner. 1989. "Image and Agenda in Urban Politics." Paper presented at A Tiger by the Tail Conference, Albany, New York, April 7–8, 1989.

Judd, Dennis R., and Michael Parkinson. 1989. "Urban Revitalization in America and the U.K.: The Politics of Uneven Development." In *Regenerating the Cities: The U.K. Crisis and the U.S. Experience*, ed. Dennis R. Judd, Bernard Foley, and Michael Parkinson. Glenview, Ill.: Scott, Foresman and Company.

Kasarda, John D. 1980. "The Implications of Contemporary Redistribution Trends for National Urban Policy." *Social Science Quarterly* 61:373–400.

———. 1988. "Economic Restructuring and America's Urban Dilemma." In *The Metropolis Era*, vol. 1, ed. Mattei Dogan and John D. Kasarda. Beverly Hills, Calif.: Sage.

Lipietz, Alain. 1986. "New Tendencies in the International Division of Labor: Regions of Accumulation and Modes of Regulation." In *Production, Work, Territory: The Geographical Anatomy of Industrial Capitalism*, ed. A. J. Scott and Michael Storper. Boston: Allen & Unwin.

Logan, John R., and Harvey Molotch. 1987. *Urban Fortunes: The Political Economy of Place*. Berkeley and Los Angeles: University of California Press.

McGill, William J. 1983. Foreword to *Transition to the 21st Century: Prospects and Policies for Economic and Urban-Regional Transformation*, ed. Donald A. Hicks and Norman J. Glickman. Greenwich, Conn.: JAI Press.

Manners, Gerald. 1974. "The Office in Metropolis: An Opportunity for Shaping Urban America." *Economic Geography* 50(2):93–110.

Markusen, Ann. 1987. *Regions: The Economics and Politics of Territory*. Totowa, N.J.: Rowman & Littlefield.

———. 1988. "Planning for Industrial Decline: Lessons from Steel Communities." *Journal of Planning Education and Research* 7:173–84.

Molotch, Harvey. 1976. "The City as a Growth Machine: Toward a Political Economy of Place." *American Journal of Sociology* 82:309–32.

Newton, Kenneth, and T. J. Karran. 1985. *The Politics of Local Expenditure.* London: Macmillan.

Noyelle, Thierry J. 1986. "Advanced Services in the System of Cities." In *Local Economies in Transition,* ed. Edward M. Bergman. Durham, N.C.: Duke University Press.

O'Connor, James. 1973. *The Fiscal Crisis of the State.* New York: St. Martin's.

Parkinson, Michael, Bernard Foley, and Dennis R. Judd. 1989. *Regenerating the Cities: The U.K. Crisis and the U.S. Experience.* Glenview, Ill.: Scott, Foresman and Company.

Peet, Richard. 1987. *International Capitalism and Industrial Restructuring: A Critical Analysis.* Boston: Allen & Unwin.

Peterson, Paul E. 1981. *City Limits.* Chicago: University of Chicago Press.

Piore, Michael J., and Charles F. Sabel. 1984. *The Second Industrial Divide: Possibilities for Prosperity.* New York: Basic Books.

President's Commission for a National Agenda for the Eighties. 1980. *Urban America in the Eighties.* Washington, D.C.: U.S. Government Printing Office.

Sassen, Saskia. 1988. *The Mobility of Labor and Capital: A Study in International Investment and Capital Flow.* New York: Cambridge University Press.

Savitch, H. V. 1988. *Post-Industrial Cities: Politics and Planning in New York, Paris, and London.* Princeton, N.J.: Princeton University Press.

Scott, A. J., and Michael Storper, eds. 1986. *Production, Work, Territory: The Geographical Anatomy of Industrial Capitalism.* Boston: Allen & Unwin.

Smith, Michael Peter, and Joe R. Feagin, eds. 1987. *The Capitalist City: Global Restructuring and Community Politics.* Oxford: Basil Blackwell.

Stanback, Thomas M., et al. 1981. *Services: The New Economy.* Totowa, N.J.: Allanheld, Osmun.

Warsh, David L. 1988. "War Stories: Defense Spending and the Growth of the Massachusetts Economy." In *The Massachusetts Miracle,* ed. David R. Lampe. Cambridge: MIT Press.

Wolman, Hal. 1986. "The Reagan Urban Policy and Its Impacts." *Urban Affairs Quarterly* 21(3):311–35.

Wong, Kenneth K., and Paul E. Peterson. 1986. "Urban Response to Federal Program Flexibility: Politics of Community Development Block Grant." *Urban Affairs Quarterly* 21(3):293–309.

PART II

Urban Policy: National and
International Comparisons

CHAPTER 2

Political Paradoxes of Urban Restructuring: Globalization of the Economy and Localization of Politics?

Edmond Preteceille

The processes of urban restructuring that are taking place in many countries point to some paradoxical aspects of theoretical paradigms in social science, particularly when we try to examine their economic and political dimensions together. Economic change is characterized by a growing interdependence among local enterprises and increasingly international markets, financial institutions and flows, processes of technological innovation and diffusion. At the same time, most countries experience a revaluation of local politics. Local governments are promoted as major actors of urban, social and economic change, often with responsibilities and resources increased by policies of state decentralization.

Local actors, summoned to promote local economic development, are looking for pragmatic solutions, and will eventually ask researchers to help solve the dilemma of necessary but elusive local economic activity. The first responsibility of researchers is to provide theoretical tools to help in understanding the problem as a whole. And this is where the paradoxical relations between economic and political-institutional changes come in.

The most attractive and successful paradigm for the analysis of economic restructuring and its urban and regional implications, developed as part of the economic regulation theory, is the crisis of the Fordist regime of accumulation, leading to the emergence of a new flexible regime of accumulation. It is focused on industrial change and is little interested in the state, whether central or local. In parallel, regarding the renewal or rediscovery of the local dimension of social practices and of local power inside the state, two trends of analysis have developed: one focused on the dynamic of social movements and the restructuring of local communities from the base; the other looking at the politics of institutional reforms from the top. Both have few, if any, links with economic dimensions of analysis; the first eventually considers defensive reactions to the consequences of restructuring as one stimulus for the renewal of local community life, but the second leaves out in most cases the question of the relation between politics and class relations, when that question is not simply dismissed as mechanistic.

This chapter discusses how each of these perspectives, whether its main concern is economy or politics, questions the other in its capacity to provide coherent and efficient ways of understanding the various aspects of socioeconomic and urban change. Marx versus Weber, once again? It cannot be summarized that way, since theoretical elaborations derived from both traditions can be found on each side. Marxists or neo-Marxists have been criticized as economistic and mechanistic, often as a way to dismiss their work without considering it seriously.[1] Although such a critique is often accurate, social science research using Marxist concepts and hypotheses has, since the mid-1970s, paid much more attention to politics and the state and to the elaboration of more complex explanations striving to link the formerly separate spheres.

It is a difficult task. The difficulties are both theoretical and empirical in the construction of explanations recognizing at the same time the specific dynamic of the various social relations—production and political, gender, and ethnic-cultural ones—and their structural interactions.[2] Because it has become fashionable, regulation theory tends to spread out in a simplified version that promotes a recurrent form of economism where some seek a simple solution: the magic words "crisis of Fordism" and "flexible specialization" would produce a global explanation of each society deducted mostly from the restructuring of the major industrial production processes. The authors of the regulation theory, for example Boyer (1986a), are themselves much more cautious and aware of the difficulties and complexities of the necessary analyses.

Starting from a discussion of the French case, with some elements of comparison with others, I shall try in this chapter to show the necessity of systems of explanation considering the articulations between economic and political processes in their specific historical development in each social formation. Three issues will be discussed: economic restructuring analyzed according to the model of flexible specialization, the increasing economic mobilization of local governments, and decentralization trends and policies. To what extent can they be considered as related processes, contributing to the establishment of a new regime of accumulation with its new regulating mechanisms? To what extent do they reveal different or diverging trends expressing the contradictory character of social relations in our societies?

From Economic to Urban Restructuring

The economic crisis that burst out in the mid-1970s and the subsequent movements of economic restructuring have had considerable impacts on the spatial organization of economic systems, on the social structure and operation of urban systems, and, through that, on urban policies. Any attempt to analyze urban policies without taking this into consideration would ignore major components of present problems. But can economy-focused analyses give us useful propositions to deal with the more political side of those policies?

Similar economic processes are taking place in most developed capitalist countries, like the decline of sectors of traditional heavy industry and the deindustrialization of the formerly prosperous urban regions where they were concentrated. They have to do with worldwide market competition and the international diffusion of new production techniques. Their social and fiscal consequences confronting local governments, or conversely the explosive growth of new regions, point at macroeconomic processes of an international dimension.

Moving away from the essentially descriptive consideration of the emergence of new technologies or of a new international division of labor, authors of the "regulation school" (Aglietta 1976, Aglietta and Brender 1984, Boyer and Mistral 1978, Boyer 1986a, 1986b, Coriat 1978, Lipietz 1979, 1983, among others) have proposed to analyze such processes in the terms of the crisis of the Fordist regime of accumulation. In that perspective, it can be noted first that the "crisis of profitability" of those sectors most severely hit by restructuring is not seen in purely quantitative accounting terms—which limited the analysis in terms of overaccumulation of capital, in spite of the many interesting results it has produced (Boccara 1974, INSEE 1974, 1981)—or in market terms, which is the most superficial vision. The emphasis on the concrete production process makes it possible to link the study of the limits to productivity increase within one model of division of labor (Taylorism) with that of the new forms of division of labor and of the new technological processes that support and condense them. It also makes the link with two processes of present social change. On one side, it contributes to the understanding of subsequent social transformations which change the structure of the working class and of the labor force as a whole, in its various components of salaried workers (types of work and skills, positions in the labor process, new professional identities). On the other, it provides structural elements of explanation for the dismantling of former social compromises and "norms of consumption" (Aglietta 1976), which accompanied and stabilized the division of labor and distribution of the social product, thus forming key elements in the "regulation" of the reproduction of the mode of production.

The actual or potential advantages of that approach, diversified though it may be in practice, are numerous. The connection between enterprise and social structure, between micro and macro economics is one. Another, regarding more specifically urban problems, is the paths opened by the concrete analysis of production processes, with all their complexity and connections to general social conditions, to understand the new trends of location of industries, the new productive arrangements in space, the new structures of urban economies, and the relations between cities or regions, their positions and potentials in the spatial division of labor.[3] It is a way of looking at economic change as the heart of urban change which, by the attention paid to the complex spatial dimension of work processes and to the complexity of social change generated by the new productive models, can make possible a truly internal articulation of the economic, social, and political analyses of urban structures. This is all the more important since too often in urban sociology the enterprise or the workplace was seen at best as an external factor of which one had to consider the consequences, at worst as the foreign object of a different discipline. Sociologists would mostly consider social practices outside the economy, preferably those with a clear cultural dimension, whereas political scientists would focus on elections and institutions. Even the sociology of work has seldom considered the links between its object of study—concrete work relations and practices inside the firm—and the global economic interactions and stakes of enterprise operations. In urban research more sensitive to the problems of consumption and related state interventions, like the early works of Patrick Dunleavy (1980) and Peter Saunders (1979), the production issue was ignored almost completely.

Beside its advantages, which have only been partly sketched out here, regulation theory also has a number of limitations that pose specific problems when one tries to deal with urban issues. These weak points are particularly noticeable in the more simplified version, which, because it is regarded as one of today's intellectual fashions, has tended to spread.

The model of flexible specialization deals essentially with industry. It rightfully acknowledges the importance of the major social locus of production of wealth (use values and surplus value), where too many theoretical statements tend to identify economy with market, that is, circulation and exchange of commodities. But the analysis of industrial work cannot give the key to understanding the specific economic dynamics and concrete work processes in service activities. The relative share of employment in nonindustrial sectors has increased for a long time now, and many specialists believe that some of the services should be considered as contributing directly to the production of value. Services play a decisive part in the new economic structuring of many cities, particularly but not only the large metropolis. Urban economies have become in most cases a complex set of interactions between industrial and tertiary activities, of large, middle-sized, and small firms, belonging to many different sectors and branches. The idea of the Fordist city, beyond the strong image, is a misleading oversimplification of the history of most cities, even among those that were dominated by industrial activity. And the notion of "flexible specialization" can even less be applied to the complex set of economic activities of any large city without further examination of the specific characteristics of its work processes.

Even regarding industrial restructuring alone, there is an open debate on the validity of the model and the possibility of using it as the core feature of a new emerging post-Fordist regime of accumulation.[4] The model of the Fordist regime itself still poses complex problems, since the Taylorist division of labor, which is a key part of its definition, has never characterized some major production sectors, particularly those dealing with production or capital goods, since every capitalist social formation is a complex articulation of various stages and types of division of labor. Furthermore, if the diffusion of certain types of industrial and technological principles, including elements of flexibility through the adaptability of computerized processes, is a worldwide trend, it seems that the way they are actually put into action depends on specific features of the social and economic environment. Features produced by the specific history of each social formation, which tend to shape technological practices in different ways into different industrial models, are not easily exportable from one country to another. One example is that of Japanese work relations, which include a strong integration of new technologies and relations between capital and the work force that can hardly be characterized as purely flexible, since the core part of the skilled labor force tends to be attached for life to one particular firm (see Richard Hill's contribution in this volume). Another is the famous "third Italy" case, where Capecchi (1988) argues that the dynamism and flexibility of the complex network of small and middle-sized firms comes out of a long regional history of local accumulation, entrepreneurial models, and political relations in the local society, which makes it a particularly dubious case for export to other regions. Because of a too narrow industrial focus, it can be argued that the flexible specialization model also underestimates the dominance of financial forms of capital accumulation, and that this underestimation makes it difficult to cope with the consequences of that financial dominance, particularly acute for the largest metropolises.

If both models—Fordism and flexible specialization—give useful hypotheses to understand the changes in the production of consumption goods oriented toward mass markets, they seem to be less efficient for understanding other sectors. That of production goods has already been mentioned, and one could add military, aircraft, and space industries as well. But even more important for urban problems, it is also the case for a large part of the production of urban goods and services. Infrastructure and urban industrial services (roads, bridges, water and sewage networks, transportation, garbage disposal, and so on), even when produced by private firms, fit neither in the Fordist scheme for their traditional operations, nor in the flexible specialization ones for their more recent forms, even though they integrate more and more new technologies. It seems that their change has less to do with immediate restructuring of the work process than with other factors, particularly the search for an expansion of their sphere of operation and accumulation by the large firms in the field. This is in one sense a more classical response than flexible specialization to the crisis of profitability—expansion of production of absolute surplus value, to support profits by incorporating new work processes into the sphere of capitalist exploitation, as opposed to relative surplus value obtained by higher productivity in competition with other capitalist firms. But it is also at the same time not so classical, in the sense that it is largely dependent not on expropriation of smaller capital or precapitalist private production but on moving the boundaries between public and private operations. Also, it is not producing for a real market but for public authorities as immediate customers, and thus the profits are largely dependent on political factors: price policy and access to public funding for major investments. In the overall economic restructuring, these operations nevertheless constitute considerable economic stakes, related to the interest of a number of specialized multinationals, whose interests are a heavy weight on urban policies.[5]

In a different way, the whole sector of housing production, because of its form of division of labor, its organization of markets and circulation, its financing circuits, and the specific social interests invested, does not seem to fit either model. This in spite of the fact that Aglietta himself (1976, 136–7) considers housing a key element in the "consumption norm" typical of Fordist regulation.

The greater the distance from purely economic issues, the more oversimplified the theoretical statements of regulation theory seem to be. It is the case with consumption, where the theory of Fordism includes, as mentioned, the idea of a norm of consumption which, in spite of some references to social struggles and resulting compromises, appears mostly as a functional element for the reproduction of the regime of accumulation. Such a notion, and the way it is used, tends to hide the contradictions not only between accumulation of capital and reproduction of the labor force, but also within consumption relations themselves, particularly between individual-commodity and socialized-public consumption, and, finally, between state-authoritative, assistance-oriented and cooperative, self-organized, autonomous forms of socialized consumption. This discussion is critical for urban policies, considering the place that the production and management of urban services have in them.

Together with its implicit functionalism, the "norm of consumption" regarded as typical of one regime of accumulation also tends to simplify the reality of consumption, whether of market commodities or of collective services publicly financed, into one global homogeneous representation—the Keynesian welfare state for Fordism. But in spite of some common trends toward greater state intervention for collective consumption from the 1930s to the early 1970s in most capitalist countries, and the diffusion of some common intellectual models in the bourgeoisie-state elaboration of "social reform" and "urban reform" between the wars (see Magri and Topalov 1987, 1988), it seems misleading to assimilate living conditions and consumption standards in countries so different as the United States, Great Britain, France, Sweden, Italy, and Germany. This is so not only because of the quantitative differences in the degree of development of welfare intervention, but also because of the political conditions of its establishment and their impact on the actual consumption relations built into it in each of them, with all their social, economic, political, and ideological sides.

One can therefore hardly expect to be able to simply deduce determining trends of political and institutional change in urban policies from a global characterization of economic change in terms such as "the crisis of Fordism" and "the emergence of flexible specialization." Clearly, as we have seen, economic processes of change are much more complex, particularly those affecting urban economic systems. But also, political processes have impacts on economic restructuring that should not be underestimated.

The very changes in the division of labor are not independent from political relations. New technologies and new forms of organization of work are not the imposition of a previously defined system, but the hesitating invention of new practices within relations of force between capital and labor whose variations between countries, regions, sectors, even between different plants of the same firm, lead to different solutions, different uses of technologies, eventually different techniques incorporating social relations (Freyssenet 1984a, 1984b). Therefore, the possible ways out of the crisis of Fordism, when and where Fordism is the case, may vary from one country or region to the other according to relations of force at the workplace as well as in the country, city, or region. Danièle Leborgne and Alain Lipietz (1988) argue, for example, the possibility of contrasted solutions between "offensive" and "defensive" flexibility.

Collective consumption policies are another point where politics interfere with economic deductions. There are, to be sure, some general trends toward decreasing public intervention, spreading market relations, and privatizing part of public services. But the level of development of welfare states is different, and so are their political characteristics. The ways they are affected by those similar changes are also different. In housing, for example, there seems to be a general decline of public intervention for public housing, going as far as dismantling the council housing system in Britain—although France might be a case showing that we should not jump to definitive conclusions too quickly, since the present socialist government seems to be shifting back to a policy supporting a greater effort for public housing. But it is not true in the same way for other sectors. Even in Britain, authors like Patrick Dunleavy (1986) discuss the reality of a global decrease of public spending for collective consumption, and rather argue in favor of the idea of stabilizing the level of spending and reorienting its uses. In France, reorientation and some degree of privatization may be also the case, although in different directions, but the level of public spending for public health and education services has tended to increase rather than decrease. And the Swedish welfare state has maintained a magnitude and a quality unknown in most countries.

The impossibility of deducing politics and policies from purely economic processes can be discussed most clearly around economic intervention policies of local governments—the subject of the next section.

Economic Mobilization of Local Governments

During the last thirty years, urban policies have experienced a series of shifts that have complex relations with economic changes. They do not simply reflect them, they translate and specify them. Urban policies choose between various possible reactions, and they may influence economic processes in return. The case of economic intervention policies of local governments is exemplar: where a deductive logic would be expected to apply, if we look more closely we can see numerous shifts and contradictions—between discourse and practice, between local and central practices, between practices of local authorities governed by different political forces.

First, a common fact should be acknowledged. Local governments have become openly preoccupied with economic development almost everywhere, and most will say it is their first priority. It certainly is the case in France, as Hoffmann-Martinot and Nevers (1985), Becquart-Leclerc, Hoffmann-Martinot, and Nevers (1987), and Joussemet (1988) have shown, but also in Great Britain, Italy, Spain, and the United States. To understand the meaning of this present outstanding preoccupation, it is useful to place it in the historic evolution of urban policy. In France, where such a policy emerged as a relatively unified area of intervention in the 1950s, the official discourse of the state has been successively dominated by four major themes: housing, during the 1950s and the early 1960s; urban planning and public provision of services and infrastructure until the early 1970s; environment and quality of life in the mid-1970s; and since then, local economic development and the development of local responsibilities. Probably the same sequence has taken place in other countries, with perhaps different timings.

The economic crisis has not seen a new urban policy emerge immediately. Since the early 1970s, numerous fluctuations have taken place, and the present dominant themes have come out only progressively, and with some trouble and conflicts. During the first stages of economic difficulties, before the first oil crisis, the French government tried to promote a policy of quality of life and urban environment, arguing that quantitative problems had already been solved. It was partly an attempt to co-opt the demands of urban and ecology movements rapidly developing at the time, partly a first move away from its former heavy involvement in urbanization. The second aspect became more and more important as the crisis deepened and the state strived to disengage itself. But it proved insufficient to create an alternative to the previously hypercentralized form of hegemony, structured around the interventionist and planning state, responsible for the provision of welfare. That could no longer be maintained, since the hegemonic strength of centralization at a time of rapid economic growth became a weakness when centralization meant that the state was responsible for austerity and unemployment and could not control economic changes endangering the stability of social order. Decentralization emerged progressively as a possible hegemonic alternative protecting the central state, but with many difficulties, hesitations, and obstacles after 1977 caused by the political contradictions between the right-wing government at the center and the predominantly left-wing local authorities (Preteceille 1985a).

It was only progressively, and more slowly at the central than at the local level, that economic intervention became the dominant theme around which the discourse of urban policy was restructured. During the 1960s, the central state in France stressed its capacity to direct the development of society through its policy of economic planning, of structuring the productive apparatus using public investments and subsidies. In urban planning, on the contrary, economic development of cities was a blind spot. The economy was considered as being outside the urban as the planning discourse defined it, and was taken into consideration only as the exogenous engine of growth, dealt with in urban development plans through global employment forecasts (more often politically negotiated, since subsidies depended on them, than scientifically evaluated), the consequences of which in terms of housing and facilities provision, land development, and the like were to be organized in space by urban planning. Urban policy had to follow and support industrial growth by providing the necessary infrastructure as well as the means of mobilization and reproduction of the work force. In that policy, the city was seen as housing, facilities, transportation, urban centers, shops, office developments, land development—not as production, plants, work.

Today the structure of policy discourse is almost the opposite. Planning (mostly economic but also urban) has lost its hegemonic centrality, and the central state claims only a secondary role in the economy. The foremost legitimacy in the dynamic of the restructuring process is that of the enterprise, nationalized, but most of all private. This is the case in France, but even more in Britain, where the tradition of urban planning was longer and better established, and where the reversal has been even more dramatic (Ambrose 1986). Conversely, local economic development, mostly defined in the limited terms of private business, has progressively come to be the first preoccupation of local governments' urban policies.

But it has been a relatively slow and sometimes conflictual process, with various controversies. In fact, local economic intervention goes back to the 1960s, with the policy of industrial wards. More direct forms of intervention started in the early 1970s, initiated by left-wing local governments in support of workers' struggles against the dismantling of industrial plants that were major employers in the area: LIP, Rateau, Terrin, Manufrance after 1977—all were first of all strong political mobilizations of unions and parties, locally but sometimes also nationally. It was clearly a political struggle against the industrial policy of the right-wing government of the time, and those first attempts at economic intervention were done against previous advice of the Conseil d'Etat and often led to repressive measures by the prefects.

Progressively, however, in parallel to the growth of unemployment, the concern with local development and economic intervention became generalized in most cities of some size, spreading to right-wing local governments as well. It met less and less opposition from the central state until it was finally institutionalized by the left-wing government as part of the law of decentralization in 1982.

Through this quick historical survey, we can see several factors that contribute to the mobilization of local officials. The more traditional ones, related to the interests of the local bourgeoisie, are the concern with growth, economic and urban, that can stimulate local business, improve through multiplier effects the profits of existing activities, and particularly foster the profitability of the real estate and building industry in the production of housing, offices, and industrial and commercial buildings. This is typical of a certain type of urban bourgeoisie controlling those sectors. But it may eventually produce contradictions and splits between those parts of the local bourgeoisie that will be able to benefit from heterogeneous investments, and those that will suffer, to be eventually washed out in the end.[6]

The rapid growth of unemployment has introduced another factor, quite different politically but very pressing. No local politician or party can hope to maintain a position of power locally without stressing that preoccupation with economic growth, without promoting some spectacular action in the field, and eventually without getting some results that could be widely advertised. Whatever the political orientation, to do something for the economy, oriented toward the creation of jobs, has become a hegemonic obligation. It is pushed forward by a strong, explicit social demand, eventually by the pressure of social movements.

The question of jobs and economic dynamism has taken a different form, or rather found a new answer, in the last ten years. It has become, at least in words, the competition for the new technologies. Every city wants to become a "technopolis." This is a new way to deal with the hegemonic obligation, through the more ambitious and valorizing statement of becoming part of the cutting edge of modernity, of building tomorrow's more advanced prosperity.

Looking at the way those factors influence local policies according to the local political, social, and economic situation, it becomes clear that the common concern for local development and jobs hides relatively different positions and practices. The "growth machine" active in so many cities in the United States (Molotch 1976; Logan and Molotch 1987) is a combination of two factors, interests of the local bourgeoisie doing business in urban production, and an answer to the jobs problem. It can probably be found also in many Italian or Spanish cities, but it is less likely to be found in Britain or Sweden, given the local weight of the Labour or Social-Democratic parties and their political traditions, which have partly influenced the whole structure of state policies. In France, researchers have found similar coalitions of real estate agents, builders, developers, architects, lawyers, mayors, in a number of middle-sized cities held by the right (Lorrain and Barthelemy 1980). The long-time connections between the Gaullist party and a similar type of bourgeoisie have also been particularly visible and active in Paris, under the control of President Pompidou's governments, and subsequently of the local government headed by J. Chirac. But because of the strong local influence of left-wing parties, socialist and communist, a large though fluctuating proportion of urban communes do not experience such policies.[7] The political traditions of the left at the municipal level, being oriented toward public housing and public facilities, are thus opposed to "growth coalitions" of a capitalist kind, except in a few cases perhaps, such as Marseille at the time of G. Defferre (see Bleitrach et al. 1981).

Economic intervention to maintain or create jobs, even though it largely uses the same types of procedures, institutional arrangements, and resources in most cities, may in practice take different meanings.[8] This is due to the polarity in the relations between local government on one side, and capital and labor on the other side. There are cleavages in the political meaning of eventually similar subsequent institutional actions. Consider the difference between municipal mobilization to support a workers' union struggle, with occupation of the plant and public demonstrations against the management and eventually the right-wing government (Manufrance in Saint-Etienne has been a symbolic case [Kukawka 1980]), and discreet negotiations between management and a mayor.

It is interesting at this point to note the hostility of some right-wing governments toward a too-active economic intervention of local governments, particularly when they try to incorporate some minimum social concerns. As limited in the possibilities and timid in the intentions as they may be, they still represent for the right an unacceptable threat to business. The economic strategy established by the Greater London Council (GLC 1985; Mackintosh and Wainwright 1987) seems to have sufficiently displeased Mrs. Thatcher that she dismantled the GLC as a whole and the special body it had created, the Greater London Enterprise Board. In France, as mentioned earlier, right-wing governments had been reluctant, up to their defeat in 1981, to let loose the possibility of such policies for local authorities. When they came back to power after 1986, they hardly touched the decentralization reform— which might be considered as evidence of its ambiguities (Preteceille 1988)—whereas they were eager to undo many other things, starting with the nationalizations and following with the improved legal protection of tenants. But one of the few points they changed was precisely to suppress the possibilities of direct economic intervention for municipalities.[9]

The arguments put forward were that municipalities did not have the necessary technical competence to evaluate correctly the economic viability of most projects set up to save enterprises in trouble, and that they were therefore under the threat of excessive and uncontrolled financial risks. It is interesting to note, however, that the possibilities of direct intervention were maintained when it was a case of supporting local development according to the conditions stated in the national plan, or that municipalities could help private business through specialized financial institutions under the conditions that one or more private firms be also part of the capital of those institutions.

Beyond the technical argument, it is possible to give a relatively clear political interpretation of such changes. Municipalities were forbidden to oppose economic restructuring processes on their negative side (devalorization of capital, machines, and skilled labor, restructuring and dispersal of work collectives, and technological potentials). But they were welcome to contribute on their positive side (stimulation of new accumulation processes) if they would accept the objectives set up by the central government and by private business itself. There is a potential contradiction between the fact that municipalities would tend to favor strengthening certain industrial activities (particularly true of many communist municipalities) and the fact that the dominant form of capital accumulation is now financial, which triggers all sorts of speculative investments, specific service and trade activities, and office or warehouse urban development. The British case is probably the more clear-cut example of the gap between the two, with a tremendous growth of financial profits and finance-related activities but a weakening of British industry.

There is also a direct political dimension to the point: only municipalities suffered such restrictions, not the upper tiers of French local government, departments, and regions, in spite of the fact that many large cities would have more technical expertise for these matters than many departments. This is no surprise, since municipalities are the territorial institutions closest to the population, most open to demands, most related to social movements, those that have opposed most strongly the negative effects of restructuring. Departments and regions have moved very little that way and are a more isolated place of power, playing games of notables with few direct links to the population.

The fears of the right and private business about left-wing authorities intervening directly in the local economy have meant that the social ambitions put into it have always been limited, except for a few cases, and hardly subversive of the capitalist order.[10] Local governments, including those on the socialist left, can even be considered to have participated more and more over the years in the ideological glorification of the entrepreneur.

This leads us to the more socially conservative side of local economic intervention, because the widespread, and most often self-satisfied, discourse of local officials on economic policy tends to hide a number of unpleasant realities. A first one is the silence, in most cases, on the question of large enterprises and their impact. Whereas multinationals' weight in the economy has continued to increase, local economic policies seem to view development only through small or middle-sized businesses. A striking symbol can be found in a book by Xavier Greffe (1984), which makes a vibrant case for local development policies. He starts by criticizing the negative effects and numerous diseconomies resulting from the dominance and operations of very large firms, then turns to what he calls the "metaphor of local development," with no further consideration of the problems mentioned, as if large firms could be left out of the picture.

Some claim that it is the only realistic position, since nothing can be done about large firms and since small and middle-sized businesses are efficient for local development; after all, they are the only categories of firms to create a net surplus of jobs in the last ten to fifteen years. The last argument is questionable, because many small or middle-sized firms are in fact dependent on large ones, through subcontracting and externalization of certain tasks. Also many jobs in smaller businesses are unstable, low-quality, low-paid, low-skilled service jobs, whose contribution to real development are doubtful.

As to the first argument, it reveals a deep political problem: what kind of economic policy can tackle the negative aspects of large firms and multinationals? The left in France had tried to do it after its 1981 victory, through nationalizations of large industrial firms, financial institutions and banks, democratization of their management and of the state, greater possibilities of intervention for workers, new procedures of national, regional, and local planning, decentralization, and so on. The fierce resistance of national and international capital, plus its own internal political weakness and conflicts, led the left to a failure. In spite of many promising results, the socialist party decided to move back to a "realist" policy, and progressively turned to compete with the neoliberal right on its own ground: to claim economic efficiency in the terms of the financial profitability of firms, of capitalist entrepreneurship and centralized authoritative management.[11] It is thus not a surprise that the very question is now repressed, in the Freudian sense.

A second hidden problem has to do with the absence, even from the left, in most discourses on local government, of any reference to, and discussion of, the contradictory class character of work relations in local enterprises, as well as in local society more generally.[12] It works as an implicit claim of solidarity and commonality of interests between workers and managers or owners of capital. Common interests may exist to some degree (when competition or financial constraints push one firm out of the market, the capitalist may suffer along with the workers who lose their jobs, and they may want to fight together) but to a limited degree only. In small and middle-sized businesses, exploitation, domination, oppression in work relations are often harder, though less publicized because of the lower degree of unionization and the fragmentation of situations: lower wages, worse material conditions, less social benefits, greater instability, direct paternalism, or even tyranny. It is therefore surprising to see local development so often defined in the very terms of local entrepreneurs. These are, for their part, less naive or more explicitly conscious of such contradictions of interests, since most of them do not seem to be eager to take part in any common elaboration with left-wing local authorities. Some individuals may be more easily seduced or more cooperative, or may more urgently need some local support. But on the whole the experience of local committees for employment launched by the left has proved disappointing.

The last problem hidden by the dominant discourse is, at least in the French case, the gap between the insisting statement of a local priority for economic intervention, and the very limited reality, not only of its effectiveness but also of the resources devoted to it. Directly related municipal expenses represented only 2 percent of total municipal expenditures in 1986. The figure would be slightly higher if one could estimate the loss of municipal income resulting from tax abatements of *taxe professionnelle* (a local tax on business, based on capital assets and salaries). But it would still remain quite low since, in contrast with other countries, French municipalities have not, as a whole, entered a wild competition offering all sorts of subsidies to attract business. If the total product of *taxe professionnelle* has slightly receded in recent years, it is a consequence of measures decided by the central government in 1982 and 1987, and if one neutralizes their effects, the trend resulting from local decisions only is still upward (Direction Générale des Collectivités Locales 1987, 21). A few cities voluntarily decrease the rate of the tax, but these exceptions are often rich cities with a high concentration of tax base, which allows right-wing municipalities to implement locally a neoliberal fiscal policy, as in Paris.

The importance of the rhetorical side in local economics is stressed by such figures. This does not mean, however, that they are a pure illusion, a mask to hide real practices. One has to recognize the place taken today by the public relations side of politics. Policy discourse becomes part of a discourse policy, turned, through the media, toward society as a whole, whether at the national or local level, as part of the work of hegemony. It is not only propaganda, which may prove weak. Politicians and state institutions, central and local, state their capacity to recognize social problems, impose their legitimate definition and solutions, which will in turn contribute to structure the way people, as well as other economic and political actors, think of those problems and define their actions.

However, the limited effectiveness that can be achieved by one particular local authority, pushed forward locally at the same time as central states move backward, can end up as a political trap. The hegemonic obligation to pursue local economic development can result in frustration and political failure. According to some observers, many former mayors were defeated in the 1989 municipal elections because they had promised a great deal in 1983 on economic activity and jobs and achieved very little.

It is also an economic trap, since the isolated action of one particular authority cannot reasonably expect to contribute to any structural change in the economy and production relations. What is claimed to be a voluntary policy is largely a market relation where the supply side (investors) is dominant and the demand side (local governments) is fragmented and competing. Local economic development policy may modify marginally the location of plants or accelerate some investments, but studies looking at that market from the enterprise side tend to show that local incentives are only secondary criteria for business decision making. With the high level of fragmentation of local government in France, and the withdrawal of central reforms and policies that could have given a different meaning and impact to local initiatives, it is surprising that we do not observe a wilder competition between municipalities. This might be another argument in favor of the importance of politics and political traditions.

There is another paradox of the present situation. The left has resisted better in France than in Britain, it has protected much of its welfare and collective consumption-oriented urban policies, it controls the central government and half of the local ones. And yet it has been (up to now) unable to challenge the dominant representation of the enterprise focused on the capitalist entrepreneur with an alternative model able to open different economic and social perspectives. This is not simply a defeat in the face of neoliberal ideology. It is a deeper and more complex problem. The French left, having been largely maintained in the opposition, was ideologically structured around two traditions. One was opposition to the system in economic relations, refusing any kind of implication in management, unlike the German unions. This is the communist tradition, which has been on this point the dominant one in the union movement. Another was acceptance of the laws of the system, searching social justice through complementary redistribution. This is the socialist tradition, more influential in municipalities and the public sector.

The economic crisis has challenged both. Because the capitalist system could no longer be seen as efficient, the socialists had to take a step back and look for some other economic rules. Because the hegemonic crisis made it an open possibility for the left to take power, the communists could no longer refuse to participate in any kind of management. Any reference to the Soviet model was seen as less and less attractive. They had to consider setting up an alternative project for economic relations, management and policies. It could not be only an abstract statement about justice and democracy, it had also to tackle the problem of efficiency—even if the notion had to be redefined—in a complex economic system, from the shop floor to macroeconomics and international relations, from the industrial plant to the school, the hospital, the bank, the research unit.

In France and Italy, the second half of the 1970s saw many new elaborations about the possibilities of increasing productivity in different ways by liberating the creative powers of workers, about new management criteria and methods, new definitions of social efficiency integrating external economies and diseconomies (problems of training, health, safety, pollution) and new relations with users or consumers. Unfortunately, this outburst of new ideas, probably one of the most interesting and less publicized aspects of Eurocommunism, was progressively sterilized and stopped. In Italy the effort has failed up to now because the PCI (Italian Communist party) has not been able to convince the PSI (Socialist party) to take part in a united left coalition at the national level, although it exists in many places at the local level. And in France, it failed because the internal crisis of the left, after 1977, weakened such innovative trends in spite of its victory in 1981, and ended up in the socialist turn to "economic realism" already mentioned.

Such ideas have not completely disappeared in both countries; many local experiences were inspired by them. Many cooperatives have been started, and the unions have had to fight new battles and develop new forms of expertise to be able to make positive counterproposals in cases of restructuring that they criticized. In France, the presence of elected representatives of workers on the boards of nationalized firms has also stimulated such innovations. But these practices have little echo, and no longer any support in the national positions of the socialist party, fascinated as it is now by the apparent recovery and renewed dynamism of the capitalist economy. They consider the present ways of restructuring to be inevitable, if not desirable, and are mostly worried about making them socially more acceptable and less painful, and about helping workers to become more competitive themselves. A symbol of such positions can be found in the socialists' choice of Bernard Tapie, a self-made entrepreneur specialized in making money out of the collapse of industrial firms, as their candidate for a highly publicized election in Marseilles in the spring of 1989.

At the same time, the contradiction between economic and social efficiency and financial profitability has not decreased; it comes out in the open from time to time in the form of stock exchange scandals, speculative operations on industrial takeovers, or financial ventures, which are supposed to strengthen the economy. The difficulties experienced by small shareholders after the last stock exchange crisis have also raised doubts about the marvels promised by the new popular capitalism that denationalizations were supposed to promote, just as the increasing number of major ecological disasters has raised doubts about multinational firms' capacity to provide a positive future for society. But strong pressure by the media has repressed deeper economic debate, and has reduced the problem to individual scandals, of a political nature when possible. The capitalist class itself has recognized the necessity, in order to overcome the crisis of productivity, of restructuring the work process in a way that may involve workers more and gives them more opportunities for creative initiatives: quality circles, flexible working hours, and production teams managing themselves as the way to fulfill their production goals.

The debates on economic alternatives have not disappeared altogether.[13] Many local practices are attempted, but they have very little echo nationally, and no influence on the socialist government policies. The only potential force that had been able in the past to break down the consensus on such issues—the communist party—is so frozen up in its shift back to its own kind of internal conservatism that, even when they make a good point, its critiques and propositions have lost most of their credibility and receive little attention.

In contrast with an intense discourse on economic intervention corresponding to limited actions and effects, there is an area of local policies that in France is little advertised but represents a considerable share of local spending and has strong economic impacts—the production, management, and distribution of industrial urban services and facilities. In 1987 investments of local authorities represented 12 percent of the total national investment, and a little less than a quarter of the total investment of enterprises. This evidently constitutes a major economic potential, which has, over the years, been used by left-wing local authorities to achieve some degree of local social redistribution in favor of the popular classes.[14] But it has not been used very much as a tool to promote a different economic organization. On the contrary, the structure of the production of those industrial urban services, which had been an area of many innovations in the public sector since the beginning of the century, has moved toward an increasing domination of a few large firms, which tend to control the technology, the markets, the prices, and product definition. And this is not a recent privatization, like the 1986–1988 denationalizations. It is a thirty-year continuous process, which left-wing local authorities have not fought and have even taken some part in, and which has not been opposed by any counterpolicy of renationalization (or remunicipalization) from the left (Lorrain 1982). Even though these firms are essentially dependent on public funding, this huge potential is abandoned, all the more so since the fragmented system of local authorities leaves individual municipalities, most of which have little expertise, in the hands of those giant firms.

This does not take place in the same way in all countries. It seems that Germany, for example, has maintained a more public system for those municipal urban industrial services. France is even more privatized in that field than Thatcher's Britain, since the British policy of privatization of the water supply has opened the market for French firms, an unforeseen consequence of privatization that has given some trouble to the Conservatives because of its symbolic value.

Why has France gone that way in this sector? Why has the left made no move, even after 1981, to change things, to nationalize these firms that, because of their close relation to public funding and public markets and services, should have been among the first ones chosen? Beyond the ideological climate of worship of private business, it may have been a cumulative effect over time of the technical weakness of municipalities, in contrast with their capacity of innovation in public services at the beginning of the century. Another important element of explanation, however, is that the sector is in France a major source of illegal indirect funding for political parties. Several recent financial scandals have, for the first time, resulted from or led to the opening of official investigations by judges. But this illegal funding was common knowledge for everyone acquainted with the field of municipal services. To obtain a contract, any private firm would have to give back a certain percentage of the total by various channels, a classical one being to subcontract quasifictitious work to a firm indirectly owned by the party. All parties have taken large benefits, and thus the private firms involved have, in reverse, had many implicit ways to influence decisions and protect themselves. It will be interesting to see how far the present investigations regarding one of the major private firms in public works will go, and what will come out of it, since it is particularly connected to the funding of the socialist party.

Institutional Changes and Political Relations

At the same time that local governments are mobilizing for local economic development, they are also, in many countries, taken into a process of institutional change that tends to redefine their responsibilities inside the state. In most cases, this process of reorganization of the division of state labor between territorial levels has moved toward decentralization. Thus local authorities are not only pushed toward more intervention, they are also provided new institutional resources to do so.

The fact that it happens in so many different countries (France, the United States, Spain, Denmark, Mexico, Brazil, Argentina) and that it is fostered in various ways by the agencies associated with the international capitalist management of the crisis, austerity policies, and economic restructuring processes (OECD, IMF, the World Bank) supports an interpretation that considers such changing institutional arrangements as coherent with, if not necessary for, economic restructuring. The argument could be summarized in the following way.

The crisis of the Fordist regime of accumulation challenges the previous modes of state regulation, particularly those related to economic planning and to the management of the norm of consumption codified in the welfare state, which have now become an obstacle. A decentralization policy makes it possible to get rid of that norm of consumption in a flexible way, fractioning it into local social policies by moving the state responsibilities for welfare and consumption from central to local level. Such a shift to fragmented localities helps to dissolve the global social compromise as well as established class identities, which are an obstacle to the restructuring of the wage relation. It accelerates locally the dismantling of recognized social rights to public provision of collective consumption, by setting up a quasicommodity link between taxes and public provision. And finally, by fostering competition between local authorities in the race for investment in new technology firms, it helps impose "flexibility" on local economies, on local labor markets, and mobilizes local resources in favor of that flexibility. Former remarks about the stakes and privatization processes in the sphere of the production of urban industrial services can be seen as a complement to this type of interpretation more than a counterargument.

How far can such a line of reasoning explain actual institutional and policy changes? The British case presents a difficulty, since it is clearly a case of restructuring of the norm of consumption and imposition of greater flexibility and generalized market commodity relations, but through more state centralization and not decentralization. The reasons for that seem to be largely political. Many local governments, being Labour controlled, actively resist the implementation of those central policies (the Liverpool case has been one of the fiercest battles; see Parkinson 1985), and some, of the "new urban left," even strive to expand the benefits of noncommodified public provision to new categories of deprived population. These political reasons are also historical, since the decentralized form of welfare provision in Great Britain and the role of local government in the constitution of the traditional working-class identity can only be analyzed as products of a long-term history of class relations and political processes in that country.

Certainly decentralization policies in the United States fit much better with the above interpretation, or even those in Denmark, to take a contrasting case that is usually considered as part of the Scandinavian model of welfare state. In those two countries, central states reduce their share of the funding of public provision of collective consumption, and leave it up to the local authorities to maintain their chosen standard of provision, which means then raising the fiscal pressure and having to accept the political price of it. Considering the structure of the local tax system, the limited ability to redistribute resources between poor and rich localities, the pressure not to tax business for employment reasons, and thus the difficulty (or even impossibility in the Danish case, where local tax revenue comes from a local income tax on households only) to organize any local social redistribution, this can only contribute to increased social segregation. Many residents vote with their feet by moving out of localities where they would have to pay for poorer residents, and then keep the poor out of their privileged areas through real estate prices. But besides some similar features, only the United States case really seems to be an example of local policies functional to economic restructuring down to the level of state and local government policies (Fainstein and Fainstein, forthcoming). The Danish case fits in terms of trend, but not in terms of actual development of the welfare state: the national and municipal weight of the Social-Democratic party maintains a level of public provision of collective consumption services that is still quite high comparatively, and does not match the deregulated, commodified, fragmented, and competitive model of social reproduction that would be the "norm of consumption" coherent with the flexible regime of accumulation.

The French case is quite ambivalent in its own way. The incomplete definition and implementation of a decentralization reform initially launched by the left to promote a "new citizenship" has progressively resembled more and more the model adequate to flexible accumulation.[15] But again this is more true in terms of trend than in absolute level of state intervention and public provision. And the political dynamic of social movements of the 1970s, which pushed forward the decentralization issue at the same time as it contributed to the access of the left to governmental power, still shapes municipal policies in a way that should not be underestimated. Probably the same could also be said, to some extent, of decentralized policies in Italy and Spain, even if political relations are different there (see Harvey Molotch's chapter in this volume for a comparative discussion of some features of Italian urban politics).

Thus it seems unlikely that one could simply deduce the meaning of institutional changes and subsequent urban policies from only the dynamic of economic restructuring. One should rather consider this dynamic itself as shaped and channeled through political relations of power, political relations that may introduce more than secondary variations in economic and institutional arrangements and changes. More than any direct response to economic changes, and not underestimating their considerable pressure and its internationally homogenizing character, changes in state structures and urban policies are closely related to the tentative answers to the hegemony crisis going with the economic crisis. And these answers are always specified by the nationally and historically variable capacity of political forces to express the various conflicting or diverging social interests in demands, projects, or policies at the national and local level.

This argument should not, however, be understood as a mere rehabilitation of the autonomous political actor, as if politics were, contrary to economic determinism, free of any social constraint and roots in social interests. Political processes are themselves a complex expression of social relations and social interests largely structured by the economy, by production relations first of all, with their contradictory character central to the capitalist mode of production, and not only by the one-sided interests of the dominant class. It is one thing to recognize political differences and their impact, it is another to go back to an idea of pure freedom of action for politicians. There is political indetermination in the sense that even the most fundamental social relations are expressed in contradictory social processes, including political ones, the outcome of which is not predetermined elsewhere (by some economic "law," for example) but historically produced by social struggles, first of all class struggles. If alternative policies are practiced, it is not just because clever politicians have designed them, but because social forces, social movements, have opened the possibility of such alternatives and are able to give them life. Indeed at some point political elaboration of programs and solutions is needed to crystallize the potential of social forces into positive mobilization. But without social forces and movements that can make them their own, these elaborations, however brilliant, will be powerless, and either fail or fall back on the "realism" of the management of dominant interests.

In that sense, to speak of political processes also means to consider the state as part of them—not the state as an independent subject with freedom of choice and decision, but a socially and historically constituted state, a process of historical and material condensation of relations of power between classes (see Poulantzas 1978). It means that the state is simultaneously cleft by contradictions, different interests, variegated movements of change or resistance to change, and relatively unified as long as dominant interests have not been defeated in the state and in the economy.

Their relative disinterest in the state is a curious weakness of many of the regulation-theory developments. Even if the central stakes of economic restructuring are internal to production processes, they are also linked to political relations, as we have seen. And in the perspective of the regulation theory itself, restructuring the accumulation regime implies restructuring wage relations and forms of consumption, a dimension of regulation processes in which politics and the state are deeply involved. Thus economic restructuring can hardly be analyzed without considering state policies, central and local ones, in their diversities and their relative unity. The major but ambiguous changes experienced in French politics and policies over the last ten years oblige researchers to face this difficult problem. The comparison between changes experienced in different developed capitalist countries obliges us even more to accept the necessity of complexity in theoretical developments, instead of just using theory as a magic key, a simple paradigm from which everything can be derived.

NOTES

1. The influence of Marxist ideas has become so widespread and diffused, but also so diverse in its intensity, points of reference, and methods, that the designation of a Marxist "side" is mostly a political and ideological artifact. Some interpret the recession of such a block identity as a sign of the "crisis of Marxism," if not of its desired collapse, but it can also be seen as the sign of a more mature scientific attitude.

2. These issues have been the focus of the Centre de Sociologie Urbaine seminar during the last three years. A first set of the presentations can be found in Freyssenet and Magri (1989).

3. Scott and Storper (1986) are among those who have developed this more spatially concerned approach from the regulation theory.

4. See Boddy (1988) for a presentation of some of the elements in that debate, or Sayer (1989) for a closer examination of the consistency and relevance of some of the features supposed to be characteristic of the flexible organization of production.

5. For the French case on urban industrial services, see the works of Dominique Lorrain (1978, 1985, 1987).

6. Huet et al. (1977) have shown in the case of Rennes how the changes in local urban policies resulting from the increased dominance and presence of monopoly capital had accelerated cleavages inside the local bourgeoisie.

7. In 1977, 81 municipalities out of 221 with more than 30,000 inhabitants had a socialist mayor and 72 a communist one. Since the last municipal elections in March 1989, there are 132 socialist mayors in the 384 communes with more than 20,000 inhabitants and 53 communist ones.

8. See D. Lorrain and P. Kukawka (1989) for the results of a comparative analysis of 15 municipalities on the issue of local economic policy.

9. In a law significantly called "law to improve decentralization" (Law 88-13 of January the 5th, 1988).

10. Concerning interventions like LIP and Manufrance, analysts on the right have argued that workers cannot manage production themselves. LIP and Manufrance became dangerous symbols of worker management. This explains why the right was so eager to do away with them. Raymond Barre, prime minister at the time, forcefully declared, "Manufrance, c'est fini!"

11. A more detailed account of these events, and some elements of interpretation, can be found in Preteceille (1985b).

12. This problem is clearly stated by Nicole Rousier (1987), who underlines the fact that claiming economic intervention as a legitimate field of action could, perhaps should, lead local authorities to claim with it the right to contribute to the redefinition of the wage relation.

13. See Alain Lipietz's 1989 book as a recent example.

14. See our research on segregation and social access to collective consumption: Preteceille 1981b, Pinçon-Charlot, Preteceille and Rendu 1986.

15. Absence of a thorough reform of the local tax system that is needed to reduce fiscal inequalities which reproduce or reinforce social inequalities, absence of a status of public elected officials allowing modest wage earners to run for public offices, absence of mechanisms of local democracy enhancing the role and capacity of initiative of citizens (Preteceille 1988).

REFERENCES

Aglietta, Michel. 1976. *Régulation et Crises du Capitalisme: L'Expérience des Etats-Unis.* Paris: Calmann-Levy.

Aglietta, Michel, and Anton Brender. 1984. *Les Metamorphoses de la Société Salariale: La France en Projet.* Paris: Calmann-Levy.

Ambrose, Peter. 1986. *Whatever Happened to Planning?* London: Methuen.

Becquart-Leclerc, Jeannette, Vincent Hoffmann-Martinot, and Jean-Yves Nevers. 1987. *Austerité et Innovation Fiscale: Les Stratégies Politico-Financières des Communes.* Bordeaux: Institut d'Etudes Politiques.

Bleitrach, Danielle, et al. 1981. *Classe Ouvrière et Social-Démocratie: Lille et Marseille.* Paris: Editions Sociales.

Boccara, Paul. 1974. *Etudes sur le Capitalisme Monopoliste d'Etat, Sa Crise et Son Issue.* Paris: Editions Sociales.

Boddy, Martin. 1988. "Industrial Restructuring, Post-Fordism and New Industrial Spaces: A Critique." In *Reestructuraçao Economica e Formas de Urbanizaçao,* ed. Licia Valladares and Edmond Preteceille. Sao Paulo: Editora Nobel.

Boyer, Robert. 1986a. *La Théorie de la Régulation: Une Analyse Critique.* Paris: Agalma-La Découverte.

———. 1986b. *Capitalismes Fin de Siècle.* Paris: PUF.

Boyer, Robert, and J. Mistral. 1978. *Accumulation, Inflation, Crises.* Paris: PUF.

Capecchi, Vittorio. 1988. "The Informal Economy and the Development of Flexible Specialization." In *Reestructuraçao Economica e Formas de Urbanizaçao,* ed. Licia Valladares and Edmond Preteceille. Sao Paulo: Editora Nobel.

Coriat, Benjamin. 1978. *L'Atelier et le Chronomètre.* Paris: C. Bourgois.

Direction Générale des Collectivités Locales. 1987. *Guide Statistique de la Fiscalité Directe Locale 1987.* Paris: La Documentation Française.

Dunleavy, Patrick. 1980. *Urban Political Analysis: The Politics of Collective Consumption.* London: Macmillan.

————. 1986. "The Growth of Sectoral Cleavages and the Stabilization of State Expenditures." *Society and Space* 4:129–44.

Fainstein, Susan S., and Norman Fainstein. (forthcoming). "The Ambivalent State: Economic Development Policy in the U.S. Federal System under the Reagan Administration." In *State and Locality: A Comparative Perspective on State Restructuring*, ed. Christopher Pickvance and Edmond Preteceille. London: Frances Pinter.

Freyssenet, Michel. 1984a. "Division du Travail, Taylorisme et Automatisation: Confusions, Différences et Enjeux." In *Le Taylorisme*, ed. M. De Montmolin and O. Pastre. Paris: Editions La Découverte.

————. 1984b. "La Réqualification des Opérateurs et la Forme Sociale Actuelle d'Automatisation." *Sociologie du Travail* 4:422–33.

Freyssenet, Michel, and Susanna Magri, eds. 1989. *Les Rapports Sociaux et Leurs Enjeux: Seminaire du CSU, 1986–1988*, vol. 1. Paris: Centre de Sociologie Urbaine.

GLC. 1985. *The London Industrial Strategy*. London: Greater London Council.

Greffe, Xavier. 1984. *Territoires en France: Les Enjeux Economiques de la Décentralisation*. Paris: Economica.

Hoffmann-Martinot, Vincent, and Jean-Yves Nevers. 1985. "Les Maires Urbains Face à la Crise." *Annales de la Recherche Urbaine* 28:121–32.

Holloway, John, and Sol Picciotto, eds. 1978. *State and Capital: A Marxist Debate*. London: Edward Arnold.

Huet, Armel, et al. 1977. *Urbanisation Capitaliste et Pouvoir Local*. Paris: J.-P. Delarge.

INSEE. 1974. *Fresque Historique du Système Productif*. Paris: INSEE.

————. 1981. *La Crise du Système Productif*. Paris: INSEE.

Joussemet, Anita. 1988. *Services Urbains et Démocratie Locale: Compte-rendu de Recherche, Première Partie*. Paris: Centre d'Etude des Mouvements Sociaux.

Kukawka, Pierre. 1980. *Manufrance: Radiographie d'une Lutte*. Paris: Editions Sociales.

Leborgne, Danièle, and Alain Lipietz. 1988. "Flexibilité Défensive et Flexibilité Offensive: Les Défis des Nouvelles Technologies et de la Competition Mondiale." In *Reestructuraçao Economica e Formas de Urbanizaçao*, ed. Licia Valladares and Edmond Preteceille. Sao Paulo: Editora Nobel.

Lipietz, Alain. 1979. *Crise et Inflation, Pourquoi?* Paris: Maspero.

————. 1983. *Le Monde Enchanté: De la Valeur a l'Envol Inflationniste*. Paris: La Decouverte-Maspero.

————. 1989. *Choisir l'Audace*. Paris: La Découverte.

Logan, John R., and Harvey Molotch. 1987. *Urban Fortunes: The Political Economy of Place*. Berkeley and Los Angeles: University of California Press.

Lorrain, Dominique. 1978. *Le Secteur Paramunicipal: Capital et Collectivités Locales: Les Transports Urbains dans les Agglomérations de Province.* Paris: Fondation des Villes.

————. 1982. "Le Secteur Public Local entre Nationalisation et Décentralisation." *Annales de la Recherche Urbaine* 13:53–104.

————. 1985. "*L'Industrie des Réseaux Urbains en France: Des Origines Nationales à une Dynamique Mondiale.*" ISA-CUSUP Conference on The Urban and Regional Impact of the New International Division of Labour, Hong Kong.

————. 1987. "Le Grand Fossé? Le Débat Public/Privé et les Services Urbains." *Politique et Management Public* 5(3):83–102.

Lorrain, Dominique, and Jean-Roland Barthelemy. 1980. *Les Changements dans l'Amenagement et l'Urbanisme et le Gouvernement Municipal.* Paris: Fondation des Villes.

Lorrain, Dominique, and Pierre Kukawka. 1989. "Quinze Municipalités et l'Économie." *Revue d'Économie Régionale et Urbaine* 2:283–306.

Mackintosh, M., and H. Wainwright, eds. 1987. *A Taste of Power: The Politics of Local Economics.* London: Verso.

Magri, Susanna, and Christian Topalov. 1987. "De la Cité-Jardin à la Ville Rationalisé: Un Tournant du Projet Reformateur. Etude Comparative France–Grande-Bretagne–Italie–Etats-Unis." *Revue Française de Sociologie* 28(3):417–51.

————. 1988. "'Reconstruire': L'Habitat Populaire au Lendemain de la Première Guerre Mondiale. Etude Comparative France–Grande-Bretagne–Italie–Etats-Unis." *Archives Européennes de Sociologie* 29(2):319–70.

Molotch, Harvey. 1976. "The City as a Growth Machine." *American Journal of Sociology* 82(2):309–30.

Parkinson, Michael. 1985. *Liverpool on the Brink.* Hermitage: Policy Journals.

Pinçon-Charlot, Monique, Edmond Preteceille, and Paul Rendu. 1986. *Segrégation Urbaine: Classes Sociales et Equipements Collectifs en Région Parisienne.* Paris: Editions Anthropos.

Poulantzas, Nicos. 1978. *L'Etat, le Pouvoir, le Socialisme.* Paris: Presses Universitaires de France.

Preteceille, Edmond. 1977. "Equipements Collectifs et Consommation Sociale." *International Journal of Urban and Regional Research* 1(1):101–23.

————. 1981a. "Collective Consumption, the State and the Crisis of Capitalist Society." In *City, Class and Capital: New Developments in the Political Economy of Cities and Regions,* ed. Michael Harloe and Elizabeth Lebas. London: Edward Arnold.

————. 1981b. "Left-Wing Local Governments and Services Policy in

France." *International Journal of Urban and Regional Research* 5(3): 411–25.

———. 1985a. "Crise Hégémonique et Restructuration Territoriale de l'Etat: La Gauche et la Décentralisation en France." *Revue Internationale d'Action Communautaire* 13(53):49–59.

———. 1985b. "The Industrial Challenge and the French Left: Central and Local Issues." *International Journal of Urban and Regional Research* 9(2):273–89.

———. 1988. "Decentralization in France: New Citizenship or Restructuring Hegemony?" *European Journal of Political Research* 16:409–24.

———. 1989. "Rapports Politiques de Classe et Rapports Internes au Politique." In *Les Rapports Sociaux et Leurs Enjeux: Séminaire du CSU, 1986–1988*, vol. 1, ed. Michel Freyssenet and Susanna Magri. Paris: Centre de Sociologie Urbaine.

Rousier, Nicole. 1987. "L'Emploi et le Discours sur le Développement Local." *Revue d'Economie Regionale et Urbaine* 1:109–16.

Saunders, Peter. 1979. *Urban Politics: A Sociological Interpretation.* London: Hutchinson.

Sayer, Andrew. 1989. "Post-Fordism in Question." *International Journal of Urban and Regional Research* 13(4):666–95.

Scott, Allen J., and Michael Storper, eds. 1986. *Production, Work and Territory: The Geographical Anatomy of Industrial Capitalism.* London: Allen & Unwin.

CHAPTER 3

Industrial Restructuring,
State Intervention, and
Uneven Development in the
United States and Japan

Richard Child Hill

This chapter explores the interplay among industrial
production systems organized by transnational corporations, urban and regional development strategies mounted by local and
national states, and distributional outcomes for companies,
workers, and communities. The reflections and contrasts presented here stem from research on the auto industry and auto-
dependent regions in the United States and Japan.[1]

I will approach issues of economic restructuring from the vantage point of industrial production systems. Production system is
a concept for analyzing how labor processes and economic ex-
changes among firms are socially organized over space. Firms
become linked into production systems as they develop, manufac-

60

ture, and market specific commodities (see Hamilton 1981; Scott 1983; Holmes 1986).

In the automobile industry, for example, production systems involve thousands of firms, including parents, subsidiaries, and subcontractors. These firms specialize in the production of component parts (some 15,000 go into a car) or in a stage of the production process (for example, dashboard assembly). Firms ranging in size from enormous transnational companies to family workshops are interlinked in value-added hierarchies that function over regional, national, and international space with varying degrees of logistical precision and efficiency.

The spatial concentration and growth of enterprises knit together in production systems generates local employment and regional development (Jacobs 1984). Balanced development, that which passes the benefits of industrial investment onto the local population as a higher standard of living, will advance to the extent that a region's localities can maximize their share of a production system's forward and backward linkages, high value-added intermediate goods, services and components, and professional, technical, and scientific expertise (Hymer 1971; Sklair 1985). Therein lies the potential for structured conflict among the development concerns of localities, the industrial policies of nation-states, and the production strategies of transnational corporations.

Why draw comparisons between the United States and Japan? Because the two societies now intermesh in such a fashion that political-economic events in one often influence political-economic outcomes in the other. Interactions between the United States and Japan via the world market and the international relations system are transforming production organization, reordering state priorities, and posing critical urban and regional issues in each society. In the analysis to follow, I emphasize the interplay between features distinctive to each society and the commonalities the two societies share by virtue of their mutual engagement in a global political economy.

On the economic front, U.S. manufacturers are under pressure, via the competitive strength of Japanese exports from abroad and Japanese direct foreign investment at home, to restructure their

Fordist mass-production systems in the direction of Japan's Toyotaist flexible-production paradigm. Japanese manufacturers, on the other hand, are under pressure, via the U.S.-dominated international relations system, to restructure their regionally concentrated and nationally protected production systems along U.S. global production lines. In both societies, economic restructuring poses severe problems of social dislocation and challenges each nation's capacity for social reorganization.

On the national political front, many state and local governments in the United States have responded to international economic competition by altering their functional priorities—from an emphasis on regulation and social welfare to a model, strongly influenced by Japan's "developmental state," that emphasizes government-facilitated economic growth. In Japan, on the other hand, Western pressures for more domestic consumption (to reduce Japan's trade surplus) and the threat of regional deindustrialization (from the globalization of manufacturing) have recently prompted government policies more in tune with a U.S.-style regulatory state.

In both Japan and the United States, industrial restructuring and rearranged state priorities are generating new patterns of uneven development and political cleavage.

Genus and Species

> Just as two old buildings look similar until an earthquake reveals their different structures, so the similarity of the industrial societies was in part an illusion, encouraged by a world that did not test their differences. (Piore and Sabel [1984, 164])

North American social science provides a rather weak foundation for the comparative study of capitalist political economies. The problem, Chalmers Johnson has argued (1987, 1988), is that Western political economists of every stripe have been preoccupied with elaborate general theories about social processes while remaining largely indifferent to variations in the concrete institutions through which those abstracted processes are actually manifested.

At first blush, Johnson seems off the mark, at least when it comes to neo-Marxist scholarship. After all, Marxist theorists emphasize the historical specificity of capitalist institutions and they vigorously criticize neoclassical economists for their lack of interest in historical knowledge and their (fallacious) attempts to universalize what are in fact temporally bound institutional practices (see, for example, Sweezy 1953). Yet, because Marxist analysts seldom seek out comparative knowledge about capitalist institutions, they often fall into a similar analytic mold. Marxists, too, have tended to (fallaciously) generalize to all advanced capitalist societies the manner of functioning of their own society's institutions. If neoclassicists too often fall prey to the pitfalls of transhistorical generalization, then neo-Marxists too often fall prey to the pitfalls of transnational generalization. Or so it seems today.

The theoretical disinterest in comparative political economy rests on a widely shared assumption that institutions in industrial capitalist societies converge through a process of "natural" selection in the international marketplace. As Piore and Sable have observed (1984, 10–11),

> Smith saw the competitive market as the ideal system of exchange; Marx saw the market and factory as the way station to socialism. But both believed that survival in [the] economic system imposes severe constraints on the survivors. To endure, companies must adopt the unique form of social and technical organization that is most suited to the conditions of the moment. Groups, even nations, that deviate from this ideal are threatened by extinction at the hands of those who conform to it.

Once one accepts this premise, it becomes unthinkable that there could be, during any given historical epoch, equally efficient ways to organize a capitalist political economy. National and regional differences pale in theoretical significance next to the commonalities enforced by the threat of extinction in the market.

Hindsight suggests that the lack of postwar intellectual interest in comparative political economy also rested upon the material foundations of one nation's hegemony over the world system. As F. E. Wakeman (1988, 87) has recently observed,

Clear categories seem to have accompanied imperial world structures. Periods such as the late nineteenth century or the 1950s and 1960s, in which we have had clear conceptualizations of what the social sciences ought to be doing, have been periods in which the world itself appeared to be much clearer, as least in terms of architechtonic world structures. As these structures lose their clarity, so do the categories of social science lose their limpidity and rigor.

As the technological and institutional practices defining a hegemonic, capitalist world trajectory break apart, specificities in each nation's industrial and labor traditions, formerly relegated to the background, move to the forefront of theoretical concern. Nowhere is the absence of a genuinely comparative political economy more starkly visible than in the inability among Western theorists to explain the economic achievements of Japan, arguably the most advanced industrial capitalist economy in the world today. As Chalmers Johnson has observed, although "Japan is an advanced capitalist democracy, the institutions of capitalism it has built in the context of its particular experience with industrialization differ fundamentally from those encountered in American capitalism in ways that neither Adam Smith, Karl Marx nor Milton Keynes would have understood. [Institutions such as] labor unions, joint stock companies, and banking systems may have the same names in Japanese as we use in English but they function in different ways with different results" (1987, 415). What is needed, Johnson goes on to argue, is not a general theory that posits how economic forces would interact if institutions did not exist, but a comparative political economy that studies how economic objectives are actualized through institutions. For it is through institutions and struggles to institutionalize rules that are favorable to one group or another that theory is translated into practice.

Thus, to know one capitalist society is not to know them all. Or, as Piore and Sabel (1984, 162–64) put it, "Even if capitalist industrial societies are all of a genus, there are also distinct species." Species of capitalism result from the intersection of place, time, and experience. While all societies mechanize and organize production in the same world, they do so at different world-historical moments (see Dore 1973). Moreover, because some elements of an industrial production system can be substituted for others without impairing the capitalist core, shared characteristics of a common system intertwine with unique national or regional histories. Today, individual differences are shaping responses to shared crises and foreshadow possibilities for alternative forms of organization. The interplay of commonality and diversity will therefore guide the discussion that follows.[2]

Fordism and Toyotaism

Fordism

U.S. companies have excelled at organizing vertically integrated, mass production systems that turn out standardized goods with minutely specialized work forces. As exemplified in the U.S. auto industry, the so-called Fordist model of mass production assumes that industrial practices are most efficient and competitive when (1) equipment and workers are highly specialized; (2) automation is extensive; (3) goods are produced in long runs on huge machines requiring long setup times; (4) workers are kept constantly active making as many parts for assemblies as possible in a set period of time; (5) a master schedule organizes the manufacture and delivery of parts, a schedule designed to keep machines running despite problems that might develop at a few work stations or suppliers; (6) statistical sampling techniques are used for quality control; (7) as much production as possible is done in house to ensure price, quality, and supply (Cusumano 1988).

Specific historical and institutional circumstances conditioned the emergence of the Fordist model of industrial organization in the United States. U.S. manufacturing expertise took shape between the mid-1800s and early 1900s and advanced the industrial knowhow of the day, including machines made of interchangeable parts, specialized production equipment, segmented production processes, and techniques for coordinating production flow for the high-volume manufacture of complex, standardized goods. Land, energy, and capital were cheap. A national rail system opened up huge markets and reduced the distribution costs for intermediate parts. After World War II, U.S. manufacturing companies developed a widely dispersed network of assembly plants to facilitate national distribution and supplied them from a few large-scale parts production centers exploiting economies of scale (Shimada and MacDuffie 1987).

U.S. industrial relations also shaped and were shaped by the Fordist logic of mass production. Management viewed labor abstractly, as a factor of production to be allocated efficiently. Like machines, workers performed best when they were interchangeable, replaceable, and closely supervised. Workers organized in opposition to that view. A compromise between labor and management was worked out over time. Workers protected themselves from discretionary abuses of authority and managers assured scheduled tasks were carried out without disruption through mutual agreement on a system of closely defined job classifications, task assignments, work rules, and supervision.

In sum, Fordism is a historically created and institutionalized profit logic based on economies of scale achieved through the mass production of standardized commodities by a deskilled work force. Productivity increases are generated by annexing workers to single, routine operations. Wage costs are reduced by simplifying labor. Labor control derives from management monopoly over knowledge of the production process.

"Global Fordism"—the unequal allocation of world labor and its products among various countries—is simply the extension of national Fordist regimes of "intensive" accumulation onto a global plane (Lipietz 1987). With global Fordism, the international division of labor in manufacturing is (1) increasingly subdivided into a number of partial operations that are (2) located at different industrial sites throughout the world according to (3) the most profitable combination of labor, capital, government subsidies, and transportation costs and (4) centrally coordinated through a headquarter's global strategy (Froebel, Heinrichs, and Kreye 1980; Lipietz 1986, 1987).

The world car, built out of standardized parts and designed for production in all the world's markets, illustrates global Fordism in the world automobile industry. Ford Motor Company recognized the cost advantages of global integration in Europe in the mid-1960s. This strategy, Ford concluded, would eliminate duplication of research and design staff in its German and English subsidiaries, spread design and some retooling costs over a larger volume, make possible bulk buying and longer production runs with standardized components, and give added flexibility in responding to strikes and production breakdowns (Hainer and Koslofsky 1979).

In the 1970s Ford gave birth to the Fiesta—a car designed in Europe, with engines produced in Valencia, Spain, and transaxles made in Bordeaux, France. The Fiesta was assembled in Valencia, Dagenham, England, and Saarlouis, Germany, and marketed in the EEC and North America. Ford followed the Fiesta with the Fiera, a car made in the Philippines, Taiwan, and Thailand. The Fiera's engine, transmission, and brakes came from Ford subsidiaries in England, its light rear axles and differentials from Argentina, its heavy-duty axles and some engine parts from Australia, and its steering gears, windshield wipers, and shock absorbers from Japan. Remaining Fiera parts were manufactured in the assembly plants of each producing country or purchased from local sources (Jones 1981, 9).

Spreading manufacturing and assembly plants over a number of countries gave Ford leverage over individual nations and unions. Nations desired export earnings from direct foreign investment. Unions desired local employment. Both would be less inclined to impose controls on Ford's activities if it threatened disinvestment and layoffs as it shifted production to parallel locations elsewhere. Ford's operation in Spain in the 1970s is a case in point. Ford found Spain attractive because demand was growing there, and Spanish labor was half to one-third as costly as that in the United Kingdom and West Germany. But the Spanish government had high local content and tariff restrictions. After negotiations with Spain, Ford agreed to build a plant with the capacity to turn out 225,000 cars— two-thirds targeted for export. In return, the government agreed to a lower local content requirement, a reduction in import duties, and 100 percent ownership for Ford.

Toyotaism

Japan's auto companies initiated production in the 1930s, then again in the 1950s, with technical assistance from the

United States. But it became clear to the Japanese early on that they could not be competitive in world markets simply by following U.S. footsteps. Japanese manufacturing volume and output per model were too low to compete against the economies of scale and productivity advantages accruing to the U.S. mass production system. With Toyota in the lead, Japanese car manufacturers responded to U.S. industrial hegemony by constructing a different kind of production system. The Japanese became masters at small-batch production—manufacturing a variety of high-quality models at low volumes. U.S. mass production methods lowered costs by minimizing product diversity and maximizing economies of scale. Japanese production innovations, on the other hand, improved quality and productivity through greater flexibility in the deployment of equipment and labor, lower in-process inventories, and higher turnover rates (Cusumano 1988; Friedman 1983). Over time, the higher product quality and productivity generated by Japanese flexible manufacturing methods translated into formidable global competitive power. By the early 1980s, Toyota and Nissan, insignificant companies in the 1950s, had become the world's second and third largest car makers (Cusumano 1985).

Japan's industrial production system was also conditioned by a number of historical and institutional circumstances, including a well-developed public education system, a disciplined and relatively homogeneous labor force, and a highly group-oriented network of multitiered suppliers rooted in traditional industrial communities of small firms (Shimada and MacDuffie 1987; Friedman 1988).

In stark contrast to Fordist mass production, the techniques masterminded by Toyota also required considerable cooperation among managers, workers, and suppliers. In the 1950s, Toyota managers forged a cooperative relationship with workers through a mixture of threat, persuasion, and collaboration. Toyota officials, in association with other industrialists, undercut Japan's national industrial unions and set up their own company unions dominated by white-collar workers. Toyota instigated a policy of promoting union officials to managerial positions. The company fired a large number of workers, then offered lifetime employment to a select group of employees in return for cooperation. Toyota promoted a system of worker participation and self-inspection and reduced the number of job categories in order to shift workers easily and expand job routines (Cusumano 1985, chapter 5).

In organizing its transnational system, Toyota opted for a horizontal rather than a vertical strategy (Porter 1986; Gilpin 1987, chapter 6; Hill 1989a). Rather than dividing the manufacturing process into multiple pieces, spreading the pieces over many regional locales, and coordinating relationships among the pieces from specialized centers of control, Toyota organized a spatially concentrated and integrated manufacturing complex at a strategic regional location. Over 80 percent of its worldwide production capacity is concentrated in one satellite community, Toyota City, located on the periphery of the Nagoya metropolitan area, in Aichi Prefecture, Japan.

Toyota's flexibly specialized production system is a "post-Fordist" model of industrial development that combines the advantages of craft flexibility with the most advanced information processing and telecommunication technology.[3] Toyotaism's profit logic is based on innovations and efficiencies achieved through spatial agglomeration, flexible specialization, and just-in-time delivery logistics (Cusumano 1988). Productivity and savings are enhanced through just-in-time synchronization of delivery to the assembly line. Inventories, waste, plant size, and energy costs are considerably reduced. Corporate welfare programs and an "enterprise as community" ideology dampen labor strife. Rising wage costs are countered by reducing labor content through automated production methods and by a tiered wage system among regional suppliers based upon firm size and value added to the final product (Luria 1986). Companies organized into Toyotaist production systems possess the capacity to respond to economic problems and market uncertainties by continuously reshaping productive processes through the rearrangement of component activities.

The Regulatory and the Developmental State

So long as U.S. companies dominated domestic markets and enjoyed technological superiority over their competitors, the Fordist system of mass production seemed the quintessence of late-industrial capitalism. But as the technological gap between the United States and Japan closed, and as competition from Japan in the U.S. market increased, the Fordist plateau proved illusory. The sharp decline in market share and employment accruing to U.S. companies, in relation to Japanese, indicated that Fordist mass production was a poor match for Toyotaist flexibility in an advanced capitalist environment marked by increasingly segmented markets and innovations in microelectronic technologies and production organization.[4]

The ever-stronger international showing by Japanese companies contributed to a global overproduction crisis in the 1970s. U.S. companies initially perceived the challenge from Japan through Fordist lenses (mainly as a threat from low wage producers) and they responded by running faster along the path they had already charted. They further extended their production apparatus abroad and further automated their production facilities at home. Global glut and the intensification of Fordism proved disastrous for the U.S. manufacturing belt. Between 1979 and 1985, for example, the Great Lakes region (defined as the eight states bordering the Great Lakes) lost 1,371,000 manufacturing jobs, over 16 percent of the industrial base. Nearly 50 percent of those jobs disappeared from the region's major lakefront cities, which lost over one-quarter of their manufacturing employment (Hill and Negrey 1987).

Japan's challenge from abroad and the ravages of deindustrialization at home ignited a debate in the United States over the role government should play in responding to economic crisis and facilitating economic restructuring. Industrial policy issues, as it turned out, were to hold greatest sway with state governments. Constitutionally dependent upon the states, U.S. municipalities had limited resources to combat their economic traumas. The federal government, on the other hand, was dominated by conservatives with an active distaste for national industrial strategies. And since the nation covered a broad and diverse economic terrain, federal policymakers could politically "aggregate out" data indicating regional industrial decline by lumping them with growth indicators elsewhere in the nation.

But industries are structured regionally, not nationally. As Jane

Jacobs (1984) has argued, industrial production systems emerge in cities and fan out into regional economies. Because states are the closest approximation to regional units of government in the United States, officials in the industrial states confronted deindustrialization and the imperatives of economic restructuring with an immediacy lacking in Washington, D.C. With or without support from the federal government, officials in many states had to act.

As economic crisis gradually focused attention on differences in the way Japanese and U.S. companies organized production systems, so the industrial policy debate began to shed light on differences in the way the state meshes with the economy in the United States and Japan.

Contrasting patterns of state economic intervention in the United States and Japan, like differences in their production systems, are linked to the timing of each nation's industrialization effort. An early industrializer, the U.S. government took little direct part in generating new economic activity. Instead, the U.S. state assumed regulatory responsibilities. As competition and labor mobility undermined traditional ways of life, the state intervened to protect the individual. In late industrializing Japan, by contrast, the state assumed developmental functions and led the drive to industrialize the nation (Dore 1973; Johnson 1982; Morishima 1982).

These contrasting state orientations toward private economic activity—regulation versus development—are associated with different kinds of relationships between business and government in the United States and Japan. According to Chalmers Johnson (1982, 18–19), a "regulatory" or "market rational" state is concerned with forms and procedures—the rules of economic competition—but not with substantive matters (antitrust laws but not industrial targeting, for example). The "developmental" or "plan rational" state sets sight on substantive economic goals and takes a strategic approach to the economy. Industrial policy, the promotion of industrial structures that will enhance a nation's international competitive power, takes priority. The market rational state, in contrast, does not have an industrial policy, or at least it doesn't explicitly recognize and attempt to legitimate its policies as such. Domestic and foreign economic policy stresses rules and reciprocal concessions (Johnson 1982, 18–19).

Regulatory and developmental states also differ in patterns of economic and political decision making. In Japan, the strategic importance of economic policy is reflected in the high positions garnered by economic bureaucrats. Members of Japan's bureaucratic elite number among the most talented individuals in the society. They tend to be educated in law and economics and are recruited from the best schools of policy and management. While pressured by political claimants, these technocrats nonetheless make most of the major decisions, draft most of the legislation, and control the national budget. After retiring at age fifty-five or sixty, government bureaucrats move into powerful positions in private industry and the "third sector" world of public/private corporations.

Public service seldom attracts the most capable individuals in the United States. National decisions are made by elected representatives, usually lawyers, rather than by bureaucrats. The movement of elites is from private sector to government rather than vice versa. Government officials usually gain their position through political appointment—a relatively rare occurrence in Japan. Congress controls the budget in the United States, reflecting once again the emphasis on procedures rather than outcomes in a regulatory state (Johnson 1982, 19).

In Japan's state-guided, high-growth system, business ownership and management are left in private hands, thereby maintaining competition, while state officials set goals and shape market behavior through incentives. The chief industrial policy mechanisms are (1) selective access to government financing; (2) targeted tax breaks; (3) government-supervised investment coordinated to keep all parties profitable; (4) equitable government allocation of burdens during adversity; (5) government assistance in the commercialization of products; and (6) government assistance to declining industries (Johnson 1982, 310–11).

Aichi Prefecture: 1950s

While most writing on business-government relations in Japan has focused upon the connections between large companies and the central state (Johnson 1982; Pemple 1982), research on Toyota Motor Corporation suggests that the "local developmental state" has also played a significant role in the creation of Japanese-style industrial production systems (Fujita and Hill 1988).

As noted above, Toyota City and surrounding Aichi Prefecture house all of Toyota Motor Corporation's major production plants and most of its employees and major suppliers. Western analysts usually attribute agglomeration tendencies in the automobile industry to "natural" market forces (Hurley 1959). But in Toyota's case, industrial concentration was also the political outcome of local industrial policies.

After the defeat of national industrial unions in the early 1950s, Toyota Motor Corporation formed a local electoral alliance with its union, a bond that helped translate the company's economic interests into Toyota City's industrial policies. Identifying closely with the company, and bent upon seeing their city grow, Toyota City officials designed policies that were instrumental in Toyota Motor Corporation's ability to locate all of its major production plants in the area.

In the late 1950s, officials at Toyota Motor Manufacturing, Toyota City, and Aichi Prefecture combined forces to promote an "industrial city." They made a proposal to the Ministry of Agriculture, Forestry, and Fishery to build their city on government land. Gaining permission from the ministry, they used the public land to extend existing assembly facilities and to make adjoining sites available for Toyota's major subcontractors. Toyota City's industrial location laws—including city land provision for plant sites, city construction of supporting infrastructure, and tax abatements—helped entice the corporation's principal suppliers and subcontractors to the region, enabling Toyota to establish its vaunted just-in-time production system.

Toyota City later gave tax incentives for plant expansions as well as first-time projects. The duration of tax incentives was lengthened from three to five years and various site improvements were included. These public benefits were also made available to Toyota suppliers wishing to build in the city, and city officials created industrial parks designed for small and medium-sized Toyota subcontractors. Toyota City also built highways to smooth the flow of goods between Toyota's satellite plants and suppliers and new railroad connections to speed the company's shipments to domestic and international markets. Each time Toyota Motor Corporation decided to build a new plant on the city's periphery, Toyota City annexed the area to ensure a predictable political environment for the company.

Michigan, USA: 1970s and 1980s

Perhaps the most striking change in the U.S. intergovernmental system over the past twenty years has been the shift in state and local government priorities—from regulation to development—a transformation linked to stiffening international economic competition, particularly from Japan (Osborne 1988).

In Michigan, political fallout from the record losses and layoffs in the auto industry during the deep 1979–1983 recession pressured for a reorientation in state priorities. When Democrat James Blanchard took over as Michigan's governor in 1983, the state's unemployment rate was over 17 percent and the state treasury faced a $1.7 billion deficit. Blanchard's early actions, including a tax increase and maintenance of welfare outlays, led to a taxpayers' revolt and recall elections in several districts. Michigan Democrats lost their majority in the state senate and the governor's regulatory programs were stymied. The Blanchard administration retreated on taxes and welfare and began constructing a developmental agenda.

The state's developmental vision, as defined in its principal economic strategy report, *The Path to Prosperity* (State of Michigan 1984), is for Michigan to become an international center for the production of the "factory of the future"—the hardware (such as robotics and machine-vision equipment) and the software (such as Manufacturing Automated Protocol) for computer-integrated, flexible manufacturing systems. Because Michigan is home to the auto industry, companies experimenting with these technologies already have a considerable presence in the state.

Michigan's officials have buttressed their strategic vision with an array of development initiatives, including (1) the standard tax, loan, land, and infrastructure incentives; (2) supply side, "business climate" improving measures, like reduced workers' compensation levies and less paperwork; and more far-reaching neocorporatist initiatives, including (3) a targeted industries program, (4) public/private "centers of excellence" for high-tech research and development; (5) a strategic investment fund; (6) a venture capital fund stocked with 5 percent of the state's pension funds; and (7) various (weakly organized) job retraining programs.

New, and potentially more far-reaching, are recent attempts at direct state intervention into Michigan's auto production system. The Auto-in-Michigan project (AIM), housed in the Industrial Technology Institute (an Ann Arbor–based "center of excellence"), is the best illustration. AIM researchers, policy analysts, and consultants are developing strategies for (1) business retention through restructuring (such as Buick City–type projects in Flint); (2) state recruitment of new domestic and foreign investment for strategically defined niches in the production system (advanced assembly, engine production, galvanized steel, plastics); (3) product conversion (from iron and steel to aluminum, for example); (4) development infrastructure, including monitoring and early-warning systems for plant closings, technology deployment for small and medium-sized businesses, a just-in-time training service, and a computer integrated manufacturing skill training program; and (5) fostering institutional mechanisms for restructuring based upon a three-sided bargained redevelopment model involving labor, business, and government.

On the model of industrial regionalism in Japan (Friedman 1988), the core of Michigan's "Path to Prosperity" strategy is the deployment of new technology into a massive network of smaller manufacturing companies—some 15,000 manufacturers employing more than half a million workers, about half of whom are in industries linked to automobile production, such as plastics, primary and fabricated metals, and machinery (Osborne 1988, 165). The state characterizes these manufacturers as "foundation firms" because they make up the supplier network that supports the major auto assemblers. In an effort to help foundation firms adjust to advanced manufacturing technologies and procedures, state officials have recently created a comprehensive industrial extension service, called Michigan Modernization Services (MMS).

MMS also provides assistance with worker retraining and the restructuring of labor-management relations.

Industrial City and Technopolis

High-technology enterprises, like the Factory of the Future activities Michigan officials are promoting to restructure the state's industrial economy, increasingly cluster in "science cities" or "technopolises" of which there are now a large number worldwide. Technopolises are government-stimulated attempts to gain a competitive locational edge on research, new technology, and product development. Technopolises have in common strong business-university ties, large concentrations of scientific and engineering talent, heavy government research subsidies, and lush, greenfield locations on the periphery of large urban areas (Castells 1984; Fujita 1988). Because high-technology industries are not locating in the same places where traditional manufacturing industries are declining, state-supported restructuring strategies, like Michigan's, are fostering new patterns of uneven urban development.

In Michigan, high-tech entrepreneurs and state development officials are promoting a suburban corridor in the Detroit metropolitan area, running from Ann Arbor on the southwest to Auburn Hills on the northwest, as a "Silicon Valley" in southeastern Michigan for suppliers of durable-goods equipment (Osborne 1988, 162). Dubbed "Automation Alley" by state officials, the corridor already hosts the largest concentration of machine-vision and robotics firms in the United States. According to a recent study by the state's Industrial Technology Institute, 76 percent of Michigan's high-tech automation companies are located in just four Detroit area counties; the vast majority of those cluster in Automation Alley; and only 6 percent are located inside the central city of Detroit (McAlinden, Luria, and Everett 1988).

Oakland Technology Park anchors the northwest pole of Automation Alley. Linked to Oakland University, spanning 1,800 acres and housing $2 billion in research and development facilities for robotics, engineering, automation, and advanced manufacturing applications, Oakland Technology Park numbers among the largest and fastest-growing research and development sites in the United States. It will generate an estimated 52,000 jobs by the mid-1990s.

Oakland Technology Park is located in suburban Auburn Hills. A township until 1984, Auburn Hills has since grown to 16,000 residents. By the mid-1990s, according to planning projections, it will have as many jobs downtown as the city of Detroit. By that time, the community will also have more public revenue per capita than any city in the state. Criss-crossed by rolling woodlands, streams, and the Clinton River, Auburn Hills is a mecca for yuppies. The suburb is also strategically located at the intersection of a major north-south U.S. freeway and one of the state's principal east-west transportation arteries.

Contrasting Auburn Hills with Highland Park (a municipality inside the boundaries of the central city of Detroit) conveys the connection between industrial restructuring and uneven development in the Detroit metropolitan area. Highland Park in the 1920s was home for Henry Ford's Crystal Palace, the world's showplace for mass production. Called the "City of Trees," Highland Park possessed beautiful neighborhoods and vibrant institutions. The community's schools were so good that suburban students flocked in to attend. Chrysler Motor Corporation has long been headquartered in Highland Park and the city is now dependent upon the corporation for half its income taxes and one-third of its property taxes. Chrysler recently moved its 5,000-strong engineering division to Auburn Hills and the company's whole headquarters operation is likely to follow eventually. Forty-five percent of Highland Park's residents now receive some form of public assistance. The city has received four emergency loans from the state just to keep barebones public services alive.

The contrast between Highland Park and Auburn Hills also reveals how economic restructuring is redirecting the flow of capital—away from Detroit's central city and into the northwest Oakland County suburbs. In 1960, the city of Detroit held 50 percent of the region's assessed valuation; Oakland County's share was 14 percent. By 1980, the city's share had plummeted to 18 percent while Oakland County's had grown to 38 percent. Industrial restructuring has transformed Detroit into a polycentric regional economy where multiple divisions demarcate unequally competitive places (Darden, Hill, Thomas, and Thomas 1987).

Ironically, as Michigan officials attempt to counter deindustrialization by facilitating a restructuring of the state's auto production system from global Fordism to regional Toyotaism, officials in Aichi Prefecture are facing the threat of deindustrialization brought on by the globalization of their regionally organized production system. Japanese manufacturers and public officials have been under considerable political pressure from the United States and other Western powers to restructure their regionally concentrated and nationally protected production systems to reduce Japan's trade surplus with the rest of the capitalist world. The principal pressure point has been adjustment in currency exchange rates.

In September 1985, financial ministers from the five major industrialized countries (the "G5") met in New York and agreed to increase the value of the yen against the dollar. Since then, the yen has steeply appreciated from 265 to the dollar in summer 1985 to 130 in spring 1989. As the rising yen reduced Japan's export competitiveness, industrialists accelerated overseas production. Japanese corporations had been locating production sites abroad since the 1960s and they stepped up direct foreign investment in the early 1980s to circumvent trade barriers. But in speed and scale, the transnationalization of Japanese firms since the G5 meeting in 1985 is unprecedented in Japan's postwar history.

Toyota responded to the yen appreciation with a shift in strategic emphasis—from a horizontally organized, regional production strategy to a vertically organized, international division of labor. There are two dimensions to Toyota's current global strategy. The first is a Pacific Rim division of labor whereby Toyota is using newly industrialized countries of East Asia as export platforms for low value-added parts and economy cars targeted principally for markets in Japan and the United States. The second is Toyota's transplant production strategy in North America and Western Europe (Fujita and Hill 1989).

The globalization of Toyota Motor Corporation poses a potentially serious employment issue for Aichi Prefecture. A recent survey of Japanese car companies estimated that a 2 million decline in motor vehicle exports to the United States could result in the loss of nearly half a million domestic jobs.

Toyota's factories in Aichi Prefecture have remained busy thus far supplying engines and transmissions to the company's North American transplants. But as stiffening competition in the North American market has led to more U.S. plant closings and laid-off workers, the United Auto Workers and American supplier associations are challenging the low local content of Japanese transplants (United Automobile Workers 1987). To maintain access to the North American market, Toyota and other Japanese auto companies eventually will have to produce engines and transmissions in the United States and Canada.

Toyota's first-tier, transplant suppliers are also under pressure to increase North American content. The Toyota group must either recruit more second-tier suppliers from Japan or increase their use of indigenous North American companies. Either way, Aichi-based suppliers will lose export orders and face production cutbacks. And by channeling parts produced in Mexico and Asia into its North American operations, Toyota is even further reducing business for lower-tier, Aichi-based suppliers.

How are Japan's public officials responding to the deindustrialization threat? The national government has recommended a reorientation in Japan's growth strategy from export- to domestic-led expansion. To reduce the trade surplus, the government is encouraging firms to set up more transplants abroad and consumers to spend more money on imports at home. To spur domestic consumption, the government has emphasized new land use and housing construction policies, shortened working hours, and modifications in food import controls. The government has backed these policies with an emergency expenditure package of 6 trillion yen, including 5 trillion in public works and 1 trillion in individual tax reductions.

To soften the pains of restructuring, the state has recommended priority allocation of public works projects to structurally depressed regions. Japan's Ministry of International Trade and Industry (MITI) also has proposed regional development centers to attract investment in information and related service industries. The plan requires local governments to construct "core" industrial parks and facilities in the targeted areas. Companies locating in the target areas are to receive tax breaks and other public subsidies.[5] MITI has also set up "relocation centers" in each prefecture's chamber of commerce and industry to exchange information on job opportunities and to mediate employment transfers between different companies and regions (Fujita and Hill 1989).

Japan's Ministry of Labor estimates that as many as 1.65 million workers may be forced to leave the manufacturing sector between 1986 and 1993. But there is no sign yet of a hollowing out of the Aichi regional economy, as indicated by deep production cuts or large-scale layoffs. Increased domestic sales spurred by an expansionary government fiscal policy have kept Aichi's economy buoyant thus far. Toyota and local supplier companies are also increasing outlays on research and development in an effort to create new products for the domestic market, to compensate for the contraction in overseas industrial exports.

Conclusion

In closing, it seems fitting to return to the issue that frames the book as a whole. What role do local governments play in the industrial development process? Can something be learned from a cross-national comparison between the United States and Japan?

Governments have a stake in advancing the net wealth and the standard of living of the citizenry residing within their borders. In the auto-producing regions of Japan and North America, subnational governments have similar interests: they want to attract and retain high value-added activities and foster intraregional linkages among firms in their auto production systems. Government officials in both parts of the world are attempting to advance those objectives by developing industrial strategies and making social investments in supportive infrastructure, technical services, and training programs.

Governments can have an "independent impact" on the development process. Toyota City's role in the growth of Toyota Motor Corporation's production system evidences a local developmental capacity in late industrializing Japan.[6] Strategic interventions of a similar nature are increasingly evident in the United

States (Osborne 1988). Industrial policies prompted by Michigan officials, the U.S. example highlighted in this chapter, are having a demonstrable effect on that state's auto production system (Hill, Indergaard, and Fujita 1989).

It is a misnomer, however, to speak of an "independent" local development policy if that implies cities are somehow separate and autonomous from other levels of government. Local autonomy may prevail with respect to some urban activities—probably more so in the United States than in Japan—but where economic development policy is concerned, it is the relationships among levels of government in both societies that stand out.[7] Intergovernmental relations are evident, for example, in Toyota City's use of national public lands and industrial location laws to facilitate the development of a regional auto production system in Aichi Prefecture. Likewise, officials in cities dotting Michigan's fast-growing Automation Alley have worked in tandem with state government and benefited considerably from Michigan's strategic development policies.

The impact of intergovernmental relations on local development extends to the international arena. Japan's current industrial restructuring is more the result of Western political power, exerted through the international relations system, than comparative economic efficiency, exerted through the market. While industrial organization and state policies in the United States and Japan do seem to be converging today, the forces promoting that convergence are more complex and discontinuous than market-focused "natural selection" theories imply.

The rhetoric of market determination dominates today's political discourse. Yet public officials in capitalist states have a demonstrable capacity to shape economic development. Patterns of urban growth and decline therefore reflect public choices. As government interventions contribute to new trajectories of uneven development in the United States and Japan, the groundwork for tomorrow's urban politics is being laid.

NOTES

1. This research is reported in Fujita and Hill 1988, 1989; Hill 1989a; and Hill, Indergaard, and Fujita 1989.

2. Theda Skocpol's argument has merit: "Neo-Marxists have too often sought to generalize—often in extremely abstract ways—about features or functions shared by all states within a mode of production, a phase of capital accumulation, or a position in the world capitalist system. This makes it difficult to assign causal weight to variations in state structures and activities across nations and short time periods, thereby undercutting the usefulness of some neo-Marxist schemes for comparative research" (1985, 5). The capitalist world system approach, championed by Immanuel Wallerstein (1979), evidences a similar weakness. Students of the world system analyze dynamic relations among system properties over time but the distinctiveness of economic and political institutions in specific capitalist societies (like Japan) and the transformative influence on the structure of the whole system that individual nations can at times exert (like Japan today) seem to fall outside the world system frame of reference. Skocpol's "state-centered" approach, however, seems to err on the side of national distinctiveness. By attempting to establish cause and effect among variables through selected comparisons of properties of individual historical cases, Skocpol assumes (as in all correlational analysis) independence among the cases she is investigating. Underplayed, therefore, is the interdependence among nations and the systemic character of the world capitalist system. In this chapter, I emphasize the interplay between commonality and diversity, an approach that is well articulated in the work of Piore and Sabel (1984).

3. Whether Japanese production methods represent merely a refined version of Fordism ("neo-Fordism") or something qualitatively different ("post-Fordism") as argued here is still a matter of some debate. Compare for example Dohse, Jurgens, and Malsch (1985) with Kenney and Florida (1988).

4. I stress "advanced capitalist environment" here because the logic of mass production is still applicable to the poorer countries of the world and what seems to be emerging is an international division of labor than combines both mass- and flexible-system techniques and organization (see Hill 1989b).

5. Japan, of course, has its own technopolis plan—a central state commitment to building nineteen science cities within a systematically applied policy framework (see Fujita 1988).

6. The relationship between Toyota Motor Corporation and Toyota City may appear to American eyes as a simple case of company domination over a community; in fact, it is a more complex and institutionally balanced form of political corporatism. For further discussion of this point see Fujita and Hill 1988. For a discussion of Japanese corporatism that brings labor back in, see Garón (1987). Samuels (1983) explores the connection between corporatism and intergovernmental relations in Japan.

7. The conflictual relations between central and local government

imbedded in Britain and France, as analyzed by Parkinson and Preteceille elsewhere in this volume, attest to the same conclusion.

REFERENCES

Braverman, Harry. 1974. *Labor and Monopoly Capital.* New York: Monthly Review Press.
Castells, Manuel, ed. 1985. *High Technology, Space and Society.* Beverly Hills, Calif.: Sage.
Cusumano, Michael. 1985. *The Japanese Automobile Industry.* Cambridge, Mass.: Harvard University Press.
———. 1988. *Manufacturing Innovation and Competitive Advantage: Reflections on the Japanese Automobile Industry.*
Darden, Joe, Richard Child Hill, June Thomas, and Richard Thomas. 1987. *Detroit: Race and Uneven Development.* Philadelphia: Temple University Press.
Dohse, Knuth, Ulrich Jurgens, and Thomas Malsch. 1985. "From 'Fordism' to 'Toyotaism'? The Social Organization of the Labor Process in the Japanese Automobile Industry." *Politics and Society* 14(2):115–46.
Dore, Ronald. 1973. *British Factory—Japanese Factory.* Berkeley and Los Angeles: University of California Press.
Friedman, David. 1983. "Beyond the Age of Ford: The Strategic Basis of the Japanese Success in Automobiles." In *American Industry in International Competition,* ed. John Zysman and Laura Tyson. Ithaca, N.Y.: Cornell University Press.
———. 1988. *The Misunderstood Miracle: Industrial Development and Political Change in Japan.* Ithaca, N.Y.: Cornell University Press.
Froebel, Folker, Jurgen Heinrichs, and Otto Kreye. 1980. *The New International Division of Labor.* Cambridge: Cambridge University Press.
Fujita, Kuniko. 1988. "The Technopolis: High Technology and Regional Development in Japan." *International Journal of Urban and Regional Research* 12(4):566–94.
Fujita, Kuniko, and Richard Child Hill. 1988. "Toyota's City: Corporation and Community in Japan." Paper presented at the American Sociological Association annual meeting, August 26, 1988.
———. "Global Production and Regional 'Hollowing Out' in Japan." 1989. *Comparative Urban and Community Research,* vol. 2, ed. Michael Smith. New Brunswick, N.J.: Transaction Books.
Garon, Sheldon. 1987. *The State and Labor in Modern Japan.* Berkeley and Los Angeles: University of California Press.
Gilpin, Robert. 1987. *The Political Economy of International Relations.* Princeton, N.J.: Princeton University Press.
Hainer, Marge, and Joanne Koslofsky. 1979. "Car Wars." *NACLA Report on the Americas* 13(4):3–9.

Hamilton, F. E. Ian. 1981. "Industrial Systems: A Dynamic Force Behind International Trade." *Professional Geographer* 3(1):26–35.

Hill, Richard Child. 1989a. "Comparing Transnational Production Systems: The Case of the Automobile Industry in the United States and Japan," *International Journal of Urban and Regional Research* 13(3): 462–80.

———. 1989b. "Divisions of Labor in Global Manufacturing: The Case of the Automobile Industry." In *Instability and Change in the World Economy*, ed. Arthur MacEwan and William K. Tabb. New York: Monthly Review Press.

Hill, Richard Child, Michael Indergaard, and Kuniko Fujita. 1989. "Flat Rock, Home of Mazda: The Social Impact of a Japanese Company on an American Community." In *The Auto Industry Ahead: Who's Driving?* ed. Peter Arnesen. Ann Arbor: University of Michigan, Center for Japanese Studies.

Hill, Richard Child, and Cynthia Negrey. 1987. "Deindustrialization in the Great Lakes." *Urban Affairs Quarterly* 22(4):580–97.

Holmes, John. 1986. "Organization and Locational Structure of Production Subcontracting." In *Production, Work, Territory*, ed. Allen J. Scott and Michael Storper. Boston: Allen & Unwin.

Hurley, Neil. 1959. "The Automotive Industry: A Study in Industrial Location." *Land Economics* 35(1):1–14.

Hymer, Stephen. 1971. "The Multinational Corporation and the Law of Uneven Development." In *Economics and World Order*, ed. J. W. Bhagwati. New York: Macmillan.

Jacobs, Jane. 1984. *Cities and the Wealth of Nations*. New York: Random House.

Johnson, Chalmers. 1982. *MITI and the Japanese Miracle: The Growth of Industrial Policy, 1925–1975*. Stanford, Calif.: Stanford University Press.

———. 1987. "How to Think About Economic Competition from Japan." *Journal of Japanese Studies* 13(2):415–27.

———. 1988. "Studies of Japanese Political Economy: A Crisis in Theory." *The Japan Foundation Newsletter* 16(3):1–11.

Jones, Daniel T. 1981. *Maturity and Crisis in the European Car Industry: Structural Change and Public Policy*. Sussex European Research Centre, Sussex European Papers No. 8.

Kenney, Martin, and Richard Florida. 1988. "Beyond Mass Production: Production and the Labor Process in Japan." *Politics and Society* (16)1: 121–58.

Lipietz, Alain. 1986. "New Tendencies in the International Division of Labor: Regimes of Accumulation and Modes of Regulation." In *Production, Work, Territory*, ed. Allen Scott and Michael Storper. Boston: Allen & Unwin.

———. 1987. *Mirages and Miracles: The Crises of Global Fordism.* London: Verso.

Luria, Daniel D. 1986. "New Labor-Management Models from Detroit?" *Harvard Business Review,* Sept.–Oct., pp. 22–29.

McAlinden, Sean, Dan Luria, and Mark Everett. 1988. "Michigan's Automation Supply Sector: A Resource for Automobile Suppliers." *AIM Newsletter* 3(1):1–8.

Morishima, Michio. 1982. *Why Has Japan Succeeded?* Cambridge: Cambridge University Press.

Osborne, David. 1988. *Laboratories of Democracy.* Boston: Harvard Business School Press.

Pemple, T. J. 1982. *Policy and Politics in Japan: Creative Conservatism.* Philadelphia: Temple University Press.

Piore, Michael, and Charles Sabel. 1984. *The Second Industrial Divide.* New York: Basic Books.

Porter, Michael, ed. 1986. *Competition in Global Industries.* Boston: Harvard Business School Press.

Samuels, Richard J. 1983. *The Politics of Regional Policy in Japan.* Princeton, N.J.: Princeton University Press.

Scott, Allen. 1983. "Industrial Organization and the Logic of Intra-Metropolitan Location: 1, Theoretical Considerations." *Economic Geography* 59:233–50.

Shimada, Haruo, and John Paul MacDuffie. 1987. "Industrial Relations and 'Humanware': Japanese Investments in Automobile Manufacturing in the United States." A Briefing Paper for the First Policy Forum, International Motor Vehicles Program, MIT, May 4.

Sklair, Leslie. 1985. "Shenzhen: A Chinese 'Development Zone' in Global Perspective." *Development and Change* 16:571–601.

Skocpol, Theda. 1985. "Bringing the State Back In: Strategies of Analysis in Current Research." In *Bringing the State Back In,* ed. Peter B. Evans, Dietrich Rueschemeyer, and Theda Skocpol. New York: Cambridge University Press.

State of Michigan. 1984. *The Path to Prosperity.* Lansing: State of Michigan, Department of Commerce.

Sweezy, Paul. 1953. *The Present as History.* New York: Monthly Review Press.

United Automobile Workers. 1987. *U.S. Auto Jobs: The Problem Is Bigger Than Japanese Imports.* Detroit: UAW Research Department.

Wakeman, F. E. 1988. "Transnational and Comparative Research." *Social Science Research Council ITEMS* 42(4):85–89.

Wallerstein, Immanuel. 1979. *The Capitalist World Economy.* Cambridge: Cambridge University Press.

CHAPTER 4

Political Responses to Urban Restructuring: The British Experience under Thatcherism

Michael Parkinson

Britain has undergone a profound urban transformation during the past two decades. The restructuring of the international economy, the emergence of highly mobile finance capital, the decline of manufacturing industry and its export to low-wage economies, and the rise of the service sector with its dual labor market have created in Britain, as in other advanced economies, a pattern of intensely uneven urban development. The impact of this unevenness upon different social and economic groups and segments of the labor force is well known: growing regional and individual economic inequality, the emergence of core and peripheral workers, the marginalization of particular social groups. The purpose of this chapter is less to explain those processes than it is to explore Conservative political responses to them and the related themes of economic change, urban decline, and the prospect of urban regeneration.

The evolution of urban policy in Britain during the 1980s under the Conservatives perfectly illustrates one of the themes of this book: politics, not economics, dominates national responses to urban restructuring. The economic problems facing British cities may have intensified during the 1980s but they did not substantially change their nature. But a decade of Conservative rule dramatically changed the way in which government responded to those problems. Indeed during this period there was a sea change in the way British cities were governed. Most crucially, the radical shifts in policy under the Conservatives were not economically determined but the result of conscious political choice. Change was primarily ideologically, not economically, driven.

The ideological shift that took place in urban policy remains imperfect and incomplete. But its essential features are clear. In the litany of Conservative measures, markets replaced politics as the primary response to urban decline. The values of urban entrepreneurism replaced those of municipal collectivism. Private-sector leadership replaced public intervention. Investment in physical capital displaced investment in social capital. Wealth creation replaced the distribution of welfare. Most ironically, a regime committed to decentralizing power in fact weakened alternative local power bases. Britain's response to urban decline under Mrs. Thatcher may be characterized as the centralization and privatization of power. And the effect was to increase, rather than reduce, the pattern of uneven urban development (Hamnett, McDowell, and Sarre 1989). This chapter explores these issues by examining the evolution of government policy for British cities. Its primary focus is the 1980s but it also examines the historical context from which that policy emerged.

Urban Policy and the Rise of Privatism

From the late 1960s, when the Labour government "rediscovered" the problem of the inner cities, until Mrs. That-

cher's accession to power in 1979, government policy under both
political parties rested on two shared assumptions. First, policy
was as much designed to provide social and welfare support services to the victims of economic change in the cities as it was to
create wealth in those areas. Second, since disinvestment by the
private sector was seen as the cause of many cities' economic
decline, the public sector was regarded as the natural agency to
lead urban reconstruction (Edwards and Batley 1978; McKay and
Cox 1979; Lawless 1979; Higgins et al. 1983; Robson 1988).

In the 1980s, however, the Conservative government increasingly defined the public sector, especially profligate expenditure
and bureaucratic planning by local authorities, as the cause of
inner cities' problems and the private sector as the solution. Apart
from morally exhorting the private sector to increase its involvement in the inner cities, the government introduced a wide range
of initiatives designed to give the private sector a lead role in urban
policy—city action teams, task forces, enterprise zones, free ports,
urban development grants, urban regeneration grants, city grants,
and urban development corporations. In the late 1980s urban "regeneration" became the Conservative government's goal, as
wealth creation replaced the distribution of welfare as the primary
aim of urban policy. Equally important, the government decided
that local authorities were unable to lead the economic regeneration of their cities and gradually cut many of their traditional
powers and resources.

This Conservative effort to restructure urban policy must be
seen in a larger context: its attempt to change the ideological
climate of Britain by creating an enterprise culture and replace
state action with market forces. This desire to roll back the fron-
tiers of the state underpinned the government's efforts to cut
public spending, taxation, and employment; to substitute private
for public provision; to increase individual choice in the provision and consumption of collective services; and to charge consumers the full economic price for those services. The Conservative effort at retrenchment was not confined to urban policy
narrowly defined but extended to a wide range of other policy
arenas with a decisive impact upon cities' fortunes: education,

housing, welfare, finance, transportation, and planning (Parkinson 1987; King 1987).

Lessons from America?

One of the sources of the Conservative government's reliance on market mechanisms rather than public intervention to regenerate its cities was the United States, which during this period increasingly served as a model for British social policy (Parkinson, Foley, and Judd 1989; Boyle 1989; Hambleton 1989). This was not an entirely new phenomenon. In the 1960s when a Labour government first attempted to address the "social" problem of British cities—the threat of racial disorders—it was heavily influenced by the U.S. administration's War on Poverty programs. In the 1980s British governments turned to the United States for inspiration once again. However, this time a Conservative administration was looking for a solution to the "economic" problems of British cities. The apparent economic renaissance of East Coast cities like Boston, New York, Baltimore, Pittsburgh, and Philadelphia as the revitalized centers of service-sector economies had a powerful attraction for a British government forced to respond to the restructuring of the international economic order and the rapid decline of its older industrial cities.

The apparent success of such U.S. cities in restructuring their economies attracted the Conservative government to an American reliance upon the marketplace, with its relaxed planning regime, extensive use of fiscal incentives to attract private investment, focus upon the small-firm sector, and privatization of service provision. The government was also attracted by the model of the "entrepreneurial" American city, which was supposed to respond to economic adversity by creating new political arrangements, especially the much-vaunted public-private partnerships, to develop regeneration strategies. Such partnerships were widely promoted by the Conservative government as one important way British cities could positively respond to economic decline (Harding 1990; Lawless 1988b; Stoker 1988).

Inevitably, the very different institutional, financial, and political contexts into which these ideas were imported affected the way they operated in Britain. In contrast to the fragmented American federal system, Britain was more centralized—politically, economically, and financially. Also the two countries' party systems were quite different. America lacked a disciplined party system, and federal policy for the cities was shaped by a wide variety of interest groups. In Britain political parties, not pressure groups, dominate urban policymaking.

The different ideological traditions of the parties were also important. The political control the Labour party exercised over many cities helped ensure that the urban underprivileged were better represented in British cities (Sharpe 1973). This in part explains why they received more generous levels of public housing, welfare, and education than their American counterparts, where those services frequently remained outside cities' control and underfunded. Although it was partially eroded during the 1980s, the British welfare state historically provided a safety net for the poor that was absent from American cities. Equally important, cities in the two countries have traditionally had different fiscal powers and responsibilities. British cities had more limited sources of taxation and income than American cities and did not have the same financial flexibility to pursue economic development. Historically, however, this weakness was compensated for by the fact that British cities received more generous levels of financial support from national government than did their American counterparts.

These institutional and ideological differences were important. They meant there was no simple translation of American experience into the British context. But a decade of Conservative government in the 1980s eroded some of those traditional differences and in some respects "Americanized" British urban policy. However, despite evidence of a policy convergence, there was one fundamental difference in the two countries' experience. The American conservative strategy led to a decentralization of federal power and a shift of responsibility to the states and cities (Fainstein and Fainstein 1989). But the Conservative British strategy had exactly the reverse effect: increased centralization of power and a loss of local control. This requires some explanation.

The Conservative Paradox: Centralization versus Decentralization

The centralization of power that took place under the Conservatives was a paradox (Parkinson 1987). The government's original strategy for the regeneration of cities involved a major redistribution in political power—but not centralization. One element of the strategy was to decentralize power and shift control of policy from central to local level. The second strand was to use private markets to break the control of monopoly public suppliers at city level and liberate consumers. Producer groups—central government, local government, their employees, and their trade unions—were to lose power. Consumers—voters, rate payers, tenants, parents and pupils, welfare clients, as well as the voluntary and private sectors—were to gain.

In principle, the Conservative government's plan to reduce the overall size of the public sector was not incompatible with local authorities and city governments retaining a major role. They were the lowest tier of government, closest to local consumers, often seen as meeting their needs better than national government. Indeed, the attempt to decentralize state power might have increased the responsibilities of city governments. This was, for example, the effect of the new federalism practiced in the United States from the 1970s.

However, a different, more powerful, pressure pushed the Conservative government in a quite different direction—toward the increased centralization of state power. The pressure to centralize was driven primarily by the government's macroeconomic strategy and in particular its view that in order to regenerate the British economy, overall public-sector expenditure had to be cut to encourage a recovery led by private-sector investment. Despite this belief, however, the Conservative government faced a dilemma in cutting public spending. Many of its own programs were growing during this period. For example, it was unable to contain the cost of welfare benefits for the growing number of unemployed produced by its deflationary policies at the beginning of the 1980s. Also it had an electoral commitment to sustain spending on defense and law and order, as Table 4-1 shows.

TABLE 4-1.   Changes in Public Expenditure Priorities, 1978–79
Through 1989–90

	1978–79	1986–87	1989–90
Employment and training	1.6%	2.7%	2.7%
Health and personal social services	13.9	15.1	16.0
Law and order	3.7	4.8	5.0
Defense	11.3	12.6	12.1
Other	10.5	8.8	8.6
Agriculture, fisheries, and food	1.5	1.6	1.8
Transport	4.8	4.0	3.9
Industry, trade, and energy	5.1	2.1	0.9
Housing	7.6	4.1	3.9
Education and science	14.3	13.1	13.1
Social security	25.6	31.1	31.6

Source: White Paper on Public Expenditures (London: HMSO, 1989); Public
Expenditure Plans, 1989–90 through 1990–91 (London: HMSO, 1989).

These constraints forced the government to look beyond its
direct spending programs to other parts of the public sector. And
spending by local governments, cities in particular, became the
Conservative government's prime target, even though city governments had limited their expenditure more than central governments during the previous ten years. Table 4-2 shows that, in
contrast to the postwar boom period, between 1970 and 1980 local
authority spending actually fell as a proportion of gross domestic
product and as a proportion of total government spending.

In some respects the structure of the welfare state made conflict
between the central and local state inevitable. Although it determines the shape of and directly finances much of the welfare state,
central government plays a minor role in providing it. Local governments are the primary suppliers of services, which are labor-
intensive and expensive. They, not the national government, employ the workers and spend the money. Any effort to restrict public
spending was guaranteed to produce conflict between central and
local government, particularly the cities. This structural division
exaggerated the existing tension between the government's philo-
sophical commitment to decentralize power and its need to intervene in local affairs to achieve its more important ideological goal
of controlling public spending and to centralize state power.

During the 1980s the Conservative government devoted more

TABLE 4-2.   Local Government Spending in the United
Kingdom, 1950–1985

	As percentage of gross domestic product	As percentage of total government expenditure
1950	9.9%	16.7%
1960	9.9	23.3
1965	13.4	30.6
1970	14.9	31.5
1975	17.6	29.5
1976	17.0	28.2
1977	15.1	27.0
1978	13.0	24.0
1979	14.2	25.6
1980	14.7	25.3
1981	14.4	23.7
1982	13.9	22.9
1983	14.7	23.9
1984	14.6	23.8
1985	13.7	22.9

Source: UK National Accounts (Central Statistical Office, London).

attention to the cities than virtually any other domestic policy issue. It used three methods to reduce their powers. The most direct was to impose strict limits on their revenue and capital expenditure. A second method was to privatize or deregulate many urban services, either by forcing the sale of city assets or by opening up the supply of local services to increased competition from private suppliers. The third method was to audit cities more extensively and make more information about their performance available, in the hope that better informed local taxpayers would, through the ballot box, curtail city spending.

The impact of these measures was dramatic. The Conservatives radically restructured and restricted the way in which central government financed cities. They abolished cities' own source of income, the rates or property taxes, and replaced it with a community charge or poll tax. In the six largest urban areas the government eliminated a complete tier of elected government, the metropolitan county councils. Many local-authority services, for example housing and social services, were privatized. Tenants in public housing and parents of children in public schools were given the right to vote to leave the local government sector and to choose private provision at least partially funded by central government. The government argued that it was transforming an expensive, inefficient bureaucracy into an organization more accountable to its citizens and more democratic. Cities, by contrast, argued that individual consumer choice was being reduced and the central government's determination to bypass local authorities left them reduced to mere functionaries of an increasingly powerful and undemocratic central state (Blunkett and Jackson 1987). Whoever was right, an extraordinary change in national policy for the cities took place in this decade. How did this occur?

National Policy for the Cities, 1968–1989

Britain did not have an explicit national urban policy until the late 1960s, when the Labour government placed the cities near the top of the domestic political agenda. They rarely lost that position during the subsequent twenty years. However, during that period governments changed their response to the "problem" of cities several times. Although not mutually exclusive, three broad eras of urban policy can be identified: 1968–1976, 1976–1979, and 1979–1989 (Lawless 1986, 1987, 1988b; Solesbury 1986, 1987). This chapter concentrates on the last period but examines the first two briefly, since much Conservative policy after 1979 was a reaction to the alleged policy failures of those earlier areas.

1968–1976: The Social Pathology of the Ghettos

Cities first emerged as a major political issue in British politics in the late 1960s. Until then it was commonly assumed that the welfare state and the planning system that had been built during the long postwar boom addressed the needs of cities and individuals. But during the 1960s growing evidence of the extent of poverty within the welfare state, compounded by growing political uneasiness about the consequences of black immigration into many older British cities, reinforced by the race riots in America, led the Labour government in 1968 to introduce a program targeted specifically at Britain's cities.

However, although it was sustained on a bipartisan basis by the succeeding Conservative government, Labour's original urban program was limited in several crucial respects. The resources allocated to it were modest, never rising beyond £30 million a year. There was little discussion between the two levels of the government about the policy priorities of the program. It essentially adopted a social pathological model of the cities which assumed that there were relatively limited numbers of people who lacked the capacity to succeed economically and who needed social support. Also, the policy was controlled not by the government department with primary responsibility for urban affairs, but by the Home Office, which administered Britain's immigration policy and was regarded as responsible for the country's black population. In more than one sense, the original urban program ghettoized the problem. During this first period of policy until the mid-1970s government commitment to the cities was at best tentative.

1976–1979: Facing Urban Economic Change

By the mid-1970s the limitations of government policies were growing increasingly obvious. In particular it had become clear that the dramatic structural economic changes taking place in the cities, especially the process of disinvestment by the private sector, which underlay many of the social problems, were almost entirely ignored by government policy. When Labour returned to government in the mid-1970s it made significant changes in urban policy. The sociopathological view of the inner-city problem, which concentrated on the failings of individuals, was abandoned. Instead the new approach emphasized the significance of the economic changes that were taking place, leaving many victims in their wake. Labour's policy focused on the economic as well as the social causes of decline and accepted the need to create wealth in the cities to form a platform for urban regeneration. But the program also retained its commitment to deliver welfare services to those left outside the economic mainstream in the cities. Labour also planned substantial shifts in government resources. The urban program funds were expanded and the much larger main program budgets of government departments were intended to be bent in favor of cities.

There were substantial organizational changes. The urban program was placed in the hands of the urban affairs department, the Department of the Environment. Most important, the policy created in the six largest cities in Britain new institutions, inner-city partnerships, that were intended to link central government, local government, the private sector, and community groups in a novel partnership with collective responsibility for developing innovative policy responses to decline in the cities (Parkinson and Wilks 1983, 1986; Hambleton 1981).

1979–1989: Municipal Socialism versus Urban Entrepreneurism

Despite shifts in emphasis there were several continuities in government policy between 1968 and 1979. Welfare remained a central goal. Public expenditure was seen as crucial. City governments were regarded as important actors in urban regeneration. After the election of the Conservative government in 1979, however, this bipartisan consensus disintegrated as those key assumptions were fundamentally challenged. During the next decade the institutional and policy framework that they underpinned was slowly eroded as the Conservative government attempted to substitute its new strategic response to urban decline—urban entrepreneurism led by the private sector.

During the same period, however, this central government policy impulse was matched by a rather different reaction in many cities. Just as the Conservative government drew the lesson from the 1970s that the public sector had failed the cities and that the private sector was the solution, many large Labour-controlled cities drew the diametrically opposite conclusion. In their view, the public sector was the only institution capable of staunching the hemorrhaging caused by private-sector disinvestment from the cities. During the 1980s, many cities adopted strategies that attempted to give local authorities the lead role in economic development. For a brief period at the beginning of the decade, the rise of the government's new urban entrepreneurism was complemented in the cities by the rise of municipal socialism (Gyford 1985; Boddy and Fudge 1984).

Indeed the history of urban policy in the decade after 1979 constituted a struggle between these two tendencies, as the Conservative government used its legal, financial, and political resources to reduce the ability of Labour-controlled cities to pursue their alternative ideological agendas. By the late 1980s the ideological imperative to eliminate the spectre of socialism in the cities had become at least as important for the Conservative government as its original, more pragmatic concerns: to reduce public expenditure, improve urban services, and protect consumer interests. When the Conservatives took control of government they were committed to decentralizing power. But they were also committed to reducing public expenditure and pursuing a clear ideological vision of the future of Britain's cities. By 1989 it was evident how that internal tension would be resolved, which layer of the state and which ideological tendency would win the political struggle. Power was being both centralized and privatized. City governments were losing even their limited capacity to shape their economic fates.

Labour Cities' Response to Economic Crisis: The Politics of Municipal Socialism

British cities have traditionally exercised some control over their own economic welfare, but their capacity has always been limited in a financially, economically, and politically centralized state. At the beginning of the 1970s most cities' economic development policies were confined to providing land for industry and building manufacturing premises. However, the election of the Conservative government in 1979 led to significant growth in local intervention in economic development.

The explanation for this increased intervention was part economic and part political (Lawless 1987). After 1979 many cities found that their traditional manufacturing bases were rapidly disappearing, a process dramatically exacerbated by the government's macroeconomic policies, especially its cuts in public expenditure. Many Labour cities felt obliged to make some response to these local economic crises, which had been induced by Mrs. Thatcher's policies. However, there was also a more directly political explanation for the growth in municipal intervention: the rise within the Labour party of a new urban left. In the 1980s many city Labour parties, both dissatisfied with the failures of the earlier 1970s Labour governments to pursue full-blooded socialism and opposed to Mrs. Thatcher's new free-market priorities, adopted more left-wing economic development programs. Under the influence of a new generation of younger, more radical political activists, often middle-class professionals employed in the public sector themselves, many cities determined to become testing grounds for the development of alternative socialist economic strategies that could be used both to resist the market-led strategies of central government and to offer a lead to the national Labour party.

Labour's urban agenda of the early 1980s had several strands: a major stress on the role of the public sector in urban regeneration, especially public-sector employment; intervention in the private market to strengthen the position of workers and encourage more democratic forms of ownership and control; efforts to provide long-term employment in indigenous enterprises; attempts to promote equal opportunities in employment and support the supply of "socially useful" goods and services; and the promotion of community involvement in economic planning (Harding 1989).

During the 1980s cities engaged in a wide range of economic development activities: promotional policies, physical redevelopment, new enterprise development, cooperative and community development, intervention in the labor market, and fiscal innovations. Some cities created new enterprises in managed workspace and incubator units where new companies could begin in a protected environment. Others attempted to create science parks. Many cities encouraged cooperative and community enterprise to provide permanent local jobs in socially useful products for people marginalized by market forces. The most interventionist cities moved into direct economic development, providing grants and loans to firms. Some directly invested in local companies by creating enterprise boards, which could take equity shares in local firms lacking investment capital (Lawless 1987).

These Labour city initiatives during the 1980s were politically important and represented a coherent alternative to the Conservative government's strategy. Nevertheless, the impact of these economic development programs upon the underlying economies of their cities was debatable. On balance such local initiatives remained peripheral to market forces. Restricted in the amount of taxation they could raise, even very large cities had such meager resources that their programs had a limited effect on production, output, employment, or profits. In addition, the leading role in local economic development in the 1980s had been taken by the regional governments in the largest cities, the county councils. But these institutions were abolished by Mrs. Thatcher in 1986, at least partly because they played this role. Inevitably, this substantially reduced the scope for innovative economic development programs in the big cities.

Conservative Urban Entrepreneurism in the 1980s

The significance of Labour cities' municipal socialist strategies of the early 1980s remained essentially ideological rather than economic. Despite their policy efforts, many cities struggled unsuccessfully to resist the restructuring of national and international capital during this period. Power to resist those forces, if it lay anywhere in government, lay with the central, not local, state. However, the Conservatives assumed that such market-led restructuring should be encouraged, not discouraged. Even if government could control the movement of capital, it was not desirable. And its urban policy reflected this belief. The Conservatives adopted a very different view of the role of government, which meant that the innovative, albeit economically marginal, policies of Labour cities were overshadowed during the 1980s by the financial and legal powers the government gave to the private sector and to some government agencies.

The Conservatives' first step was to revamp their predecessors' policies. For example, the primary piece of machinery the Conservatives inherited from Labour was the inner-city partnerships, a potentially innovative relationship between national and local government, the community, and the private sector. The Conservatives distanced themselves from the Labour legacy, minimizing local government's role in the partnerships and increasing the contribution of the private sector and central government. Indeed throughout the 1980s government increasingly marginalized the partnerships so they finally ceased to play a significant part in the decision-making machinery (Lawless 1988b). The ideological priorities of the urban program were also substantially changed as the government encouraged expenditure on projects with a narrow economic rather than a broader social focus. Resources were also targeted upon capital rather than revenue projects, since the latter tended to increase the numbers of local government employees—a trend opposed by the government. The private sector, in the shape of the local chambers of commerce, was given a larger role in the choice of urban program priorities. Table 4-3 shows the growing importance of economic priorities in the urban program.

The Conservatives also introduced a variety of new initiatives designed to impose their own ideological priorities upon urban policy. The enterprise zones created in over twenty cities were one obvious example. Enterprise zones rested on the premise that economic development was prevented by bureaucratic city planning and high local taxation imposed by Labour politicians. If physical and financial controls in specific areas of cities were eliminated, the government argued, enterprise, investment, and new jobs would be created. Hence in the zones land use controls and occupational safety regulations were relaxed. More important, firms locating in them were given exemption from local property taxes for ten years and 100 percent capital allowances on commercial and industrial buildings.

In fact the enterprise zones had mixed results and did not substantiate the government's views about urban regeneration. Twenty thousand jobs were created but the most successful were those with the greatest public-sector rather than private-sector investment. Also, 80 percent of the jobs created were not new but transferred from other parts of the city to take advantage of the tax breaks and created few new opportunities elsewhere. Since the program cost £180 million in the first five years, the jobs it created were expensive and heavily subsidized (Lawless 1987; National Audit Office 1988).

In the light of these criticisms in 1988 the government announced that no new zones would be created. Nevertheless the

TABLE 4-3. The Balance of Priorities of the Urban Program

	Economic	Environmental	Social
1981–82	32%	27%	41%
1982–83	38	29	33
1983–84	36	25	39
1984–85	36	21	43
1985–86	32	26	42
1986–87	42	25	34
1987–88	42	20	38
1988–89	55	20	25

Source: Public Expenditure Plans, 1981–82 through 1988–89.

principle of loosening city control over planning was extended in the simplified planning zone system. Although they did not provide financial benefits to private developers, the zones reduced local government control and increased that of the private sector and central government over development. In this way, government attempted to bend the planning process so there was a "routine presumption in favor of development" (Harding 1989).

The fiscal initiatives for urban redevelopment introduced by the Conservative government during the 1980s—urban development, urban regeneration, and city grants—displayed similar features. The urban development grants, based on the American Urban Development Action Grant model, were intended to give local authorities incentives to collaborate with the private sector in development projects. Central government paid 75 percent of the grant made by local authorities to the private sector for development projects that would not otherwise proceed without public-sector support. Between 1982 and 1986 almost two hundred schemes were initiated (Boyle 1985; Department of the Environment 1988). However, in 1986 the government, not satisfied that Labour cities were collaborating sufficiently with the private sector, introduced an urban regeneration grant that eliminated the local authority completely and offered central government funds directly to the private sector for development projects. The principle was extended in 1988 when a new system of city grants replaced the two original arrangements and eliminated entirely the local-authority role in the development grant process (Lawless 1988b). Table 4-4 shows the dramatic increase in city grants during the 1980s.

TABLE 4-4. Government Expenditure on City Grant
(£ at constant 1989 prices)

Year	Cost	
1983–84	£11,000	
1984–85	21,000	
1985–86	29,000	
1986–87	28,000	
1987–88	30,000	
1988–89	37,000	(estimated)
1989–90	63,000	(planned)
1990–91	70,000	(planned)

Note: City Grant includes Urban Development and Urban Regeneration Grant.
Source: Public Expenditure Plans, 1989–90 through 1990–91.

Other institutional innovations also attempted to increase central government's control over urban redevelopment and reduce
that of city governments. For example, the government created
city action teams in the six largest cities, which were intended to
give the central government a lead role in guiding and coordinating
redevelopment. Also task forces consisting of small teams of officials from central government departments, bolstered by representatives from the private sector, were set up in twelve areas to
encourage redevelopment projects. Although the resources of such
teams were modest, amounting to approximately £20 million annually, and the impact of projects sometimes marginal, the inten-
tion was to put central government and the private sector at the
leading edge of redevelopment. At best the notion of a partnership
with local authorities was weakened; at worst the local authorities
found themselves being bypassed.

These trends can be found in other policy areas that affected
cities. Perhaps the two most important examples were finance and
housing. In finance, for example, the Conservative government
created increasingly complex and punitive grant mechanisms that
were intended to restrict cities revenue and capital spending. It not
only substantially reduced the level of resources it provided to
cities and made them tax their own ratepayers more, but it also
restricted cities' ability to raise their own resources or spend those
they already possessed. The effect was to reduce the coherence of
the financial system, induce fiscal stress, and make it increasingly

TABLE 4-5.   The Contribution of Government Grant and Rates
to Local-Authority Income (£ in constant 1989 prices)

	Government Grant	Rates	Total
1979–80	£23,800	£12,400	£36,200
1980–81	23,800	13,500	37,300
1981–82	21,600	14,600	36,200
1982–83	20,300	15,200	35,500
1983–84	21,900	14,800	36,700
1984–85	22,200	15,300	37,500
1985–86	20,000	16,800	36,800
1986–87	22,200	17,400	39,600

Source: Public Expenditure Plans 1979–80 through 1986–87.

difficult for cities to control their environment and deliver services (Parkinson 1985; Travers 1987; Davies 1987; Newton and Karran 1985). The impact can be seen in Table 4-5. Government support fell in less than a decade by 7 percent and the local property taxes, the rates, were increased by 40 percent.

There were similar shifts in housing. National government increased its control over decisions about levels of investment in the ownership, pricing, and maintenance of public housing. Public investment in housing was dramatically reduced during the decade, so that there was essentially no longer a public house building program, as Tables 4-6 and 4-7 demonstrate. Cities were forced to sell off much of their best housing but prevented by the government from using their own resources to replace or improve their remaining stock. Some consumers benefited from the privatization of public housing, especially those who bought public housing at substantial discounts. But the contraction and impoverishment of the public housing sector meant that the poor and the powerless lost out (Murie 1987).

However, the two most distinctive examples of the Conservatives' urban strategy during the 1980s were their support for public-private partnerships and urban development corporations. In many respects they were different kinds of initiatives, but they shared many of the same ideological characteristics: an emphasis on private-sector leadership, a concentration on physical regeneration, and a diminished role for city government.

TABLE 4-6. Local Authority Investment in Housing
(£ at constant 1989 prices)

Year	Amount
1979–80	£3,648,000
1980–81	2,476,000
1981–82	443,000
1982–83	87,000
1983–84	1,080,000
1984–85	1,320,000
1985–86	1,406,000
1986–87	1,169,000
1987–88	899,000

Source: Social Trends 1989 (London: HMSO).

Public-Private Partnerships

The public-private partnerships that emerged in British cities during the 1980s are difficult to define precisely since as informal associations that varied widely in different settings, they lacked well-defined legal, organizational, or financial status. But in a number of cities the public and private sectors formed agreements to jointly promote and encourage physical redevelopment projects. Whatever precise form it took, the model was clearly imported from the United States. It also echoed the golden age of privately led urban development found in Victorian Britain in which "a romanticized view of Victorian urban society is offered which stresses the philanthropic leanings and civic pride of local economic elites and the benefit of their actions which allegedly filtered down to other groups in the locality" (Harding 1990, 111).

Both those historical and comparative contexts vary significantly from those in which public-private partnerships had to operate in Britain the late 1980s. The conditions underpinning the Victorian urban economy had been transformed by a number of key developments: the extension of the franchise, the rise of a working-class political party, the suburbanization of economic elites, the development of the welfare state and local government's role within it, the professionalization of both public and private sectors, the development of limited companies and their extension into national and multinational operational spheres. And there were significant differences between the United States and

TABLE 4-7.   Annual Construction of New Houses in United
Kingdom

	Local Authorities	Private Sector	Total
1961–1970	152,000*	198,000*	350,000*
1971–1980	111,000*	161,000*	272,000*
1981	58,000	119,000	177,000
1982	36,000	128,000	164,000
1983	37,000	151,000	188,000
1984	35,000	163,000	198,000
1985	29,000	159,000	188,000
1986	24,000	170,000	194,000
1987	21,000	178,000	199,000

*Annual averages.
Source: Social Trends 1989 (London: HMSO).

Britain that made it difficult to import the model, most obviously
including spatial differences in the organization of capital, governmental structure, intergovernmental fiscal relations, party systems, and ideological characteristics (Harding 1989).

Despite those constraints, the Conservative government stren-
uously encouraged the incipient movement toward such alliances
during the 1980s. Two trends were visible. The first was the
growth of national-led partnerships responding primarily to the
impulse of corporate responsibility. This was especially true of the
best-known and best-established example, Business in the Community (BIC), which had Prince Charles as its patron. BIC grew out
of an Anglo-American conference held after inner-city riots took
place in several British cities in 1981. A national umbrella organization for large corporations, BIC, with the support of staff from
central government and the private sector, government grants, and
tax exemptions for company contributions, created a national
network of enterprise agencies and trusts whose primary aim was
to encourage small-business development. BIC also moved into
training initiatives and was responsible for importing into Britain
the school compact model from Boston, which linked local business to local schools and which was subsequently endorsed by the
government as a demonstration project in fourteen cities.

The second wave of partnerships that emerged during the
mid-1980s, reflecting the government's interest in physical re-

generation, were more obviously local property-based schemes, with construction interests playing a leading role. The two most important were the Phoenix initiative and British Urban Development (BUD). Phoenix, which was formed in 1986 and primarily drew upon a report of the U.S. experience, was a national organization that acted as a lobbying agent and broker to central government and promoted particular development schemes. BUD was established in 1988 with equity contributions from eleven major building and property development corporations who used their resources to assemble and service land which was then resold to targeted developers. Significantly, the first chief executive of BUD was a former policy adviser to Mrs. Thatcher.

One of the Conservative government's goals during the 1980s was to encourage local authorities to collaborate more willingly with the private sector in development. In its early period of office, this was mainly achieved by the use of sanctions that severely restricted local authority powers. But in its later years, especially after its election to a third period in office in 1987, the government moved toward the use of incentives to encourage local-authority collaboration in private sector–led urban regeneration. This strategy appeared to have some political success at least. Several Labour-controlled industrial cities, including Newcastle, Glasgow, Sheffield, and Birmingham, realizing that resistance to the government's strategy had failed, allied themselves with the private sector and formed public-private partnerships to lead the physical and economic regeneration of their cities.

However, the impact such partnerships would have upon regeneration was unclear. The evidence of such experiments from the United States was mixed and indicated that major issues of political accountability and equity remained even when there was some evidence they encouraged economic growth. However, the politics of the process were clear in 1980s Britain. Realpolitik dictated that many Labour cities assume the role of urban entrepreneurs preferred by Mrs. Thatcher's government if they were to attract private-sector investment or public-sector approval (Harding 1990). Whether the initiatives would flourish and bring economic prosperity back to those provincial cities in the face of the flight of mobile capital remained, at best, uncertain.

Urban Development Corporations

The most dramatic illustration of the Conservative government's vision of urban regeneration in the 1980s was the urban development corporations (UDCs) (Parkinson 1988; Parkinson and Evans 1990; Lawless 1988a). The first were created in London and Liverpool in 1981, but eight were subsequently established in the core of economically stressed cities mainly outside the booming southeast. Development corporations were designated, empowered, and financed by, and directly accountable to, central government and they were given substantial powers to regenerate their areas. They were appointed rather than elected bodies intended to eliminate the political uncertainty produced by local democracy, which the government regarded as a major deterrent to private investment. Government financial support for the development corporations increased throughout the 1980s just as its support for other parts of the urban program was cut, along with as well as main local-authority services: education, housing, and transportation. Table 4-8 shows the shifting importance of development corporations within the urban program.

UDCs were given extensive powers over land acquisition, finance, and planning. In some cases, the UDCs were actually given direct ownership of land. Even where this did not happen they were given the powers of compulsory purchase (eminent domain). And UDCs were made the planning authority in their area. Cities lost their customary powers to control development and decide planning applications within UDC areas. The boards of UDCs typically had heavy representation from local business, especially construction interests. Local politicians were invited to be members, but not as official representatives of their cities, and many refused to join. The UDCs had substantial budgets from the government, varying between £20 and £60 million annually, which, in keeping with government philosophy, were primarily intended to provide incentives to private-sector investment in the cities by reducing the costs and risks.

The UDCs adopted a different redevelopment strategy from local government, emphasizing a property-led form of urban regeneration that diluted wider social goals of urban policy. They

TABLE 4-8. Government Expenditures on Urban Program and Urban Development Corporations (£ at constant 1989 prices)

	Urban Program	Urban Development Corporations
1979–80	£169,000	—
1980–81	194,000	—
1981–82	145,000	£59,000
1982–83	228,000	91,000
1983–84	212,000	127,000
1984–85	229,000	114,000
1985–86	208,000	105,000
1986–87	186,000	105,000
1987–88	184,000	149,000
1988–89	197,000 (est.)	252,000 (est.)
1989–90	166,000 (planned)	252,000 (planned)

Source: Public Expenditure Plans 1989–90 through 1991–92.

also adopted a more relaxed, entrepreneurial approach to planning, in contrast to allegedly bureaucratic local-authority style, with its traditional emphasis on planning as development control. In keeping with the property-led model of regeneration, heavy emphasis was placed on immediate action and visible results, often prestige "flagship" redevelopment projects, which were intended to improve the environment and image of an area and generate the confidence needed to attract private-sector investment.

The significance of the UDCs lay less in their scale than in their policy implications during the 1980s. Their experience raised three broad questions: How successful were they in creating private-sector investment and jobs in the cities? How accountable were they to their surrounding communities? To what extent were the benefits of regeneration equitably shared?

The records of the first two UDCs were mixed and revealed many of the problems of the government's strategy. Both used their extensive powers and privilege—direct access to central government resources and freedom from local political accountability—to achieve many of their goals. In particular, both did a great deal to physically regenerate their docklands areas. Substantial public pump priming, in the form of major infrastructure investment, transformed the London and Liverpool docklands from derelict areas to desirable environments. For example, London reclaimed more than two square miles of derelict dockland in six years. It was estimated that £440 million in public funds attracted more than £4.4 billion in private-sector investment—a gearing ratio of 1 to 10. A new airport, a new railway system, five million square feet of office and retail floor space, and 8,800 new houses were built. The largest redevelopment project in Europe, which could create 50,000 new service-sector jobs, was begun in London docklands.

Obviously the UDCs efficiently encouraged the physical regeneration of their area. However, on the equity and accountability criteria, their records were much more uneven. The benefits of much of regeneration—new jobs, new houses, and environmental improvements—did not go to the original docklands low-income community. Instead the jobs were created at the top end of the labor market in the skilled-services sector, just as the houses were built at the top end of the private housing market. Especially in London, little attention was paid to providing the training, jobs, or low-income housing to meet the needs of the original residents, who paid many of the economic, social, and environmental costs of regeneration while deriving relatively few of the benefits (House of Commons 1988; National Audit Office 1988; Church 1988; Docklands Consultative Committee 1988).

Indeed, regeneration in many respects increased inequality in access to private and public goods in the area. There were financial inequalities as well. As we showed earlier, UDCs were allocated substantial public resources at the same time that government financial support for city governments in the area was reduced. This not only caused political resentment, it also heightened the danger that the UDCs would regenerate their own narrowly defined areas while the surrounding neighborhoods deteriorated from lack of public funds, creating islands of private excellence amidst seas of public squalor.

A further difficulty with the government's UDC model of urban regeneration gradually emerged through the decade. The first wave of UDC policies concentrated virtually exclusively upon physical regeneration, with little attention paid to social provision or to the development of human capital. In keeping with government philosophy, wealth creation was the goal. Trickle-down would redistribute that wealth. However, in the late 1980s the UDCs found that physical regeneration required major social infrastructure and investment in human capital and turned their attention to the provision of low-income housing, community facilities, education, and training programs. The UDCs realized that if they did not make that provision, it would be difficult to attract workers who could afford to live or who were sufficiently trained to take the new service-sector jobs in the regenerated areas. This underlined a larger point about Conservative government strategy. By the end of the decade many cities were arguing that urban regeneration required a wider vision and a broader package of programs for finance, education, training, enterprise development, and social provision than an agency singlemindedly devoted to physical regeneration of a narrowly defined area could achieve.

Urban Regeneration under a Conservative Regime: An Assessment and a Prognosis

What was the impact of the shift in urban policies and priorities under Mrs. Thatcher? Which groups benefited and which lost? What does it tell us about the future economic regeneration of British cities? During the 1980s the Conservative government clearly restructured state power. It also enhanced the role of the private sector in urban policy. And it encouraged initiatives that provided increased incentives for entrepreneurial behavior by individuals, cities, and regions. In this process cities obviously lost power over economic development. The major gainers were the private sector and central government. There was little evidence that the government's economic development policies during the decade helped the urban underprivileged, however. Main programs in housing, education, and social services were reduced, and there was little targeting of programs that would specifically aid vulnerable groups.

Indeed, one effect of the government's strategy was to reinforce or increase unevenness in the distribution of economic rewards between regions, cities, and individuals. Many specific area-based initiatives like the development corporations or enterprise zones brought regeneration to limited parts of cities but left other parts unimproved. In some cases the policies produced very uneven benefits for different social groups—the underprivileged lost out at the expense of the affluent.

Of course, these forces were not confined to Britain. Cities in many advanced industrial economies are undergoing a wave of crucial and occasionally dramatic economic and social changes. The restructuring of the international economy has undermined the Victorian urban hierarchy and is creating new patterns of exchange and dominance. All cities are seeking, and some are finding, new economic niches as local, national, and international capital discovers that profit once again can be made in some, if not all, parts of cities. New actors, especially in the financial, construction, and property development sectors are taking the lead in regeneration. Governments are creating new institutional and fiscal mechanisms to encourage, control, or contain the rapid changes that are taking place. A variety of new political alliances between the public and private sectors are emerging to steer this uneven process of urban regeneration. For cities in Britain and elsewhere, the 1980s has become the decade of entrepreneurial urban mercantilism and aggressive place marketing.

Some cities are simply unable to compete in this rapidly changing economy and are falling behind in the economic race. Many individuals, firms, and communities find it equally hard to survive in the abrasive competition. However, some regions, cities, and indeed parts of cities are able to respond to and exploit the changes. But even where "successful" regeneration is taking place, different economic groups and neighborhoods benefit from, or lose out, in the process. Paradoxically, urban regeneration is occurring at the same time, often in the same place, as is decline. But whether cities are succeeding or failing, the economic and social consequences are highly uneven. Each process has different winners and losers.

This pattern of uneven urban regeneration has been perhaps most marked and most discussed in the United States in the past ten years. The experience of many cities has demonstrated that traditional manufacturing cities can regenerate by shifting their economic base and moving into new service industries. However, the experience also indicates that affluence and poverty increase at the same time in the city as a consequence of the bifurcated labor market typical of the service sector. American cities have had relatively little success in linking the benefits of regeneration to excluded social groups. City centers and neighborhoods remain in unequal competition for public and private resources. Office- and leisure-led development booms downtown and on the urban waterfronts, while neighborhoods often languish without resources. The resulting physical juxtaposition of extreme wealth and poverty, both of people and places, can be found in many cities. Such features are now emerging in the British cities that have experienced regeneration in the later part of the 1980s. The classic example, as we have seen, is London docklands, where the process of market-driven economic restructuring, physical renewal, and community displacement is most clearly visible. But the pattern can be seen in many British cities where development pressures are less intense.

These changes raise a series of questions about urban strategy that must be addressed during the next decade in Britain. Is investment in physical, as opposed to human, capital the best way of ensuring urban regeneration? Can the market and the private sector address issues of equity and fairness as well as those of efficiency and wealth creation? What will be the consequence of the growing centralization of government power, the rise of appointed development agencies, and the loss of direct local accountability? Are the public-private partnerships now growing in some cities mechanisms that can genuinely share as well as help create the benefits of growth in cities? The experience of the 1980s is that urban regeneration is not impossible, but it is uneven and partial. If Britain does not address those issues and the questions they raise in the next decade, the social price it pays may be very high indeed and the tentative economic benefits that have so far been achieved may be lost.

Just as important as the debate over uneven urban development is the debate over the future of local government in the United Kingdom. Throughout the decade the Thatcher government made increasingly strident efforts to deal with what it regarded as a crucial problem—the level of local authority spending, in particular the level of spending by Labour-controlled cities. Between 1979 and 1990, in an effort to cut city spending, the government made over 100 major and minor changes to the grant regime. They ranged from reducing the level of support for city spending to actively penalizing those cities that spent more than the government felt they should. The strategy had two consequences—one fiscal, the other political. The fiscal consequence was that the system of financing cities became increasingly complex and uncertain, encouraging cities to engage in perverse forms of financial behavior as they attempted to evade government controls. The political result was that public opinion eventually united with party political and professional opinion that the government's policy was damaging local democracy as well as local administration.

The apotheosis of this trend came at the end of the decade as the Conservatives introduced their most controversial measure: abandoning the rates or property tax system and replacing it with a community charge. Popularly known as the poll tax, this was a flat rate charge on all people over the age of 18. The government intended the system to make all adults pay for local services and as a result encourage them to vote against high-spending Labour authorities. But the change had precisely the reverse effect. It led to public outrage directed not at the cities who had to levy the tax, but at the government who had created it. The principled public objection was that the tax, failing to distinguish between the prince and the pauper, was even more regressive than the rates. The instrumental objection was to the level of taxes the system produced as individuals and families found their local tax bill trebling or quadrupling in the spring of 1990.

The change proved politically explosive for the government. Echoing the peasants' revolt in the fourteenth century, the last time a government attempted to introduce such a tax, the poll tax led to massive public protests across the country, scenes of violent disorder in the capital, and substantial Conservative losses in the local elections in May 1990. By this time the issue was threatening to undermine the prime minister's position and cast doubt over the government's ability to win another general election. It began to retreat from its original position and started a rapid review of the policy to minimize public opposition. By mid-1990 the details of that review were unclear, but the poll tax had made Mrs. Thatcher's urban policy the most highly politicized issue in the country. The cities, the last stronghold of Labour support in the country only five years earlier, may prove to be the cause of the government's, or Mrs. Thatcher's personal, downfall.

REFERENCES

Blunkett, David, and Keith Jackson. 1987. *Democracy in Crisis: The Town Halls Respond.* London: Hogarth Press.

Boddy, Martin, and Colin Fudge, eds. 1984. *Local Socialism? Labour Councils and New Left Alternatives.* London: Macmillan.

Boyle, Robin. 1985. "UDAG: The Urban Development Action Grant." *Policy and Politics* (13):27–41.

———. 1989. "Private Sector Urban Regeneration: The Scottish Experience." In *Regenerating the Cities,* ed. Michael Parkinson, Bernard Foley, and Dennis Judd. Glenview, Ill.: Scott, Foresman.

Church, Andrew. 1988. "Urban Regeneration in London Docklands: A Five Year Policy Review." *Environment and Planning C: Government and Policy* 6(2):187–208.

Davies, Harry. 1987. "Capital Spending." In *Reshaping Local Government,* ed. Michael Parkinson. New Brunswick, N.J.: Transaction Books.

Department of the Environment. 1988. *An Evaluation of the Urban Development Grant Programme.* London: HMSO.

Docklands Consultative Committee. 1988. "Six Years in London Docklands." London.

Edwards, John, and Richard Batley. 1978. *The Politics of Positive Discrimination: An Evaluation of the Urban Programme 1967–77.* London: Tavistock.

Fainstein, Susan, and Norman Fainstein. 1989. "The Ambivalent State: Economic Development Policy in the U.S. Federal System in the Reagan Years." *Urban Affairs Quarterly* (25):41–62.

Gyford, John. 1985. *The Politics of Local Socialism.* London: Allen & Unwin.

Hambleton, Robin. 1981. "Implementing Inner City Policy." *Policy and Politics* 9:27–41.

———. 1989. "Urban Government Under Thatcher and Reagan." *Urban Affairs Quarterly* 24:359–88.

Hamnett, Chris, Linda McDowell, and Phillip Sarre. 1989. *Restructuring Britain: The Changing Social Structure.* London: Sage.

Harding, Alan. 1989. "Central Control in British Urban Economic Development Programmes." In *The New Centralism,* ed. Colin Crouch and David Marquand. Oxford: Basil Blackwell.

———. 1990. "Public-Private Partnerships in Urban Regeneration." In *Local Economic Policy,* ed. Michael Campbell. London: Cassell.

Higgins, Joan, et al. 1983. *Government and Urban Poverty.* Oxford: Blackwell.

House of Commons, Employment Committee. 1989. "The Employment Effects of the Urban Redevelopment Corporations," vols. 1 and 2. London: HMSO.

King, Desmond. 1987. *The New Right: Politics, Markets and Citizenships.* Chicago: The Dorsey Press.

Lawless, Paul. 1979. *Urban Deprivation and Government Initiative.* London: Faber.

———. 1986. *The Evolution of Spatial Policy: A Case Study of Inner City Policy in the United Kingdom, 1968–81.* London: Pion.

———. 1987. "Urban Development." In *Reshaping Local Government,* ed. Parkinson.

———. 1988a. "Urban Redevelopment Corporations and Their Alternatives." *Cities* 5(3):277–89.

———. 1988b. "British Inner Urban Policy Post 1979: A Critique." *Policy and Politics* 16:261–75.

McKay, David, and Andrew Cox. 1979. *The Politics of Urban Change.* Beckenham: Croom Helm.

Mackie, Peter. 1987. "Transport." In *Reshaping Local Government,* ed. Parkinson.

Murie, Alan. 1987. "Housing." In *Reshaping Local Government,* ed. Parkinson.

National Audit Office. 1988. "Department of the Environment: Urban Development Corporations." London: HMSO.

Newton, Kenneth, and Terrence Karran. 1985. *The Politics of Local Expenditure.* London: Macmillan.

Parkinson, Michael. 1985. *Liverpool on the Brink.* Hermitage: Policy Journals.

———. 1987. *Reshaping Local Government.* New Brunswick, N.J.: Transaction Books.

———. 1988. "Urban Regeneration and Development Corporations: Liverpool Style." *Local Economy* 5:109–19.

Parkinson, Michael, and Richard Evans. 1990. "Urban Development Corporations." In *Local Economic Policy,* ed. Michael Campbell. London: Cassell.

Parkinson, Michael, Bernard Foley, and Dennis Judd. 1989. *Regenerating the Cities: The UK Crisis and the US Experience,* Glenview, Ill.: Scott Foresman.

Parkinson, Michael, and Stephen Wilks. 1983. "The Politics of Inner City Partnerships." *Local Government Studies* 11:63–81.

———. 1986. "Testing Partnership to Destruction." In *New Relations in Central-Local Research,* ed. Michael Goldsmith. Aldershot: Gower.

Robson, Brian. 1988. *Those Inner Cities.* Oxford: Oxford University Press.

Sharpe, L. J. 1973. "American and British Democracy Reconsidered." *British Journal of Political Science* 10:21–53.

Solesbury, William. 1986. "The Dilemmas of Inner City Policy." *Public Administration* 64:32–47.

———. 1987. "Urban Policy in the 1980s: The Issues and the Arguments." *The Planner* 73:110–23.

Stoker, Gerry. 1988. *The Politics of Local Government.* London: Macmillan.

Travers, Tony. 1987. "Current Spending." In *Reshaping Local Government,* ed. Michael Parkinson.

PART III

The Limits and Possibilities of Local Policy

CHAPTER 5

Economics, Politics, and
Development Policy:
The Convergence of
New York and London

Susan S. Fainstein

During the 1980s two global cities, New York and London, have shown a remarkable convergence in public policy and development patterns. Where previously they had followed quite different planning traditions, their governing regimes have recently
responded similarly to world economic forces that have heightened
the importance of financial control centers while diminishing the
significance of manufacturing locations. The question for analysis
here is the linkage between the pressures of world economic transformation, on the one hand, and political and ideological forces on
the other in determining the character of development.

By raising this question, I do not intend to imply that underlying economic forces were not the primary mechanism in shaping

these cities. Nevertheless, within the context of contemporary economic change there are alternative paths that policymakers can follow, involving more or less comprehensive planning, more or less citizen participation, more or less redistribution of the growth divided. The governments of New York and London opted for the route of minimal planning, dampened participation, and market distribution. These policies have contributed to highly uneven development, severe shortages of affordable housing, congestion, and environmental deterioration. Given the capitalist framework and economic situation in which the two cities were situated, government could not have created a vastly different form of development. It could, however, have broadened the decisional process and mitigated development's negative effects. This chapter explores the interaction that produced the extant outcome.

The Theory of Economic Restructuring and the Role of Development Policy

The last fifteen years have been a period of extraordinary change in the world economic system, usually captured under the rubric *economic restructuring* (see, among others, Frobel, Heinrichs, and Kreye 1980; Harvey 1987; Kasarda 1988). "Restructuring" refers to the transformation of the economic bases of cities in the advanced capitalist world from manufacturing to services; the rapid growth of the producer services sector within cities at the top of the global hierarchy; the simultaneous concentration of economic control within multinational firms and financial institutions, and decentralization of their manufacturing and routine office functions; the development of manufacturing in the Third World; and the rise of new economic powers in the Pacific Rim.

Economic change has in turn produced spatial change (see Castells and Henderson 1987; Gregory and Urry 1985; Markusen 1987; Storper and Scott 1988). The common perception is of highly decentralizing tendencies among both production and consumption units along with the clustering of certain specialized functions in nodes. Spatial decentralization is paradoxically made possible by economic concentration: "We find a tendency both toward the delocalization of the logic of the economic process and toward the concentration of decision-making units in a few commanding heights of the international economy" (Castells 1985, 30). The great size of the modern corporation permits it to break up its component parts into separate operating units; the large costs of financing giant enterprises, the negotiations involved in acquiring and recombining them, and the necessity of coordinating their far-flung parts require spatial concentration for deal making and control. "Key cities throughout the world are used by global capital as 'basing points' in the spatial organization and articulation of production and markets" (Friedmann 1986, 71; see also Sassen-Koob 1986).

Implicit in much of the literature is a direct attribution of the changes in spatial and social forms to economic causes. At the same time, however, numerous authors make explicit pleas that due deference be paid to the forces of historical contingency and political struggle in causing social outcomes (see, for example, Massey 1984; Sayer 1982; Parkinson and Judd 1988; Logan and Molotch 1987; and the introductory chapter to this volume). Several recent books comparing American cities have contended that variation results not just from their economic situation but also from their political histories (Stone and Sanders 1987; Jones, Bachelor, and Wilson 1986; Cummings 1988; Beauregard 1989). Internationally, cursory examination indicates that land use and development policy constitute one of the crucial policy arenas in which nations vary. As a consequence of economic situation and political interaction, countries have distinct traditions of state activity, and within those traditions the level and character of public intervention oscillate (Gough 1975; Marcuse 1982).

There are a number of different interpretations of the meaning of the varying levels and content of development policy. Marxist critics of the state role in planning have contended that it necessarily serves business interests, both because of the political power of business elites and because of the structural position of the state (see Offe 1975; Panitch 1977; Harvey 1978). According to this analysis, because the continued authority of the state requires economic growth, the state must constantly subsidize capital accumulation to ensure the conditions for profitability and further private investment (Przeworski and Wallerstein 1988). Moreover, to avoid a crisis of legitimacy, the state must compensate for the social outcomes of market processes by offering income support and public services, including housing, to people unable to achieve a subsistence wage within the market system (Offe 1984; Clark and Dear 1984). According to this view, then, the state is structurally dependent on capital and therefore must act in its interests regardless of the intentions of public officials. The extent to which the state *also* acts in the interests of other classes depends on their capacity to mobilize themselves and threaten the legitimacy of ruling groups.

Another group of theorists within the state managerialist school locates the thrust for state intervention in the independent power of political leaders and state bureaucrats seeking to enlarge their areas of autonomy (Saunders 1981: chapter 4; Pahl 1975; Gurr and King 1987; Evans, Rueschemeyer, and Skocpol 1985). Most histories of the welfare state in Europe emphasize the role of public officials, often conservative in ideology, in enlarging the state's role (Flora and Heidenheimer 1981; Rimlinger 1971; Ashford 1986). This perspective stresses the motivations of state personnel rather than business elites in state intervention. It leaves open, however, the question of the resulting distribution of benefits among the population; a state-led system need be no more egalitarian than a capitalist-led one. Government officials can stipulate only limited policy alternatives even if other social groups cannot easily impose their desires either.

Although state theory attributes the welfare state to governmental initiatives, it does not specify how far the capitalist state can go in opposing business interests or in pressing for redistribution. Capitalist governments usually find it easier to foster accumulation or provide security to the middle class than target expenditures to the deprived. Thus, tax subsidies typically assist investors and property owners, while the largest state welfare programs—health insurance and old-age pensions—are normally self-financing and largely based on taxation of the same groups that receive benefits. This is both because the economic power of capital gives it disproportionate political influence and because in democracies the middle strata, which possess the bulk of electoral power, do not benefit from highly redistributive programs.

In the realm of urban development the debate between the Marxist and managerialist schools of thought concerning the autonomy and effectiveness of the capitalist state raises three crucial issues for empirical investigation: (1) Is there a necessary relationship between capitalist economic development and state-sponsored development policy? (2) How does the ideological and institutional setting in which development policy takes place affect the role definitions of public decision makers and the character of their activities? (3) Whose interests does planning serve, and is its distribution of benefits predetermined?

Most of the literature has assumed irresolvable differences between the basic theoretical approaches; this chapter instead takes a synthesizing viewpoint. Its premise is that the relationship between state policy and capital is not fixed but changes over time in relation to political forces. These political forces are themselves ultimately rooted in the relations of production, but they are also shaped by ideological formulations that develop relatively autonomously and are affected by noneconomic factors. This analysis accepts the influence of popular interests on policy and, as in the state managerialist position, allows state capacity to vary historically while rooting politics more strongly in economics than that tendency does. It implies that the social impact of policy is not clear-cut and is at least potentially redistributive although limited by structural bias (see Castells 1977).

Comparison of two cities with long but changing histories of state activism allows the formulation of an argument concerning the forces generating development policy, the strategies of planners within similar economic but differing political contexts, and the consequences of public policy aimed at urban redevelopment. The reliance on just two cases does not permit the testing of any hypotheses generated across a statistically significant number of instances, in contrast to studies that test the association between certain structural characteristics of countries and cities and public expenditures (see Wilensky 1975, for example). On the other hand, it does permit a close examination of the dynamics of policy development and an evaluation of policy outcomes (see Levy, Meltsner, and Wildavsky 1974).

This chapter examines the reasons why, in two cities that long had similar economic structures and have undergone a comparable restructuring, formerly dissimilar public policies have increasingly converged. The next sections set forth the broad similarities and differences between New York and London and look at recent development in both cities. The conclusion discusses the role of the state in affecting development and the relation between state policy, economic and social structure, and politics.

The Comparison

London and New York are generally considered to be cities that perform unique functions within the world economy (Los Angeles and Tokyo occupy similar places at or near the top of the global hierarchy). As well as being the locations of the principal world financial institutions and markets, they are international centers of advanced services like law, accounting, advertising, public relations, insurance brokerage, and management consultancy. Moreover, their cultural influence, their attraction to tourists, and their reception of immigrants give them a worldwide prominence that transcends their purely economic role.

Theorists who have studied the character of world cities contend that the opportunities they provide for face-to-face negotiation and upper-class consumption make them necessary locations in the management of international power and financial relations (Sassen-Koob 1984; Friedmann and Wolff 1982; Thrift 1987). They point to commonalities in the physical development of these cities that result from their economic and cultural importance: very high spatial centrality of commercial activity; enormous expansion of office space, dwarfing their national competitors; growth of tourist facilities and specialty retailing; gentrification and conversion of manufacturing to commercial and residential structures.

The theoretical literature, however, is incomplete. It does not fully address certain questions about the activities that have pro-

TABLE 5-1.   New York Employment by Industry, 1950–1987 (thousands)

	1950	1960	1970	1980	1987*
Manufacturing (including mining)	1,041	949	768	497	387
Construction	123	125	110	77	112
Transportation and utilities	332	318	323	257	216
Wholesale and retail trade	755	745	736	613	633
Finance, insurance, and real estate	336	386	460	448	532
Services	508	607	785	894	1,106
Government	374	408	563	516	589
Total Employment	3,468	3,538	3,745	3,302	3,575

*March 1987.
Source: Temporary Commission on City Finances, The Effect of Taxation on Manufacturing in New York City, December 1976, Table 1; Real Estate Board of New York, Fact Book 1983, October 1982, Table 56; U.S. Bureau of Labor Statistics, Employment and Earnings, May 1987.

duced the phenotypical world city (see Friedmann and Wolff 1982). Questions requiring further investigation include the specific effects of local government policy in both encouraging and moderating the consequences of economic change; the political and ideological forces that make this policy; and the importance of national and regional political factors in determining the global city's development and role.

London and New York are a particularly useful source for comparative study because their common attributes permit the identification of a limited number of variables to explain their differences. They both developed as great ports; their roles as centers of international trade, and the requirements for financing that trade, caused them to develop the world's most important financial markets (Vogel 1988). Each has been the financial capital of the dominant global economic power, and each faces increased competition from other world centers. While the United Kingdom's international economic position has declined, London continues to hold its place as a financial capital. In both cities, although far more dramatically in New York, manufacturing employment diminished by half since the middle 1960s while office employment increased (see Tables 5-1 and 5-2). The changes in employment are signified spatially in an expansion of office space, including major government-sponsored development schemes, and pressure on conveniently

TABLE 5-2. London Employment by Industry, 1960–1980 (thousands)

	1960	1980
Manufacturing (including mining and agriculture)	1,468	690
Construction	281	165
Transportation, utilities, wholesale distribution	740	663
Retail trade	506	300
Finance and business services	462	593
Services	384	265
Government (health, education, welfare, public administration)	606	890
Total Employment	4,447	3,566

Source: Derived from Nick Buck, Ian Gordon, and Ken Young, *The London Employment Problem* (Oxford: Clarendon Press, 1986), Tables 4.1, 4.2.

located housing (Fainstein, Fainstein, and Schwartz 1989; Marcuse 1986). Both cities have inner-city concentrations of poverty and are surrounded by affluent suburban rings. In both, manufacturing jobs have moved out of easy access for the inner-city poor.

Some political and social characteristics also are similar. Government agencies in each city actively pursue private investment and have met strong opposition from neighborhood and preservationist forces. Borough councils in London and community boards in New York are comparable forums in which planning issues are first debated (Marcuse 1987; Saunders 1979, chapter 5). In both cities, ethnic divisions exacerbate conflict over turf. While systems of local finance differ, they are becoming more similar in requiring increased dependence on locally raised revenue. Both cities have a majority of renter households and systems of rent regulation; however both, especially London, have increasing levels of owner occupancy. Each exists in a national context of conservative, market-oriented ideological ascendancy but has strong political forces demanding continued state intervention within a significant tradition of state-sponsored social service and housing provision. Indeed, New York has been the most "European" of American cities in the historic activism of its government. The two cities also have experienced important changes in gender relations rooted in economic transformation, new family structures, and changing consciousness that both affect and are affected by spatial outcomes (Matrix 1984; Birch 1985; Redclift and Mingione 1984).

New York and London, however, have strikingly different political institutions. The mayor determines New York's political direction; no similar executive authority exists in London. On the other hand, the London borough councils are much more powerful than New York's community boards. London is organized by competing political parties with articulated programs; New York is virtually a one-party city, but the governing Democratic party has no machinery for enforcing a program and, in reality, has no program to impose. Essentially party officials act autonomously of party control (see Shefter 1985). Politics and historical precedents thus differentiate the two cities, although both operate within an original common ideological tradition of Lockean liberalism (Hartz 1955).

Development Politics in New York City

New York within the last forty years has undergone reversals in both its economic and political trajectories. The two cycles, however, have not been wholly synchronous; New York's oscillation between regular and reform politics has not fully coincided with swings of the economic pendulum (Shefter 1985). If economics did not immediately determine the city's politics, neither is it evident that politics and consequent policy affected economic development. At best we can chronicle the city's recent history and try to discern the forces that underlie its changing character.

New York entered a period of state-directed redevelopment (Fainstein and Fainstein 1986, 1989a) earlier than other U.S. cities.[1] Under the leadership of Robert Moses, who headed powerful independent authorities, New York's regime rapidly transformed the spatial character and living conditions of the city in the decade and a half following World War II (Caro 1974). Moses constructed the bridges and circumferential highways that modernized the city's transportation system while simultaneously weakening its transit services. He mounted a vast program of slum clearance and public housing, establishing a pattern whereby the government provided leadership in close collaboration with private developers and to the exclusion of community groups. The period, nevertheless, was one of substantial prosperity for New York's working and middle class. Moreover, while particular working-class elements suffered displacement as a consequence of city transportation and slum-clearance programs, many benefited from the construction of new low- and moderate-income housing. The continuation of the wartime rent-control program and the introduction of rent stabilization for new construction in 1969 kept housing costs low for the more than 70 percent of households that rented. Manufacturing and service sectors both prospered, and New York was exceptional among old American cities in enjoying considerable commercial and residential construction independent of government stimulus.

A number of factors, however, undermined the city's apparent stability and became glaringly obvious by the mid-1960s. As in most American cities population composition shifted dramatically between 1950 and 1970, as white middle-class people departed for the suburbs and Puerto Ricans and southern blacks replaced them (see Table 5-3). New York's extensive array of social services, including its famous public hospitals, free City University, and especially its school system, could not adapt sufficiently to the demands of the new clientele. The city became increasingly segregated, partly because its urban renewal program eliminated pockets of black population scattered throughout Manhattan and partly because white flight emptied many middle-class neighborhoods. Demands by racial and ethnic minorities for school desegregation, the ending of job discrimination, and improved services met resistance from the predominantly white city bureaucracy. The various subsidized housing programs foundered over the racial issue, as white voters refused to support programs that they saw as primarily benefiting minorities.

The progressive alliance that had existed between middle-class Jews, public- and private-sector trade unions, and elements of the political leadership broke down. It had formerly championed an active government engaged in social spending, as well as redevelopment, making New York the most liberal city in the United States. This coalition underlay the election of John Lindsay in 1965. The Lindsay regime, while continuing to promote the development of the Manhattan central business district as the key to

TABLE 5-3.   New York City Population, 1940–1984 (thousands)

	1940	1950	1960	1970	1980	1984
New York City	7,455	7,892	7,782	7,895	7,072	7,165
Percent white*	94	90	85	62	51	NA
Manhattan	1,890	1,960	1,698	1,539	1,428	1,456
Percent white	83	79	74	54	50	NA
Brooklyn	2,698	2,738	2,627	2,602	2,231	2,254
Percent white	95	92	85	60	48	NA
Bronx	1,395	1,451	1,425	1,472	1,169	1,173
Percent white	98	93	88	50	34	NA
Queens	1,298	1,551	1,810	1,986	1,891	1,911
Percent white	97	96	91	78	62	NA
Staten Island	174	192	222	295	352	371
Percent white	98	96	95	90	85	NA

*Before 1970, "white" includes individuals of Hispanic origin who are defined as Puerto Ricans.

Source: U.S. Bureau of the Census, State and Metropolitan Area Data Book 1986, 202, Table A; New York City Council on Economic Education, 1986 Fact Book on the New York Metropolitan Region, 1; L. C. Rosenwaike, Population History of New York City (Syracuse: Syracuse University Press, 1972), 121, 133, 136, 141, 197.

the city's economic future and doing little to stem the outflow of manufacturing and port-related jobs, devoted the bulk of its resources to efforts at improving conditions in low-income neighborhoods. Lindsay's response to minority protest groups was largely conciliatory, and during the first term of his mayoralty various anti-poverty and neighborhood improvement programs proliferated (Morris 1980).

The extreme racial antagonism that followed the 1968–69 battle over community control of schools, however, doomed further concessions (Fainstein and Fainstein 1974, chapter 2). In addition, the public service unions, which formerly had joined forces with their clienteles to press for the enlargement of social programs, now regarded their vociferous clients as hostile—and vice versa. The unions continued successfully to demand salary and pension improvements, thereby increasing pressure on the city's treasury. The ostensible beneficiaries of their activities, however, no longer necessarily saw themselves gaining from budget increases for salaried city workers.

The waning of the concessionary period in New York in the

early 1970s paralleled events in other cities. The decline of the national civil rights movement, racial backlash, and the Nixon presidency produced a context hospitable to the ascendancy of local conservative forces. New York had been unusual in the strength of its working-class movement during the nationally conservative period of the 1950s and in the extent of incorporation of minority interests into the regime of the mid-1960s. Municipal expenditures continued to grow rapidly in real dollar terms and in the percentage spent on education and social welfare purposes until the fiscal crisis in 1975; after that point, however, the budget contracted sharply in overall, constant dollar spending, and the proportion of this smaller expenditure directed to low-income people diminished (Brecher and Horton 1988).[2]

Neither the rise nor the decline of New York's proactive, liberal coalition can be explained by purely economic events. The city's and nation's economies, of course, underlay the social structure from which New York's unusual politics derived. New York's role as principal entry point for European immigrants and its rapidly growing economy, which kept many of them within the city, produced the conditions that generated political radicalism in much of this century. It was, however, political activity rather than either economic prosperity or downturn that stimulated state interventionism; sometimes this political activity, as in the 1950s, was against the national tide.

The growth of an unusually active governmental sector, embodied in state as well as city programs, had roots in a strong labor movement concerned with community as well as bread-and-butter issues and a long tradition of paternalism and civic activism by New York's upper classes. When racial and neighborhood militance divided the city in ways that crosscut old allegiances, the progressive coalition collapsed. The fiscal crisis of 1975 administered the *coup de grâce*. The freezing of social welfare expenditures and virtual termination of the capital budget that followed ended the distributional programs about which otherwise feuding interests could make common cause. The 1977 election of Edward Koch signaled the empowerment of a regime with little practical or symbolic commitment to low-income minorities, one which, once prosperity returned, continued to emphasize economic development rather than social welfare activities (Mollenkopf 1989). The mayor summed up his attitude: "I speak out for the middle class. You know why? Because they pay the taxes; they provide jobs for the poor people" (Koch 1984, 221).

The recasting of New York's objectives as achieving fiscal integrity and economic development rather than fighting poverty and obtaining federal funds transformed the thrust of city programs. During the bleak years after 1975 when New York nearly went bankrupt, almost the only investment activity that took place within the city involved the renovation and conversion of existing residential and factory buildings into middle- and upper-income domiciles. These took advantage of tax subsidy programs that substantially reduced costs to new occupants and resulted in the gentrification of parts of Manhattan and Brooklyn (Sternlieb, Roistacher, and Hughes 1976; Zukin 1982; Tobier 1979). The single major effort toward providing low-income housing consisted of the *in rem* program for buildings seized for tax delinquency. This program used federal Community Development Block Grant funds for maintenance and rehabilitation. At the same time large numbers of units dropped out of the housing stock as a consequence of landlord abandonment, condemnation, and fire. New York appeared hostage to financial institutions and economic forces well beyond its control (Tabb 1982; Alcaly and Mermelstein 1976). Contrary to many predictions (O'Connor 1973), however, retrenchment led low-income groups to moderate their claims rather than create a legitimation crisis.

To almost everyone's surprise, by 1980 New York's economy had reversed direction and was speeding toward recovery. Developers, responding to demand from financial institutions for expansion space and using city tax-abatement programs, began building millions of square feet of office space. Whereas only 4 million square feet of office space were added between 1975 and 1980, 23 million square feet were constructed in the next five years (Real Estate Board of New York 1985, Table 154). The city government did everything within its powers to encourage development, acting through quasi-independent development corporations which played an entrepreneurial role in spurring construction. Despite a revival of its capital budget, New York relied heavily on private developers to construct public infrastructure, offering zoning bonuses in return. The Department of City Planning kept a low profile and devoted itself mainly to a research and narrow regulatory function (Fainstein and Fainstein 1987, 1989b).

As New York became wealthier in the aggregate and despite a substantial drop in unemployment, income distribution worsened and the housing crisis became ever more acute (Stegman 1985, 1988). Poverty and homelessness, however, produced merely limited protest, primarily among advocates for affordable housing. Only after the boom began to taper off in 1987 did the mayor present a substantial housing program, relying in large part on the expected $1 billion income stream generated by the Battery Park City project, a giant complex of upper-income residential and blue-ribbon commercial structures developed by a semi-independent public authority.

What can we say in general about the relationship between economics, politics, and social welfare in New York's recent history? New York City's government obviously did not control the forces that caused manufacturing decline and advanced service growth in the U.S. economy. As the traditional center for financial, legal, accounting, and management consulting firms, New York was in a good position to capture the expansion resulting from the 1980s stock market boom, the explosion of mergers and acquisitions, and the internationalization of the country's economy.

The continued location of financial institutions and advanced services in New York, however, was not an automatic outcome of their growth. The decline of San Francisco relative to Los Angeles indicates the possibility of shifts in momentum. The increased competitiveness of New Jersey, furthermore, meant that the city had to bid to keep firms within its taxing jurisdiction. New York's notoriously complex regulatory system, very high taxes, and heavy energy costs act as constant deterrents to business growth. Even while the city government deserves criticism for the environmental harm caused by massive increases in density and the social degradation resulting from housing crisis and inadequate welfare spending, it also can be credited for policies that fostered economic development. There is no clear method by which to settle the dispute over whether public policy played a significant role in causing the boom of the 1980s. This observer accepts that the speedy resolution of the fiscal crisis and the promotion of physical development did make an important difference in the city's fate (although the region's trajectory might have remained the same). Agreeing that public programs stimulated growth, however, does not resolve whether the costs of development to lower-income people could have been mitigated through more enlightened policy.

One way of answering this question is to determine whether, given its fiscal precariousness and the high costs of doing business in New York, the city had any choice. In other words, was it wholly susceptible to blackmail by development capital, and could it not afford to be more generous with the gains of growth? Another way of looking at the issue is to inquire whether an organized working-class or community-based force limited its freedom of action. It was, in fact, the absence of any popular mobilization pressing for redistribution that made the city hostage to developer interests. Indeed the maintenance of rent regulation despite the sustained and bitter opposition of landlords implies that the power of property can be effectively opposed.

The Koch regime itself was not simply the passive consequence of an increasingly assertive stratum of capitalists and a declining progressive movement. The mayor, within the setting of national ideological conservatism, actively shaped his political context, giving voice to but also influencing his middle- and working-class supporters. Economics alone did not shape their perceived interests; rather the mayor's followers were persuaded that a more generous city government would siphon off hard-earned dollars to welfare payments and would cause jobs to leave the city.

Development Politics in London

London like New York experienced a postwar history marked by an initial period of growing prosperity, followed by decline then recent boom. Its decline, however, as represented by loss of jobs and population, was longer and steadier than New York's and its contemporary affluence less substantial as measured by physical development and employment. In both cities poverty and minority status became concentrated in particular neighborhoods (Stegman 1987, chapter 5; Townsend 1987, chapter 4). In London, however, the smaller size of the minority population and the existence of council housing in every borough precluded the racial homogeneity and extensive blight found in much of New York. The large-scale abandonment that occurred in many of New York's poor areas never happened in London. Although London experienced extensive suburbanization, the flight of the middle class from the central city did not take place at New York's scale.

Although both cities have significant immigrant communities, the rate of immigration into New York has surged in the last decade (Bogen 1987), while it has shrunk substantially in London (Jones 1988). London's population, like New York's, became increasingly composed of racial and ethnic minorities, but again there was a large difference of degree, with foreign born constituting about 18 percent of London's population in 1981 (see Table 5-4) as compared to New York's near 50 percent minority proportion in the same year. Thus, London's ethnic neighborhoods are largely composed of second-generation immigrants, while parts of New York are being transformed by the new influx. New York's nonwhite electorate is represented by a number of officials of shared ethnicity at the municipal, state, and national levels; nonwhite representation on governing bodies is far less in London.

One cannot talk about a politics of London in the same way as New York, since London does not have its own political regime. First the London County Council, then the Greater London Council (GLC), acted as the city's general-purpose government. Even at the height of the GLC's ascendancy, however, it never possessed the authority of New York City's government since budgetary and ultimate decision-making power rested with the central government, while housekeeping functions and primary responsibility for publicly provided housing and most land use planning rested with the boroughs. The elimination of the GLC in 1986 demonstrated the ultimate control exercised by the Cabinet and Parliament over the city (O'Leary 1987; King 1989; Game and Leach 1988). London's limited governmental autonomy, combined with the role played by nationally constituted parties with specified

TABLE 5-4.   Greater London Population, 1940–1984 (thousands)

	Population	Percent Born in New Commonwealth* and Pakistan
1931	8,110	NA
1951	8,197	NA
1961	7,992	NA
1971	7,452	13
1981	6,696	18
1986 (est.)	6,775	NA

*Includes Caribbean, India, Bangladesh, Cyprus, Gibraltar, Malta, Gozo, and the Far East.
Source: Great Britain, *Annual Abstract of Statistics* (London: H.M.S.O., 1987), Table 2.8; Hugh Clout and Peter Wood, eds., *London: Problems of Change* (London: Longman, 1986), Table 18.1.

programs in shaping local councils, means that national not local politics determines the broad outlines of public policy. In many ways, however, the ideological and practical impact of the successful Conservative attack on a governmental body that was viewed as free-spending and too radical resembled that of the fiscal crisis in New York—it dampened opposition and made proposals for redistributional measures seem far-fetched.

While there is no parallel set of regime types to define a set of stages like those of New York, there remain striking similarities between the development-policy history of London and that of New York. London in the immediate postwar period, of course, underwent enormous redevelopment under government auspices as public officials sought to reconstitute the war-damaged city. Efforts centered particularly on the construction of council housing estates and continued through both Conservative and Labour governments. As in New York governmental activity strongly affected infrastructure and land uses, but the focus was different. Nothing comparable to Robert Moses's arterial system for New York was developed; on the other hand, investment in public transit continued, with both modernization of existing lines and extensions into the outer boroughs. Little public effort was directed toward the development of commercial property; in fact, a deliberate attempt was made to decentralize industry to the new towns (Buck, Gordon, and Young 1986, chapter 2). There was a privately inspired commercial property boom in the 1960s, although of far less scope than New York's. The emphasis of planning was on the creation of an orderly environment; regulation was much stricter than in New York; and the preservation of the greenbelt around Greater London constituted one of the cardinal principles on which planning was based.

Despite these similarities, important variations exist and form the basis of comparative analysis. Although both governments have sponsored significant housing and redevelopment programs, in London these programs have functioned within an articulated planning framework that has no American counterpart (Savitch 1987, 1989; Clawson and Hall 1973; Foley 1972). Not only has there been a plan for the development of London, but it was framed within a national development scheme. Even the Thatcher government, with its stress on market determination, has maintained elements of the original physical plan, including the greenbelt (Jones 1988). In contrast, there is no overall planning for the New York region, and within the city economic development agencies rather than physical planning bodies determine redevelopment planning (Fainstein and Fainstein 1987). While London has seen a notable relaxation of planning controls in the last decade, environmental concerns still play a much greater role in restricting speculative development than in the New York region (Savitch 1989).

During the 1970s Labour dominated London's politics at both the national and local level. It developed an inner-city strategy similar to the War on Poverty and Model Cities programs of New York (Lawless 1987). Under the leadership of Ken Livingstone, the GLC of the 1980s sought to fuse an industry-based economic development strategy with urban radicalism (Mackintosh and Wainwright 1987). It went much further than did the comparable Lindsay regime of the previous decade in New York in seeking to combine enhanced collective consumption, community participation, and economic revitalization developed through a bottom-up rather than trickle-down approach. It established the Greater London Enterprise Board (GLEB) as its major instrument for this purpose. In the docklands it sought to foster manufacturing, in contrast to the later London Docklands Development Corporation's emphasis on office construction (Marris 1987).

The difficulties of London's economy in the last two decades, however, far more than was true of New York at the same time, reflected national economic malaise. Thus, job loss was much more severe than in New York (see Tables 5-1 and 5-2). The Conservative victory of 1979 did not stimulate a national economic boom, as did Reagan's 1980 triumph; consequently London's struggle to rebuild its economy was far more arduous than New York's. As in New York, manufacturing jobs disappeared by the hundreds of thousands, but so far they have been only partially replaced by service-sector employment (see Table 5-2).

London like New York has undergone fiscal stringency, although not as a consequence of the free-spending pattern of earlier regimes or the changing composition of its population. Even under the Labour government of the 1970s, the central government sought to deal with its budget deficits by reducing grants to local governments; under Margaret Thatcher this necessity has become a principle (Glassberg 1981; Parkinson 1987, 2–7; Pickvance 1988). Consequently the London authorities like most other municipal governments throughout the United Kingdom have confronted social deterioration with diminished resources and have been forced to reduce their staffs. Central government restrictions on local-authority spending mean that even greatly heightened prosperity in the city would not allow it to increase its spending dramatically, although presumably it would reduce demands on the public fisc.

The problem of inner-city poverty and job loss ultimately caused the government to reverse its policy of supporting decentralization of population and employment (Manners 1986). It now actively promotes commercial expansion within the city core. As in New York, megaprojects for first-class office and upper-income residential construction have become the order of the day. The docklands redevelopment project, under the supervision of an urban development corporation unbound by the planning regulations that restrict borough councils, is the largest such enterprise in the world (Parkinson and Evans 1989; Potter 1988; Church 1988). The designation of part of docklands as an enterprise zone frees developers from many taxes and environmental regulations. Another gigantic commercial development is planned for the King's Cross area in the heart of London. As in New York, there is skepticism over the market's capacity to absorb all this new office space and criticism that the jobs created will require skills not possessed by the inner-city unemployed (*Economist* 1988). The government, as in New York, assumes that office space generates jobs and that the multiplier effects of advanced services industries will produce employment opportunities for the less qualified.

In the 1970s London presented a model of greater state intervention in the provision of social welfare than did New York; now there is remarkable convergence in both the content of state policy and its justification. In an article written over a decade ago, Norman Fainstein and I (1978, 139–42) attributed the greater governmental contribution to egalitarian living conditions in London than in New York at that time to three factors: (1) the existence of a capitalist class that construed its interests collectively and held a paternalistic vision of its role in society; (2) the political capacity of the state to establish a sphere of autonomy for itself; and (3) the political capacity of subordinate classes to influence state policy in their own interests. Since the Conservative victory of 1979, development and welfare policy in London increasingly resembles New York's, with similar processes of massive commercial development, gentrification, and increasing income inequality occurring (Rees and Lambert 1985; Buck, Gordon, and Young 1986; Townsend 1987). The explanation for this shift lies in the reformulation of capitalist ideology that Thatcher has led and in the accelerating weakness of subordinate classes in developing an effective counterprogram (Krieger 1986).

Restructuring and Political Restoration

Throughout most of the twentieth century the United States and the United Kingdom implemented differing policies of planning and social welfare. Within the social science literature policy differences have been variously attributed to different institutional structures (centralized versus decentralized; elite versus nonelite selection to the bureaucracy); party systems (mass or cadre; ideological or nonideological); class systems (presence or absence of an aristocracy; traditions of deference; levels of social mobility); dominant ideology; level of working-class mobilization; and cultural traditions. The parallels between London and New York in the last decade point to the elimination of some of these variables as explanators of convergence and divergence and illuminate the close interconnectedness of others.

Dissimilar institutional structures clearly can be the vehicle for quite similar substantive policies. The systems of local government in the United Kingdom and the United States have become less alike in the recent past. The elimination of the metropolitan layer of government in Britain's largest conurbations has partly recapitulated the American situation in which regions consist of numerous, uncoordinated municipalities. Nowhere in the United States, however, do agglomerations exist on the scale of London's core area without an overarching general-purpose government. In addition, the move by central government to exert ever greater fiscal and policy control over local government restricts municipal autonomy to an extent unimaginable in the United States. Just a short while ago Labour control of the GLC allowed it to pursue a course sharply at variance with national policy, indeed one that probably exceeded the leeway available to New York. Now the possibility of deviation is totally blocked.

During the same period the British party system has also diverged from the American one. It remains much more programmatic and has become even more centralized. At the national level it has become a three-party system, and at the local level there is not the single-party dominance that characterizes most American big cities and has shaped New York politics during the postwar years. The elimination of the metropolitan level of government has meant no one party governs London; rather, party control varies among the thirty-three borough councils. The real authority over London policy, however, resides in the central government.

The high stakes involved in controlling the national party program have exacerbated the divisions within the Labour party. In contrast, conflict within the New York Democratic party results not from efforts to determine its program but from contests for the party nomination that usually assures elected office. The minority status of the Labour party within the British national government means that, with the elimination of the GLC, it can do little to determine London's course. The majority status of the Democrats in New York, despite Republican ascendancy in Washington, means that theoretically they could impose a Democratic program on the city. The atomistic nature of the party, however, means they have no program to impose.

Despite these differences the actions of public officials determining local initiatives became more the same. Using the tools of development corporations, tax subsidies, advertising and public relations, and financial packaging, officials have stressed the economic development function of government to the detriment of social welfare and planning. Margaret Thatcher, in the name of freeing up the market and stimulating an enterprise culture, has reduced redistributive governmental programs and forced the borough councils to make land available for private developers. Edward Koch, without endorsing the laissez-faire mentality of the Republican national government, has similarly cozened developers in the name of the middle class.

The crux of the increasing resemblance of New York and London lies not in political institutions but in social relations and the way in which those relations are interpreted. The occupational structures of the two countries both reflect a "postindustrial" economy, although the United Kingdom continues to have a larger proportion of its population engaged in manufacturing and extractive industries. In André Gorz's phrase, both nations have said farewell to their working classes, at least as traditionally defined. The growth of service-producing strata, divided into a prosperous technical, managerial, professional grouping on the one hand, and a poorly paid clerical and service proletariat on the other, has transformed political cleavages. The upper stratum, even if it does not wholly identify with Reaganite-Thatcherite conservativism, finds little in either the traditional Democratic or Labour parties to capture its enthusiasm. The lower end has largely failed to organize itself around a coherent political program as the unionized, blue-collar working class had done. While members of this grouping share a collective interest in higher wages and protective legislation, they differ markedly in the types of work they do, the situations under which they do it, the kinds of employers they have, and their attachments to their jobs. A middle-aged nurse's aide in a public hospital has little in common with a teenage boy flipping hamburgers. Moreover, the low-wage service stratum finds itself in a minority, particularly among voters.

The shift from manufacturing to service dominance has certainly not resulted in greater equality, and much evidence points to increasing social polarization within both London and New York. Objectively, therefore, the bottom half of the population has fared relatively poorly during the recent period of growth and might be expected to rebel. In a time of intense international competition, however, where national stagnation results in absolute, not just relative, deterioration of living standards and in which disillusion with the capacity of socialist economies to produce prosperity is complete, the left has not been able to present a convincing alternative to the doctrine of growth at any price. The programmatic failure of the left and the resurgent market ideology of the right combine in both New York and London to produce the phenomenon of the missing political actor—a unified counterforce to finance- and development-led capital. The common lack of this political force, rather than the institutional structure of the two metropolises, accounts for their policy similarities.

A causal linkage can be traced from economic restructuring to the changes in social structure discussed above to the absence of a strong political force pushing for egalitarian measures. Nevertheless, economic restructuring does not simply create politics. The electoral triumph of conservative regimes in New York and London has not, for the most part, been replicated elsewhere, and it is the political-ideological dominance of these regimes that is the direct cause of state policy.

At the national level within both the United States and Great Britain, the left has not persuaded the voting public that it has a formula for economic expansion. New York's political trajectory during prosperous times moved somewhat independently of national trends; in the present period, however, recent memories of lagging growth have combined with racial division to preclude ideological autonomy. In London the absence of a governing regime separate from the national government makes autonomy impossible. In both cities, therefore, the failures of the left nationally have reduced local opposition to relatively narrow issues and a primarily negative stance.

This situation may be simply cyclical, in which case convergence around a pro-growth, antiplanning, antiwelfare program may cease. More likely, however, it results from the aforementioned social divisions as well as from the difficulties at the national level of devising a program whereby capital is publicly controlled yet remains internationally competitive. In a chicken-and-egg conundrum, reduction of private control of investment requires an effective political movement for its attainment; such a movement, however, seems to require that private capital be less convincing in persuading the public that it represents its interests and in pressing government to nurture its ambitions.

This conclusion pushes the question of the relative influence of politics and economics back another step and in some sense makes the question unanswerable. Within an intellectual framework that accepts economic determination as a premise, whether it be a conservative analysis of market forces or a Marxist view of the requirements of capital accumulation, there is, in fact, no basis for the formulation of a positive (rather than critical) argument for economic transformation under capitalism that will also produce more equality.[3] In such a framework no nation has sufficient autonomy to slacken in its effort to accumulate capital without bearing the substantial costs of disinvestment.

Acceptance of this reasoning, however, reflects the hegemony of the ideology of private capital accumulation but not necessarily its validity. If, in fact, a unified egalitarian movement organized itself politically with sufficient force to direct policy, then the very character of international competition would change. The absence of such a force is in part the product of the recomposition of the class system resulting from economic restructuring. It is also, however, the result of political-ideological factors that have undercut mobilization and thereby rendered the left ineffective.

Growth with equity requires the development of a program for a more publicly oriented yet market-based system with greater democratic control of capital investment than currently exists in either Britain or the United States. It remains for the left to devise such a program that the majority of the public identifies as not simply benefiting only labor unions or ethnic minorities. Rather its premise must be universalistic, promising growth and benefits for the middle class, accepting the new flexibility of production and the inevitability of internationalization of local economies. Only such a program carries the potential to make common cause between the two segments of the service-providing strata, allowing the new social relations of production to result in a progressive political force rather than division among its various elements.

NOTES

Acknowledgment: I am grateful to Susana Fried for her research assistance and to Norman Fainstein for his comments. Support for the research herein was provided by the Rutgers University Research Council and the Rutgers University President's Council on International Programs.

1. In *Restructuring the City* (1986, chapter 7) Norman Fainstein and I distinguish three types of local regimes and three stages in the postwar politics of urban redevelopment. From the mid-1940s until about 1965, urban regimes emphasized large-scale development projects, which were initially sponsored directly by government. During this *directive* period, local regimes operated with little effective popular opposition. They were succeeded by *concessionary* regimes, which responded to the urban disorders of the 1960s by making concessions to minority-group and community demands. The third period, extending from 1975 to the present and marked by the heightened influence of business interests and the muting of popular demands, is *conserving* in the sense of stressing fiscal stability but still retaining some of the institutions and programs born in the concessionary period. New York City entered and emerged from the directive period earlier than most American cities but otherwise conforms to this pattern.

2. The impact of these spending cuts was compounded by the simultaneous growth in the poverty population. It is extremely difficult to compare New York's pattern and level of expenditures to that of other large cities. New York's municipal budget includes spending for education, public health, and public assistance while elsewhere these functions are part of independent school district and county budgets.

3. Progressive programs at this time tend to focus on specifics like affordable housing, affirmative action, and balanced development rather than more global strategies.

REFERENCES

Alcaly, Roger E., and David Mermelstein, eds. 1976. *The Fiscal Crisis of American Cities.* New York: Vintage.
Ashford, Douglas E. 1986. *The Emergence of the Welfare States.* Oxford: Basil Blackwell.

Beauregard, Robert A., ed. 1989. *Atop the Urban Hierarchy.* Totowa, N.J.: Rowman and Littlefield.

Birch, Eugenie, ed. 1985. *The Unsheltered Woman.* New Brunswick, N.J.: Center for Urban Policy Research, Rutgers University.

Bogen, Elizabeth. 1987. *Immigration in New York.* New York: Praeger.

Brecher, Charles, and Raymond D. Horton. 1988. "Politics in the Post-Industrial City." Paper presented for the Social Science Research Council Dual City Working Group Meeting, February.

Buck, Nick, Ian Gordon, and Ken Young. 1986. *The London Employment Problem.* Oxford: Clarendon Press.

Caro, Robert. 1974. *The Power Broker: Robert Moses and the Fall of New York.* New York: Knopf.

Castells, Manuel. 1977. *The Urban Question: A Marxist Approach.* Cambridge: MIT Press.

———. 1985. "High Technology, Economic Restructuring, and the Urban-Regional Process in the United States." In *High Technology, Space, and Society,* ed. Manuel Castells. Beverly Hills, Calif.: Sage.

Castells, Manuel, and Jeffrey Henderson, eds. 1987. "Technoeconomic Restructuring, Socio-political Processes and Spatial Transformation: A Global Perspective." In *Global Restructuring and Territorial Development,* ed. Jeffrey Henderson and Manuel Castells. Beverly Hills, Calif.: Sage.

Church, A. 1988. "Urban Regeneration in London Docklands: A Five-Year Policy Review." *Environment and Planning C: Government and Policy* 6:187–208.

Clark, Gordon L., and Michael Dear. 1984. *State Apparatus.* Boston: Allen & Unwin.

Clawson, Marion, and Peter Hall. 1973. *Planning and Urban Growth: An Anglo-American Comparison.* Baltimore: Johns Hopkins University Press.

Cummings, Scott, ed., 1988. *Business Elites and Urban Development.* Albany: SUNY Press.

Economist, The. 1988. "London Docklands." Feb. 13.

Evans, Peter B., Dietrich Rueschemeyer, and Theda Skocpol, eds. 1985. *Bringing the State Back In.* Cambridge: Cambridge University Press.

Fainstein, Susan S., and Norman I. Fainstein. 1974. *Urban Political Movements: The Search for Power by Minority Groups in American Cities.* Englewood Cliffs, N.J.: Prentice-Hall.

———. 1978. "National Policy and Urban Development." *Social Problems* 26 (December): 125–46.

———. 1986. "Regime Strategies, Communal Resistance, and Economic Forces." In *Restructuring the City: The Political Economy of Urban Redevelopment,* rev. ed., ed. Susan S. Fainstein et al. New York: Longman.

————. 1987. "The Politics of Land Use Planning in New York City." *Journal of the American Planning Association* 53:237–48.

————. 1989a. "Governing Regimes and the Political Economy of Re-development in New York City." In *Power, Culture, and Place: Essays on the History of New York City,* ed. John Hull Mollenkopf. New York: Russell Sage Foundation.

————. 1989b. "New York City: The Manhattan Business District, 1945–1988." In *Unequal Partnerships,* ed. Gregory D. Squires. New Brunswick, N.J.: Rutgers University Press.

Fainstein, Susan S., Norman Fainstein, and Alex Schwartz. 1989. "Economic Shifts and Land Use in the Global City: New York, 1940–1987." In *Atop the Urban Hierarchy,* ed. Robert Beauregard. Totowa, N.J.: Rowman and Littlefield.

Flora, Peter, and Arnold J. Heidenheimer, eds. 1981. *The Development of Welfare States in Europe and America.* New Brunswick, N.J.: Transaction.

Foley, Donald L. 1972. *Governing the London Region: Reorganization and Planning in the 1960's.* Berkeley and Los Angeles: University of California Press.

Friedmann, John. 1986. "The World City Hypothesis." *Development and Change* 17:69–83.

Friedmann, John, and Goetz Wolff. 1982. "World City Formation: An Agenda for Research and Action." *International Journal of Urban and Regional Research* 6 (September): 309–44.

Froebel, F., J. Heinrichs, and O. Kreye. 1980. *The New International Division of Labor.* Cambridge: Cambridge University Press.

Game, Chris, and Steve Leach. 1988. "The Abolition of Metropolitan Governments: An Interim Assessment of the Abolition of the English Metropolitan County Councils." Paper presented at the annual meeting of the American Political Science Association, Washington, D.C., September.

Glassberg, Andrew D. 1981. "Urban Management and Fiscal Stringency: United States and Britain." In *Urban Political Economy,* ed. Kenneth Newton. New York: St. Martin's.

Gough, Ian. 1975. "State Expenditures in Advanced Capitalism." *New Left Review* 92:53–92.

Gregory, Derek, and John Urry, eds. 1985. *Social Relations and Spatial Structures.* New York: St. Martin's.

Gurr, Ted Robert, and Desmond S. King. 1987. *The State and the City.* Chicago: University of Chicago Press.

Hartz, Louis. 1955. *The Liberal Tradition in America.* New York: Harcourt, Brace.

Harvey, David. 1978. "Planning the Ideology of Planning." In *Planning Theory in the 1980s,* ed. Robert Burchell and George Sternlieb. New Brunswick, N.J.: Center for Urban Policy Research, Rutgers University.

————. 1987. "The Geographical and Geopolitical Consequences of the Transition from Fordist to Flexible Accumulation." Paper presented to the Conference on America's New Economic Geography, Center for Urban Policy Research, Rutgers University, Washington, D.C., April.

Jones, Bryan D., and Lynn W. Bachelor, with Carter Wilson. 1986. *The Sustaining Hand.* Lawrence: University of Kansas Press.

Jones, Emrys. 1988. "London." In *The Metropolis Era*, vol. 2, ed. Mattei Dogan and John D. Kasarda. Beverly Hills, Calif.: Sage.

Kasarda, John D. 1988. "Economic Restructuring and America's Urban Dilemma." In *The Metropolis Era*, vol. 1, ed. Dogan and Kasarda.

Katznelson, Ira. 1978. "Considerations on Social Democracy in the United States." *Comparative Politics* (October):77–99.

King, Desmond S. 1989. "Political Centralization and State Interests in Britain: The 1986 Abolition of the GLC and MCCs." *Comparative Political Studies* 21 (January):467–94.

Koch, Edward. 1984. *Mayor.* New York: Simon and Schuster.

Krieger, Joel. 1986. *Reagan, Thatcher, and the Politics of Decline.* New York: Oxford University Press.

Lawless, Paul. 1987. "Urban Development." In *Reshaping Local Government*, ed. Michael Parkinson. New Brunswick, N.J.: Transaction.

Levy, Frank S., Arnold J. Meltsner, and Aaron Wildavsky. 1974. *Urban Outcomes.* Berkeley and Los Angeles: University of California Press.

Logan, John R., and Harvey Molotch. 1987. *Urban Fortunes: The Political Economy of Place.* Berkeley: University of California Press.

Mackintosh, Maureen, and Hilary Wainwright, eds. 1987. *A Taste of Power.* London: Verso.

Manners, Gerald. 1986. "Decentralizing London, 1945–1975." In *London: Problems of Change*, ed. Hugh Clout and Peter Wood. London: Longman.

Marcuse, Peter. 1982. "Determinants of State Housing Policies: West Germany and the United States." In *Urban Policy under Capitalism*, ed. Norman I. Fainstein and Susan S. Fainstein. Beverly Hills, Calif.: Sage.

————. 1986. "Abandonment, Gentrification, and Displacement: The Linkages in New York City." In *Gentrification of the City*, ed. Neil Smith and Peter Williams. Boston: Allen & Unwin.

————. 1987. "Neighborhood Policy and the Distribution of Power: New York City's Community Boards." *Policy Studies Journal* 16 (Winter): 277–89.

Markusen, Ann R. 1987. *Regions: The Economics and Politics of Territory.* Totowa, N.J.: Rowman and Littlefield.

Marris, Peter. 1987. *Meaning and Action: Community Planning and Conceptions of Change.* London: Routledge and Kegan Paul.

Massey, Doreen. 1984. *Spatial Divisions of Labor.* London: Macmillan.

Matrix. 1984. *Making Space: Women and the Man Made Environment.* London: Pluto.

Mollenkopf, John Hull. 1989. "Inequality and Political Mobilization in the Post-Crisis City." In *Power, Culture, and Place: Essays on the History of New York City*, ed. John Mollenkopf. New York: Russell Sage.

Morris, Charles R. 1980. *The Cost of Good Intentions: New York City and the Liberal Experiment, 1960–1975.* New York: W. W. Norton.

O'Connor, James. 1973. *The Fiscal Crisis of the State.* New York: St. Martin's.

Offe, Claus. 1975. "The Theory of the Capitalist State and the Problem of Policy Formation." In *Stress and Contradiction in Modern Capitalism*, ed. L. Lindberg et al. Lexington, Mass.: Lexington Books.

———. 1984. *Contradictions of the Welfare State.* Cambridge: MIT Press, 1984.

O'Leary, Brendan. 1987. "Why Was the GLC Abolished?" *International Journal of Urban and Regional Research* 11 (June): 193–217.

Pahl, Ray E. 1975. *Whose City?* 2d ed. Harmondsworth: Penguin.

Panitch, Leon. 1977. "The Development of Corporatism in Liberal Democracies." *Comparative Political Studies* 10:61–90.

Parkinson, Michael, ed. 1987. *Reshaping Local Government.* New Brunswick, N.J.: Transaction Books.

Parkinson, Michael, and Richard Evans. 1989. "Urban Development Corporations." In *Local Responses to Economic Development*, ed. Mike Campbell. London: Cassell.

Parkinson, Michael, and Dennis Judd. 1988. "Urban Revitalization in America and the UK—The Politics of Uneven Development." In *Regenerating the Cities: The UK Crisis and the US Experience*, ed. Michael Parkinson, Bernard Foley, and Dennis Judd. Manchester: Manchester University Press.

Pickvance, C. G. 1988. "The Failure of Control and the Success of Structural Reform: An Interpretation of Recent Attempts to Restructure Local Government in Britain." Paper presented at the International Sociological Association RC 21 Conference on Trends and Challenges of Urban Restructuring, Rio de Janeiro, Brazil, September.

Potter, Stephen. 1988. "Urban Development Corporations: Inheritors of the New Town Legacy?" *Town and Country Planning* (November): 296–301.

Przeworski, Adam, and Michael Wallerstein. 1988. "Structural Dependence of the State on Capital." *American Political Science Review* 82 (March): 11–30.

Real Estate Board of New York. 1985. *Fact Book 1985.* New York: Real Estate Board of New York.

Redclift, N., and Enzo Mingione, eds. 1984. *Beyond Employment: Household, Gender and Subsistence.* Oxford: Basil Blackwell.

Rees, Gareth, and John Lambert. 1985. *Cities in Crisis: The Political Economy of Urban Development in Post-War Britain.* London: Edward Arnold.

Rimlinger, Gaston V. 1971. *Welfare Policy and Industrialization in Europe, America, and Russia.* New York: Wiley.

Sassen-Koob, Saskia. 1984. "The New Labor Demand in Global Cities." In *Cities in Transformation,* ed. Michael Peter Smith. Beverly Hills, Calif.: Sage.

———. 1986. "New York City: Economic Restructuring and Immigration." *Development and Change* 17:85–119.

Saunders, Peter. 1979. *Urban Politics.* Harmondsworth: Penguin.

———. 1981. *Social Theory and the Urban Question.* New York: Holmes and Meier.

Savitch, Henry. 1987. "Post-Industrial Planning in New York, Paris, and London." *Journal of the American Planning Association* 80 (Winter): 80–91.

———. 1989. *Post-Industrial Cities.* Princeton: Princeton University Press.

Sayer, Andrew. 1982. "Explanation in Economic Geography: Abstraction versus Generalization." *Progress in Human Geography* 6 (March): 68–88.

Shefter, Martin. 1985. *Political Crisis/Fiscal Crisis.* New York: Basic Books.

Stegman, Michael A. 1985. *Housing in New York: Study of a City, 1984.* New York: New York City Department of Housing Preservation and Development, New York.

———. 1988. *Housing and Vacancy Report: New York City, 1987.* New York: New York City Department of Housing Preservation and Development.

Sternlieb, George, Elizabeth Roistacher, and James W. Hughes. 1976. *Tax Subsidies and Housing Investment.* New Brunswick, N.J.: Center for Urban Policy Research, Rutgers University.

Stone, Clarence N., and Heywood T. Sanders, eds. 1987. *The Politics of Urban Development.* Lawrence: University of Kansas Press.

Storper, Michael, and Allen J. Scott. 1988. "The Geographical Foundations and Social Regulation of Flexible Production Complexes." In *Territory and Social Reproduction,* ed. Jennifer Wolch and Michael Dear. London: Allen & Unwin.

Tabb, William. 1982. *The Long Default.* New York: Monthly Review Press.

Thrift, Nigel. 1987. "The Fixers: The Urban Geography of International Commercial Capital." In *Global Restructuring and Territorial Development,* ed. Jeffrey Henderson and Manuel Castells. Beverly Hills, Calif.: Sage.

Tobier, Emanuel. 1979. "Gentrification: The Manhattan Story," *New York Affairs* 5 (Summer): 13–25.

Townsend, Peter. 1987. *Poverty and Labour in London.* London: Low Pay Unit.

Vogel, David. 1988. "The Future of New York City as a Global and National Financial Center." Paper presented to the Metropolitan Dominance Working Group, Social Science Research Council Committee on New York City, May.

Wilensky, Harold L. 1975. *The Welfare State and Equality.* Berkeley and Los Angeles: University of California Press.

Zukin, Sharon. 1982. *Loft Living.* Baltimore: Johns Hopkins University Press.

CHAPTER 6

Postindustrialism with a Difference: Global Capitalism in World-Class Cities

H. V. Savitch

Since the 1970s scholars have noted a profound transformation in the content and character of capitalism. Spurred by Immanuel Wallerstein's 1974 volume depicting a world capitalist economy, scholars began to identify world-class cities as nodes for corporate distribution, exchange, and communication (Gottmann 1974; Hill 1984). World-class cities came to be seen as command posts in a global economy, which contained the wellsprings of finance, the synapses of communication, and the production centers for information and culture. New York, London, Paris, Tokyo, and Sao Paulo increasingly became great seats for corporate headquarters, radiating a web of electronic conduits and air corridors across the globe.

At the same time as capitalism was transforming, so too were world-class cities. The great migration of capital to these cities, and capital growth within them, became a crucible for determining how economics and politics would interact. As the force of economic restructuring met the object of the state, political economy became the lens through which scholars viewed the interaction.

In its simplest and most abstract form, economic restructuring is the process through which the productive base of society changes. Those changes have enormous consequences for demographic distribution, social class, physical form, and the politics of the city. More specifically, the transformation of world-class cities involved a shift from the production of goods (manufacture and assembly) to the use and manipulation of knowledge (information, finance, management, services) (Bell 1976; Fainstein chapter, this volume). White-collar workers suddenly replaced blue-collar workers, office towers sprung up where factories once stood, and fancy boutiques took the place of corner taverns. So dramatic were the changes, it was likened to the industrial upheaval a century earlier, and the phrase "postindustrial revolution" came to signify a watershed for the twentieth century (Sternlieb and Hughes 1975; Bell 1976).

From one perspective, the postindustrial revolution looked uniform, unrelenting, and clear-cut. After all, world-class cities were restructuring and the state was responding to economic imperatives (Miliband 1969; Poulantzas 1973; Offe 1972; Habermas 1973; O'Connor 1973). Scholars became interested in the role of the state, who actually ran it, how it served capital, and why state action took so many twists and turns (Block 1977; Saunders 1979; Skocpol 1980).

From another perspective, the postindustrial revolution was complex, variable, and dilatory. To be sure, world-class cities were changing. But these cities were changing at different rates, they were treating social classes differently, and they were shaping the urban landscape differently. What accounted for these differences? For one, capital was not one huge monolith that could trounce world cities. Capitalists were a competitive lot and, while they were powerful, they also could be played off against one another by clever politicians and technocrats.

Second, capitalists could not come and go as they wished. Not all capitalism is mobile. Postindustrialism has placed an enormous amount of capital (buildings, real estate, communication networks) in select cities. The more vested that capital became, the more political leverage those cities could exert on its occupants. For world-class cities, postindustrial investment is a two-way street—made by financiers, who are often anxious to set down stakes, and agreed upon by public officials who pursue different interests (Gurr and King 1987).

Third, and this is crucial to the argument, when "the state" controls something of great value, it is not always helpless. States may enjoy a significant measure of autonomy. But that autonomy is variable and depends upon political structures and cultural conditions within a particular nation. The capacity of the state vis-à-vis the influx of capitalism is contingent upon its ability to organize regional governments, raise taxes, transfer resources, intervene in the marketplace, and govern through strong institutions.

By the word *state*, I mean that entity responsible for the maintenance of order, the promotion of social norms, the exercise of political discretion, and the execution of public policy (Benjamin and Elkin 1985). The complexities that go into the making of public policy, however, cannot be captured by the concept of a single state. More often than not, public policy is the outcome of innumerable pressures and pulls from various parts of the body politic. States—especially pluralist, capitalist states—rarely act as a unitary, cohesive force. They are multidimensional and their different dimensions act upon different agendas, address different problems, respond to different pressures, and reflect different constituencies.

It may be more useful, then, to examine economic restructuring as a product of several types of "state" or semistates—the *national state*, the *regional semistate*, the *local semistate*, the *micro semistate*, and the *administrative semistate*. These types of state may be defined by depth of authority (national states are supreme), by scope of jurisdiction (local semistates exercise certain prerogatives within limited boundaries), by constituency (micro semistates service distinct neighborhoods), by function (administrative semistates are charged with specific tasks), or by any combination thereof.

The nature of semistates and their relationship to the national state portends a great deal for how cities are economically restructured. While economic restructuring is central to most types of state, that centrality is conditioned by a number of competing agendas. Put another way, economic restructuring occurs in a deeper context of problems. Invariably, that context pulls on economic questions and affects the shape and configuration of the world-class city.

Furthermore, the context of economic restructuring varies from one national state to the other. World-class cities in the United States manage policy differently than their French or British counterparts. To some extent, this is because different traditions govern relationships between the national state and semistates. Also, problems may differ in import and meaning from one culture to another. In the United States, planning is treated as a local or at most a regional problem. In France, planning has traditionally been a national issue, to be worked out between the national state and the localities. In the United States popular participation is treated as an expression of individual or interest-group behavior. In Great Britain, it is largely an ideological issue and channeled through political parties.

Since the end of World War II, world-class cities have faced sharpening issues of how to deal with a changing economy, how to improve bureaucratic performance and enhance public services, how to provide housing and sustain general welfare, and how to cope with demands for local democracy. Encapsulated, these problems read as issues of economic growth, planning, coordination or efficiency, social justice, and popular participation.

Not every state or semistate pursues every problem simultaneously, nor does every type of state choose all problems with equal fervor. In fact, the activities of semistates bump economic restructuring against other issues, impart it with variety, and make it unpredictable. As a general rule, national and local types of state are concerned with economic growth and social justice; regional and administrative semistates stress planning, coordination, or efficiency as well as economic growth; and, micro semistates emphasize popular participation and, at times, social justice.

The central proposition of this chapter is that national states set the broad contours for economic restructuring, often determining the opportunities as well as the limits of semistate action. Within these contours, however, the interaction of different types of state accounts for particular outcomes. While those outcomes are difficult to predict, they do reveal differences in the capacity of world-class cities to shape their postindustrial revolutions.

In the following sections I trace the vicissitudes of the struggle to control postindustrialism in three world-class cities: New York, Paris, and London. All three cities began that struggle with efforts to consolidate or coordinate power at the regional level. While regional power eventually gave way to fragmentation, the experiment worked differently in each city and left different legacies. These mutations are traced, as they affected the economic transformation of world-class cities, from the early 1960s up to 1990. This time frame was a critical period during which New York, Paris, and London underwent profound changes in political practice and economic life.

The Limits of Rationalized Government

The 1960s were not only an era of idealism, but a time of faith in technocracy. On both sides of the Atlantic, people believed they could plan and rationalize government.

The New York Experience

In New York, the Regional Planning and Tristate Planning Commissions began investigating problems of metropolitan imbalance and promoted ideas for areawide cooperation. New York's mayor, Robert Wagner, invited more than fifty county and municipal officials to promote regional cooperation. Under Wagner, the Metropolitan Regional Council (MRC) was formed to promote housing, rebuild infrastructure, and promote economic development (Danielson and Doig 1982). The city also created a dazzling master plan that would govern growth until the end of the century (Department of Planning 1969).

Mayor Wagner's successor, John Lindsay, followed in the planners' wake. Lindsay continued to push for regional economic development and sponsored the MRC as an official body to receive federal funds. Lindsay wanted freedom to build, to attract new business, and to keep the city vibrant. On the other hand, he wanted to reach out to the poor and to black and Hispanic communities. He wanted those dispossessed constituencies to share in the city's bounty, to receive better neighborhood services, and to continue to vote for him (Hertz and Walinsky 1970).

Caught in the dilemmas of wanting to promote economic growth, of trying to redress social ills, and of improving the bureaucracy, the Lindsay administration adopted a two-prong strategy. One prong consolidated power at the top, so that City Hall could promote and coordinate development with builders, regional and administrative semistates. The other prong radically decentralized power into a number of micro semistates that, if successful, would serve as prototypes for every neighborhood in the city. Lindsay used a number of vehicles to begin the process. These included "little city halls" to establish complaint centers in poorly serviced neighborhoods, Urban Action Task Forces (UATFs) to prevent riotous "hot summers," and Offices of Neighborhood Government (ONGs) to facilitate community participation and oversight in municipal services. The Lindsay administration also paid closer attention to neighborhood planning boards, which had been started under Wagner (Savitch and Adler 1974; Mudd 1984).

To stimulate the economy, those at the upper prong worked with state, regional, and federal officials to promote an interstate expressway that would run through central Brooklyn, connect to a bridge leading to Staten Island, and continue into central portions of Queens. The expressway was supposed to be more than just another truck route. A five-mile complex dubbed "Linear City," including residential buildings, commerce, schools, and parks, was to rise alongside the new route (Leiper, Rees, and Kabak 1970)

For Lindsay, "Linear City" was an economic spark that would ignite the moribund communities of Brooklyn and Queens. But for ordinary citizens it was an ominous conflagration, which threatened to pollute the air and destroy thousands of existing homes and businesses. Lindsay's plan was met with aggressive resistance. In the popular press "Linear City" became "Carbon Monoxide City" and no less a figure than Lewis Mumford, who called Lindsay's scheme a "planning atrocity," was recruited into the fight (Coordinating Committee of Civic Organizations 1968). Ironically, the same organizations that Lindsay created or strengthened to bring about social justice came to haunt him in the controversy over Linear City. UATFs were besieged with complaints. Planning boards in Brooklyn filed protests. At "little city halls," Lindsay staffers stood speechless in the face of irate citizens (Coordinating Committee of Civic Organizations 1968). Linear City turned into a debacle for Lindsay, and by the time he ran for a second term in 1969 he abandoned it.

By the mid-1970s new realities gripped New York. Disillusioned by Lindsay experimentation, the public lost confidence in government's ability to plan and manage urban problems. The city was in store for a new period of skepticism and a return to piecemeal administration. Lindsay's successor, Abe Beame, barely had time to disband the superadministrations and revive the old system when he was beset by fiscal crises. In the midst of this, a new city charter commission (the Goodman Commission) went about redoing the structure of city government.

In dousing the ideological flames of the Lindsay years, the Goodman Commission let a few embers burn. The experiments with neighborhood government were incorporated into fifty-nine brand-new community boards. These new micro semistates were supposed to coordinate services, comment on land use decisions, and propose capital budget expenditures (Viteritti and Pecorella 1987). Neighborhood government had taken root. New York's micro semistates would grow in the 1980s—perhaps not into mighty oaks but surely into saplings that mark the urban landscape.

Paris: Not Quite Under Chirac

Paris too, during the 1960s, was enamored with planning and the magic of technocracy. The French believed that strong administration could foster prosperity and redistribute economic growth. More than any other French city, Paris swelled with industry, business, and government. To decongest the city, the

French government sought to move factories and offices into the countryside (Sundquist 1977; Carmona 1979).

To succeed, the national state had to get a grip on more than a thousand communes, which resisted economic change. The answer lay in the creation of a political framework that consolidated central power, kept Paris under the tutelage of the national state, and shaped the political direction of other local semistates.

Through the early part of the decade, the Gaullists created a regional semistate (Ile de France) under the guiding hand of a superprefect, an agent of the central government responsible to the heads of state. Within the Ile de France eight departments (counties) encompassed the still-numerous communes. Though the communes were able to elect mayors and often chose left-wing councils, they were overseen by departmental prefects, who completed the hierarchy by reporting to the regional prefect (Alduy 1979; Dagnaud 1977, 1979).

Paris remained an exception. It alone stood as both a city and a department. It alone was run by two prefects (one solely concerned with security). It was the only municipality in France without a mayor. With all this reorganization, the Gaullists had realized some fundamental economic goals.

Beginning in the mid-1960s and through the early 1980s the region went through a massive transformation. The city of Paris lost more than 20 percent of its residents and over 40 percent of its manufacture. The tertiary sector grew, but scantily, by a mere 6 percent (INSEE 1984). What occurred was a dedensification of the city and a huge transfer of population and jobs to the rest of the region. Nearly a half million people and over 300,000 jobs moved to the hinterlands (INSEE 1984).

Under the Gaullists the national state built new towns and suburban growth poles in roughly 260 square miles surrounding the city. To the north the government planted a modern international airport, named after de Gaulle himself; to the west it laid down a giant business complex, called La Défense; and, at the epicenter of Paris it built a large cultural complex, which kept its old name of Les Halles under a radically new form.

Built in the forbidding, slab fortress style of the 1960s, La Défense occupies nearly 2,000 acres, upon which sit more than thirty office towers and 19 million square feet of office space. Only ten minutes by rail from the center of Paris, La Défense has become the city's satellite business district. An army of white-collar workers travel to it from all parts of the region and over 50,000 reside in its apartment towers (Savitch 1988).

The new Les Halles replaced the old market that once fed the city with fruits and vegetables. In its stead, the national and local state built a cultural complex that today draws millions of tourists each year and holds one of the largest mass-transit terminals in the world.

New towns, suburban growth poles, Charles de Gaulle airport, La Défense, and Les Halles are just a few outstanding examples of catalysts for reshaping the economic and physical structure of Paris. The French did not accomplish this by passively relying upon private enterprise. Instead, they aggressively orchestrated the most dramatic urban transformation in France since the day of Baron Haussmann.

An array of instruments was used to write and coproduce the economic script. One of these is the Délégation à l'Aménagement du Territoire et L'Action Régionale, or DATAR. DATAR is a bureaucracy attached to the national state with powers to withhold construction permits or induce private enterprise to move to specific locales. A special or differential tax called the *rédévance* was also applied to the most congested areas of Paris in order to discourage the growth of office space.

During the building of La Défense and the period of industrial deconcentration, DATAR withheld construction permits in the city of Paris and furnished a host of financial subventions and technical assistance to channel industry elsewhere.

Other techniques for managing economic restructuring are Zones d'Aménagement Concertée (ZACs) and Zones d'Aménagement Diferée (ZADs). ZACs are used to designate a site where the public sector can assemble land and build infrastructure. ZADs are used to freeze the price of land within or outside a specific area in order to prevent speculation. Development areas can be "ZADed" for as long as fourteen years. Les Halles as well as other areas within Paris were developed through a conjunction of ZACs and ZADs.

Still other techniques for managing economic restructuring are

Sociétés d'Economie Mixtes (mixed corporations) and Etablissements Publique d'Aménagements (EPAs). Mixed corporations are administrative semistates that combine public and private investment in particular projects. To make sure public ends are paramount, the public sector holds the controlling shares. EPAs are similar to development corporations in the United States, except they exercise stronger powers over development and hold long-term title to property. EPAs control building height, the location of major projects location, and the daily governance of newly developed localities. La Défense was built under the aegis of an EPA and is still governed by it. Mixed corporations have been used to build, own, and manage publicly assisted housing; they are relied upon to run enterprises within Les Halles and have been used extensively in the development of eastern Paris.

Unlike New York, the Parisian transformation was largely planned, produced, and to some extent owned by the national state, which operated in conjunction with local and administrative semistates. Like New York, Paris too was about to appreciate the limits of comprehensive planning. Other items pressed the agenda, namely the quest for social justice and the call for popular participation.

In Paris itself, there was a rising demand for self-government. By 1973 the municipal council was calling for greater autonomy and several bills were presented to the National Assembly. The left most energetically pressed for decentralizing power. As staunch advocates of decentralization, the communists not only pressed for an elected mayor, but wanted real power shifted to neighborhood micro semistates. The socialists also favored a strong local semistate with some authority given to micro semistates. The right was least enthusiastic about local autonomy (Townsend 1984). It had always regarded Paris as a special case, one that warranted supervision by the national state. As a compromise, it came to endorse a mayor for Paris, so long as that supervision was not undone.

As matters turned out everybody was surprised. The left never gained control of a local semistate, whose autonomy they supported. The right won control of a local semistate, whose autonomy they traditionally had opposed.

By 1977 Paris had its own mayor, the Gaullist leader Jacques

Chirac, while the presidency was in the hands of the centrist leader Giscard d'Estaing. Already there were signs that economic restructuring would be managed differently. Under Giscard, the national state was anxious to be identified as protector of the environment. Responding to Parisian demand, Giscard canceled plans for the long-awaited construction of a highway along the left bank of the Seine. Giscard also scuttled the construction of an anticipated World Trade Center in Les Halles. In its place, the President promoted (with Chirac's assent) a children's park, built squarely and conspicuously on one of the most expensive terrains in Paris. Through Giscard's tenure, there was a virtual ban on office construction in Paris. For a decade, white-collar employment went to La Défense, to the suburbs, or to the provinces.

London: Thatcher's Revenge

The British handled the planning surge of the 1960s with characteristic aplomb. Before 1965 London was little more than a patchwork of counties, a police district, urban and rural districts and boroughs. Over the years this area had begun to sprawl. Development was spotty and either intruded into historic London or ransacked the countryside. Also worrisome were the disparities between the inner areas of London and its surrounding suburbs. Class polarization and racial tensions were beginning to mount and so too was white middle-class flight. As the trek outward grew, so did commuter problems. More and more, it looked like America's urban crisis had flown across the sea and fallen on southeast England. For many the solution lay in comprehensive planning and rationalized administration. It was this chain of circumstance that made London one of the earliest world-class cities to adopt two-tier government, one tier to address metropolitan issues and another to manage community problems (Rhodes 1970; Kantor 1973; Young and Garside 1982).

At the wider tier, over 600 square miles were consolidated into greater London and represented by a Greater London Council (GLC). Placed under GLC purview were functions regarded as regional (strategic planning, land preservation, metropolitan transportation) or functions requiring capital-intensive outlays (waste disposal) or necessary to redistribute resources (taxation, "over-spill housing"). At the narrower tier, thirty-two boroughs, plus the "City of London" as a thirty-third, managed a different set of functions. Placed under the boroughs were labor-intensive functions (day care services), matters of local import (housing), or local code enforcement (parking regulations).

The GLC worked hard to conserve the environment and reduce disparities. Under GLC leadership, the greenbelt that surrounds London nearly doubled in size (Hall 1986). The GLC promoted plans for controlled growth by designating zones of greatest commercial activity in the center and developing a limited number of strategic commercial centers in outer London (Hart 1976). The GLC also worked successfully to move offices out of London, through the Location of Office Bureaus (LOB). By gentle persuasion and publicity the LOB surprisingly managed to move more than 12,000 office jobs out of central London (Sundquist 1975).

When more than the velvet glove was required, the national state stepped in to jawbone the local economy. Under Labour, strict limitations were placed on industrial and office development within central London. By 1964 the Brown Office Ban had put a virtual moratorium on further office construction. Most important, public housing was at the top of London's agenda. For a time during the 1960s, the GLC was the major provider of public housing in London and the single largest builder in Great Britain (Hebbert and Travers 1988). During the GLC period, roughly 40 percent of all housing was publicly owned, and this alleviated sharp social disparities (Greater London Council 1984). Most of this housing was low-rise and human-scaled, with adequate green space.

There were also centerpieces of economic development in London, in which the GLC played a key role. Without the GLC the boroughs were less able to plan collectively and take hold of the environment. Working with the boroughs, the GLC finally agreed on a plan to preserve London's old market at Covent Garden. This area in the center of London was eventually preserved and housing rebuilt for the great majority of its residents (Christensen 1979). The GLC also began to cooperate with five boroughs in order to rebuild the docklands. As warehouses and ports closed, the GLC and the boroughs dredged and cleared the land. By 1980 an infrastructure was prepared to accommodate more public housing, parks, and light industry (Docklands Joint Committee 1976; Select Committee of the House of Lords 1980).

For a time, it seemed as if the British had achieved a neat division of labor. But there were also serious problems with two-tier government, and the GLC ultimately fell prey to a political and social struggle. One way of interpreting the GLC's fall is to see its technical agenda (planning and coordination) displaced by a more ambitious agenda for social justice. During the later part of the 1970s, the GLC increasingly began to quarrel with conservative boroughs. The GLC mandate to build "overspill housing" had always been a source of tension, especially in outer boroughs. These tensions were exacerbated as the GLC began to spend more on public services and provide grants for voluntary organizations. Property taxes skyrocketed, while inner London might appreciate "gas and water socialism," outer London was ready to rebel. When the GLC tried to subsidize mass-transit fares with property taxes, the gantlet was laid down. One borough took up the fight and won. Others began a campaign to dump the GLC (Game and Leach 1988).

In still other ways the GLC replaced its planning and economic agendas with raw politics. Under its militant Labour leader, Ken Livingstone, London was declared a nuclear-free zone. The GLC then turned to the visible and thorny issues of racism, feminism, and gay rights. The Thatcher government shot back. By 1984 it presented Parliament with a bill abolishing the GLC along with six other metropolitan councils. By 1986 London's venture with two-tier government was over. Remaining were thirty-three micro semistates trying to find their way in the debris.[1]

Thus, during the 1960s New York, Paris, and London attempted to control their postindustrial futures through varying forms of regional consolidation. By the 1970s that consolidation either was stillborn (New York), began to lose its vigor (Paris), or became extinct (London). Despite this, consolidation produced many enduring changes in Europe—from the creation of a massive infrastructure feeding new cities in the Paris region to growth controls and land preservation in greater London.

The 1980s would yield another wave of mutations. As regional semistates were nibbled away by rivals with other agendas, centripetal capitalism would seek space in central business districts and in its adjacent neighborhoods.

Centrifugal Politics versus Centripetal Capitalism

The dismay of the 1960s left its legacy. Local and micro semistates became defensive, always guarding their prerogatives and searching for ways to enlarge their discretion. While multinational corporations and developers sought space in the central city, decision making splayed in a number of directions.

New York's community boards took their advisory powers seriously, especially on matters of land use. These micro semistates were given a formal role in a decisional chain called the Urban Land Use Review Process. The community boards were a first link in securing approval for land use changes and made the most of their consultative role. In many cases, community boards were able to stop urban development or exact from builders concessions that were so burdensome they discouraged construction.[2]

Estimates on the real clout of community boards vary, though studies indicate that compliance rates for community board recommendations are upward of 80 percent. Developers came to anticipate this, and when faced with unfriendly community boards the warning was, "Don't build, build elsewhere, or build according to the letter of the law" (Fowler 1980).

Micro semistates became sophisticated negotiators. In exchange for favorable reviews, developers found it necessary to provide communities with new libraries, ballfields, and local meeting halls. In one notorious instance, a developer gave a "gift" of $250,000 to a neighborhood chamber of commerce (Association of the Bar of New York 1988b). The practice became so flagrant that Mayor Koch took steps to enact guidelines for community boards, specifying permissible "amenities" (Office of the Mayor 1987).

Extracting concessions from builders was by no means a privilege held out to all or even most community boards. The poorest boards, whose land was under siege by crack addicts, were desperate for any kind of legitimate investment. The process of linking development to community benefits, or of exacting payoffs from developers, or of controlling growth, is something privileged jurisdictions can best execute (see Molotch chapter, this volume). This process relies on an open market, and open markets work best for those who are already blessed with desirability, affluence, or political leverage.

In still other ways centrifugal tendencies were exacerbated when a Supreme Court decision led to the abolition of New York's Board of Estimate (Supreme Court of the United States 1989). Under a new charter, most land use decisions will come under a more fragmented City Council (New York City Charter Revision Commission 1989). The council's smaller districts and more numerous membership are likely to encourage land parochialism, reinforcing community boards and strengthening fifty-nine micro semistates.

Centrifugal forces have also been felt in Paris. Upon gaining control of the national state in 1981, the socialists enacted a series of decentralizing measures. These measures sharply curbed the powers of the prefect and transferred responsibilities to departments and communes. Departments now have formidable powers over budgets and some powers of economic intervention, while communes can award construction permits and make loans to business (*Journal Officiel de la République Française* 1982; *Cahiers Français* 1985).

The most dramatic gesture toward decentralization occurred in Paris. In 1982 the socialists proposed that Parisian *arrondissements* (neighborhoods) be given the same powers as municipalities. The socialists argued that each of twenty *arrondissements* should elect its own council, each should choose its own mayor, and each should be accorded prerogatives over budget, taxation, and land use. Paris itself would become a city of federated micro semistates, its mayor selected by a council of the *arrondissements* (*Le Monde* 1 Juillet 1982).

The Gaullists were incensed and charged the socialists with seeking to control the city by cutting it up into twenty quarreling pieces. As it came to be called, "The Battle of Paris" ended when the socialists modified their proposal. A peaceful settlement was reached by allowing elected *arrondissement* councils to exercise an advisory role. The terms of settlement also allowed *arrondissement* mayors to oversee neighborhood services (Ministère de l'Interieur 1985).

Consultation, however, can be a powerful tool. In Paris this tool may be all the more cutting because a number of *arrondissement* councilors, together with *arrondissement* mayors, also sit on the municipal council. The current mayor of Paris, Jacques Chirac, already reckons *arrondissement* mayors as a real force. With one foot in the *arrondissement* and another at City Hall, *arrondissement* mayors can influence land use decisions. Research has shown that Parisian neighborhoods can be mobilized against development by a coalition of local politicians and citizens (Body-Gendrot 1987). Now that this coalition has an institutional basis, economic growth will compete with still other agendas.

After 1986 London was a different metropolis. With the GLC gone and some of its resources and staff transferred to the boroughs, government by micro semistates took on a new meaning. New symbols of autonomy now appear on London streets. Borough insignia are more evident and so are special signboards. Borough logos have been redone and borough stationery reprinted to advertise their new status. Boroughs with special status, like the "City of London," maintain business contacts with foreign embassies and the "City's" Lord Mayor is an honored guest at international banquets (Hebbert and Travers 1988).

The boroughs also have gone their own way in developing independent fiscal policies. Right-wing boroughs, like Westminster and Wandsworth, have cut spending and privatized their services. Leftist boroughs take the opposite course, trying to increase services and sponge up unemployment by adding to their staffs. Many other boroughs, among them Croyden and Islington, fund their own business enterprises.

Whatever has become of London, the central government makes sure that no single body emerges to represent the whole of it. Labour boroughs have tried to create organizations to carry out comprehensive functions—dramatized during the blitzkrieg of abolition as "GLCs in exile." But the central government has steadfastly resisted any effort to build a semblance of a regional semi-state. Instead, the Conservatives have used roughly sixty agencies to divide London into a patchwork of functional turfs. Everything from children's services to grants for voluntary organizations and waste management has been put under the jurisdiction of special authorities, joint committees, multiborough councils, and assorted boards.

Despite efforts to bring about broader collaboration, most boroughs fend for themselves (London Planning and Advisory Committee 1988). What was once a comprehensive government is now a jumble of micro semistates, occasionally trying to coordinate activities in the face of a watchful national state. As one group of London scholars put it, "ad hocery rules" (Hebbert and Travers 1988).

What can be made of centrifugal politics in the face of centripetal capital? At the simplest level of compiling a record of wins or losses, it cannot be said that capital has either clearly won or lost. There are instances where micro semistates have succeeded in putting a halt to intrusive development, just as there are instances where whole neighborhoods have been wiped away to satisfy economic growth (Danielson and Doig 1982; Hall 1980).

Looked at from the vantage of governing the urban system, ad hocery has multiplied. The rise of micro semistates as sources for popular participation has been paralleled by the expansion of administrative semistates as facilitators of economic growth and efficiency. In New York, administrative semistates can be found in public benefit corporations (PBCs), which include the Urban Development Corporation, the Battery Park City Authority, the Public Development Corporation, the Port Authority, and others. Paris relies on combining private and public capital through mixed corporations and EPAs. London uses development corporations and quasiautonomous nongovernmental organizations (Quangos).

The multiplicity of semistates has led to fights between different types of semistate. The agendas of micro and administrative semistates are not always compatible, and resolution of incremental problems often results in more serious conflicts over goals (Ferman 1989). In New York, special statutes permit administrative semistates to build where they please and accommodate builders, bankers, and entrepreneurs. In retaliation, micro semi-states have either petitioned other authorities to modify development or used the courts to stop it (Charter Revision Clearing House 1988; Association of the Bar of New York 1988a).

In London occasional sniping has now turned into open warfare. London's east end is among the better known battlegrounds. There, a number of boroughs attempted to prevent the London Docklands Development Corporation from razing and selling off the docklands to private developers (Meyer 1988).

Another way of understanding centrifugal politics is to examine how it can be organized to bring about different outcomes. Paris and London provide instructive examples. In the Paris region, the smallest of communes (aided by large subventions from the national state) have the power to keep away unwanted development. In addition to ruling on private development, mayors are not averse to routing incinerators and industrial parks away from city centers to the very periphery of their cities. Seeking to stick unwanted uses onto their neighbors, communes are partaking in a dumping contest. Thus, too much politics is creating a free-for-all and exacerbating intercommunal and regional disparities (*Le Monde* 28 Juillet 1988; IAURIF 1988).

In London, the effort to squeeze politics out of decision making threatens the power of micro semistates. In the name of economic growth, the national state not only has given authority to administrative semistates, but has taken action to curtail the boroughs (see Parkinson chapter, this volume). Some of these actions include rate capping (limiting revenue available for spending), compulsory letting (requiring private contractors to bid for public services), and the retrenchment of council housing (selling off public housing to private buyers and voluntary associations). In the extreme, the boroughs would become political holding corporations, electing local councils that have little to do but auction public services within a free market.

Thus, the proliferation of micro semistates does not necessarily mean they grow stronger. As Michael Parkinson points out in Chapter 4, abolition has become a way to recentralize power in the hands of a stronger national state. From a purely political perspective this may be true, but from the perspective of political economy it also means that thirty-three micro semistates compete with each other in a decentralized, more aggressive marketplace.

The irony of both the Paris and London examples is that marketplace power cannot be realized without political reorganization. Economic outcomes depend upon how politics is organized and how it is played. With hefty subventions from the national state and a moderate socialist government in France, local and micro semistates are capable of remaking market forces. With a radical rightist national state in Great Britain putting severe restrictions on micro semistates, the free market gets to play an altogether different role.

National Context, Semistates, and Capital

We are accustomed to viewing the national state as the supreme expression of sovereignty, and that role should be clarified rather than minimized. Indeed, the cases from New York, Paris, and London illustrate that the national state holds powerful sway over semistates and that its cooperation is necessary for semistates to be effective.

National states reflect different cultural, political, and institutional contexts, and this shapes the urban response to economic change. Americans are less inclined to take hold of the marketplace, the British are ideologically split on the issue, and the French have few qualms about it.[3] This is why New York can only resort to minimal measures like highways and zoning variances to channel capital; it is why London first builds public housing (under Labour) only to abruptly sell it off (under Conservatives); and it is why so much of Paris has been built by national, local, or administrative types of state.

The American political system is also more diffuse than British or French government. This makes it difficult for American cities to comprehensively plan or develop their land. While mayors Wagner and Lindsay unsuccessfully struggled to establish modest regional cooperation, French prefects were bringing about the most thorough revamping of Paris in more than a century and the GLC was adding a greenbelt twice the size of London.

Differences in cultural and institutional norms refract differences in outcome. Though New York, Paris, and London underwent a similar postindustrial transformation in the last quarter century, their physical and economic evolution is dissimilar. The New York region has sprawled relentlessly in all directions, and the city has been weighed down by more office towers. The Paris region was reconstructed by the hand of government—built like a wheel with Paris at the hub and fed by the spokes of mass transit. Paris itself has kept its low-rise skyline and is less dense than ever before. For all the changes Thatcher is bringing about, including a surge in office development and the sale of public resources, London still conforms to a design made fifty years ago—contained by a greenbelt and girded by spacious neighborhoods.

A quick comparison of office development within the central business cores of the three cities reveals an interesting contrast. In a ten-year period between the early 1970s and 1980s, New York's yield in office space averaged 6 million square feet per year (Port Authority of New York and New Jersey 1986). During roughly the same period, the average yield in Paris was only 1.5 million and in London 2.1 million square feet per year (APUR 1981, 1984b). All told, office space in New York grew three times as much as its European counterparts.[4]

Housing accounts for a significant component of the urban character. Public-sector housing not only determines who will inhabit the city but how its land will be apportioned and its resources used. During a crucial period of transition, contrasts in housing policy can be revealing. Between 1976 and 1982 New York City managed to reserve only 15.6 percent of its housing as publicly assisted units. The figure for Paris was 36.5 percent and for London 67.4 percent (Sternlieb and Listokin 1985; Merlin 1982; Greater London Council 1984).[5]

Even the sociodemographic complexion of these cities continues to vary because of institutional and policy differences. Manhattan has been radically transformed, it has become extraordinarily dense, and it is under severe pressure of gentrification (New York State Data Center 1980; U.S. Bureau of the Census 1980). Paris has resisted massive development and has reduced its density, though it continues to be infused with cultural centers and is undergoing *embourgeoisement* (INSEE 1984; APUR 1984a).

Inner London is still low density, still working class, and its neighborhoods are generally stable (Greater London Council 1984).

Having underlined national influence upon policymaking, we need to understand that semistates impart that policy with variety. That variety makes it difficult for capital to control anything. Trying to control a multiplicity of agendas within world-class cities is like trying to nail smoke to the wall.

Moreover, we cannot assume that capital is always mobile while states and semistates are helpless (Smith 1984, 1988). The distinction between Fordist and flexible systems of production (see Hill chapter, this volume) rests on a particular model of industrialism (manufacture and assembly). There is still another type of capital to be considered, which grew during postindustrialism (information and service). Postindustrial capital is different from industrial capital. During the last quarter century it has sunk enormous costs into the fabric of the world city—real estate, banking, investment, and development are major businesses.

Unlike Aberdeen and Houston (whose value lies in oil) or Detroit and Turin (whose value lies in automobiles), world-class cities derive their value from land. It is the strategic value of land and its dynamics of economic agglomeration that make New York, Paris, and London so different. This essential characteristic gives world-class cities real advantages vis-à-vis capital.

In some ways world-class cities are akin to Molotch's Santa Barbara writ large (see Chapter 7). Responding to an agenda for democratic participation, these cities may exact concessions from developers in exchange for allowing capital to settle in its invested terrain. Under such conditions, it will be difficult to distinguish the captive from the capturer.

NOTES

1. All in all, the micro semistates of all three cities contain populations that are somewhat comparable. New York City has fifty-nine community boards whose median population is 120,000. Paris has twenty *arrondissements* whose median population is 108,000. London is the least comparable: the median population of its thirty-three boroughs is 206,000.

2. Community boards were not effective in all types of development.

Where, for example, City Hall had a stake in a very large development, it was known to overrule community recommendations.

3. Historically the French have not hesitated to manipulate the marketplace and to take over industry. This attitude reaches back into French history. In modern times the Monnet plan, after World War II, involved public-sector direction of private enterprise and the establishment of national industrial goals. Under both the left and the right, French industry has been nationalized. Under the Gaullists roughly half the banks were placed under state control. The right may differ from the left in how intervention is undertaken, but the dichotomy between public and private sectors is altogether different from that in the United States or Britain.

4. Office development is calculated for comparable areas in New York, Paris, and London. These areas consist of Manhattan, the city of Paris, and central London (Savitch 1988).

5. The figures express the intent of government during a period of postindustrial transition. Since Thatcher's election in 1988 the Conservatives have begun to sell off public housing to existing tenants. While this can be viewed as an important change in public policy, it does not alter the socioeconomic composition of London's neighborhoods—at least not for the near future.

REFERENCES

Alduy, P. 1979. "L'Aménagement de la région de Paris entre 1930 et 1975: De la planification à la politique urbaine." *Sociologie du Travail* 21:167–200.

Association of the Bar of the City of New York. 1988a. *Testimony.* New York: Association of the Bar of the City of New York.

Association of the Bar of the City of New York. 1988b. *The Role of Amenities in the Land Use Process.* New York: Association of the Bar of the City of New York.

Atelier Parisien d'Urbanisme (APUR). 1981. *Le Bureaux à Paris, 1970–1980s.* Paris: Atelier Parisien d'Urbanisme.

———. 1984a. *Premiers Résultats du Recensement de 1982 à Paris.* Paris: Atelier Parisien d'Urbanisme.

———. 1984b. *Les Bureaux à Londre: Situation, 1983.* Paris: Atelier Parisien d'Urbanisme.

Bell, D. 1976. *The Coming of Post-Industrial Society.* New York: Basic Books.

Benjamin, R., and S. Elkin, eds. 1985. *The Democratic State.* Lawrence: University of Kansas Press.

Block, F. 1977. "The Ruling Class Does Not Rule." *Socialist Revolution* 33:6–28.

Body-Gendrot, S. 1987. "Grass Roots Mobilization in the Thirteenth Arrondissement." In *The Politics of Urban Development*, ed. C. Stone and H. Sanders. Lawrence: University of Kansas Press.

Cahiers Français. 1985. *La Décentralisation en Marche*. Paris: Documentation Français.

Carmona, M. 1979. *Le Grand Paris*. Paris: Girotypo.

Charter Revision Clearing House. 1988. *Source Book*. New York: New York City Charter Revision Clearing House.

Christensen, T. 1979. *Neighbourhood Survival*. London: Prism Press.

Coordinating Committee of Civic Associations. 1968. "Stop the Cross-Brooklyn Expressway Before It Stops You." New York. Mimeograph.

Dagnaud, M. 1977. *La Vème République et l'Aménagement de la Région de Paris*. Paris: Institut d'Aménagement et d'Urbanisme de la Région d'Ile de France.

————. 1979. "La Transformation des Institutions de Paris et de Sa Région entre 1958 et 1977." *Sociologie du Travail* 21:143–66.

Dahl, R. 1976. "The City in the Future Democracy." *American Political Science Review* 61:953–70.

Danielson, M., and J. Doig. 1982. *New York, The Politics of Urban Regional Development*. Berkeley and Los Angeles: University of California Press.

Department of Planning of the City of New York. 1969. *Plan for the City of New York*, vols. 1–4.

Docklands Joint Committee. 1976. *London Docklands Strategic Plan*. London: Docklands Development Team.

Ferman, B. 1989. "The Politics of Exclusion." Paper presented at the Annual Conference of the Urban Affairs Association, Baltimore, Md.

Fowler, G. 1980. "Community Board Wrap-up." *New York Affairs* 6:7–18.

Game, C., and S. Leach. 1988. "The Abolition of Metropolitan Governments." Paper presented at the Annual Conference of the American Political Science Association, Washington, D.C.

Gottman, J. 1974. "The Dynamics of Large Cities." Paper presented at the Institute of British Geographers and the Geographical Association at the University of Oxford.

Greater London Council. 1984. *London Facts and Figures*. London: Greater London Council.

Gurr, T., and G. S. King. 1987. *The State and the City*. Chicago: University of Chicago Press.

Habermas, J. 1973. *Legitimation Crisis*. Boston: Beacon Press.

Hall, P. 1980. *Great Planning Disasters*. Berkeley and Los Angeles: University of California Press.

————. 1986. "Reconciling Green Belt and Green Field." *The [London] Times*, p. 16.

Hart, D. 1976. *Strategic Planning in London*. London: Pergamon Press.

Hebbert, M., and T. Travers. 1988. *The London Government Handbook.* London: Cassell.

Hertz, D., and D. Walinsky. 1970. "Organizing the City: What Cities Do Is What They Think." In *Agenda for a City,* ed. L. Fitch and A. Walsh. Beverly Hills, Calif.: Sage.

Hill, R. 1984. "Urban Political Economy: Emergence, Consolidation and Development." In *Cities in Transformation,* ed. P. Smith. Beverly Hills, Calif.: Sage.

Institut National de la Statistique et des Etudes Economiques (INSEE). 1984. *Récensement de la Population: Région d'Ile de France, 1968, 1975, 1982.* Paris: Observatoire Economique de Paris.

Institut d'Aménagement et d'Urbanisme de le région d'Ile de France (IAURIF). 1988. *Ile de France 2000: Vers un Projet Regional.* Paris: Conseil Regional d'Ile de France.

Journal Officiel de la République Française. 1982. *Décentralisation.* Paris: Documentation Français.

Kantor, P. 1973. "The Governable City." *Polity* 7:14–31.

Le Monde. 1 Juillet, 1982.

———. 28 Juillet, 1988.

Leiper, J., C. Rees, and J. Kabak. 1970. "Mobility in the City: Transportation Development Issues." In *Agenda for a City,* ed. Fitch and Walsh.

London Planning and Advisory Committee. 1988. *Strategic Planning Advice for London, Draft.* London: London Planning and Advisory Committee.

Merlin, P. 1982. *Pour une Véritable Priorité au Logement Social à Paris.* Paris: La Documentation Française.

Meyer, P. 1988. "Who Should Control the Urban Economic Agenda?" Paper presented at the Annual Conference of the Urban Affairs Association, Portland, Ore.

Miliband, R. 1969. *The State in Capitalist Society.* New York: Basic Books.

Ministère de l'Interieur. 1985. *Democratie Locale.* Paris: Direction Générale des Collectivites Locales.

Mudd, J. 1984. *Neighborhood Services.* New Haven, Conn.: Yale University.

New York City Charter Revision Commission. April and May 1989. *Summary of Preliminary Recommendations.* New York: New York City Charter Revision Commission.

O'Connor, J. 1973. *The Fiscal Crisis of the State.* New York: St. Martin's Press.

Offe, C. 1972. "Advanced Capitalism and the Welfare State." *Politics and Society* 2:479–88.

Office of the Mayor. 1987. Statement by Edward I. Koch. New York.

Port Authority of New York and New Jersey. 1986. *The Regional Economy.* New York: Port Authority of New York and New Jersey.

Poulantzas, N. 1973. *Political Power and Social Classes.* London: New Left Books.

Rhodes, G. 1970. *Government of London.* Toronto: University of Toronto Press.

Saunders, P. 1979. *Urban Politics.* London: Hutchinson & Company.

Savitch, H. 1988. *Post-Industrial Cities.* Princeton, N.J.: Princeton University Press.

Savitch, H., and M. Adler. 1974. *Decentralization at the Grass Roots.* Beverly Hills, Calif.: Sage.

Select Committee of the House of Lords. 1980. *Report of the Select Committee on the London Docklands Development Corporation Area and Constitution.* London: Her Majesty's Printing Office.

Skocpol, T. 1980. "Political Response to Capitalist Crisis." *Politics and Society* 10:155–201.

Smith, M., ed. 1984. *Cities in Transformation.* Beverly Hills, Calif.:Sage.
———. 1988. *City, State and Market.* New York: Basil Blackwell.

Sternlieb, G., and J. Hughes, eds. 1975. *Post-Industrial America.* New Brunswick, N.J.: Center for Urban Research.

Sternlieb, G., and D. Listokin. 1985. "Housing." In *Setting Municipal Priorities*, ed. C. Brecher and R. Horton. New York: New York University Press.

Sundquist, J. 1975. *Dispersing Population.* Washington, D.C.: Brookings Institution.

Supreme Court of the United States. 1989. Board of Estimate of the City of New York et al. v. Morris et al.

Townsend, J. 1984. "A Mayor for Paris." *Public Administration* 62:455–72.

Viteritti, J., and R. Pecorella. 1987. *Community Government.* New York: New York City Charter Revision Commission.

Wallerstein, I. 1974. *The Modern World System.* New York: Academic Press.

Young, K., and P. Garside. 1982. *Metropolitan Government.* New York: Holmes and Meier.

CHAPTER 7

Urban Deals in
Comparative Perspective

Harvey Molotch

Even if a newly integrated global economy has produced similar restructuring challenges across nations and the localities within them, there can still be variations across places in
social and distributive outcomes of economic growth. In the
United States signs of these variations have so far stemmed from,
among other factors, the power of local governments to create
exactions out of the land development process; in other societies,
variation is produced both at the national and local levels by other
types of political forces, such as the ongoing power of left parties.
In this chapter, I illustrate how, both among countries and among
cities within countries, variation and differentiation rooted in
political response remain possible even under global restructuring.

You don't have to be a postmodernist to suspect efforts that cast
all cities as uniform in their response to larger economic changes.
Past generations of urban scholars sharply limited their own suc-

cess with that kind of generalizing. For the ecologists, regularities in physical structure and population distribution (driven by atomistic utility maximization) produced similar social and political realities across localities. Now it is clear that the ecologists' system of cities differed from country to country and subsystems varied, in both physical and social terms, even within countries.[1] For the neo-Marxists there has been a similarly grand determinism, one that viewed cities as inevitably responding to changes in the capital-accumulation system. Thus the logic of capital dictated the continuing immiseration of urban workers, another variant foretold the end of manufacturing centers within the United States, still another the inevitability of local fiscal crises. The rise of environmentalist politics, urban gentrification, and mass migrations of a new proletariat were not anticipated. For public-choice theorists (such as Peterson 1981), the need to generate revenue for services meant that cities inevitably must limit their activities to courting capital, with no running room for alternative urban agendas.

Peterson's argument can be used to show how determinists go astray. Peterson noticed an empirical pattern in the United States: cities were indeed governed by people who acted as though the only way to provide public services was to attract outside capital, that is, to increase the scale of local economic activity and hence the tax base. But Peterson's argument makes sense only if growth was indeed invariably beneficial for cities and for most of their citizens. It is easy enough to show, however, that these conditions, whether in history or contemporary society, are not met (see Logan and Molotch 1987). Cities pursued growth not because they had to, but because those who controlled their politics used them for this purpose—that is, used them as growth machines to benefit their own fortune building.

This helps sound a cautionary note about any version of economistic determinism: even if similar policies are pursued across place and time, those policies may be dictated not by underlying logics but by mundane politics. Sometimes this repetition of the same policies across places stems from pluralistic greed and similar class configurations, or more innocently because of social contagion that spreads among decision makers otherwise uncertain about how to proceed. The failure of our grand theories to explain these types of phenomena now leaves intact the task of explaining how differences in places are going to come about and how political initiatives, historic idiosyncrasies, physical constraints, or just plain luck affect outcomes.[2]

The determinism to be wary of these days, derived (as usual) not so much from theory as by projection of some recent trends, is the notion that the globalism of production patterns translates into uniform spatial and social consequences at the urban level.[3] Economies shift from heavy manufacture to services and from Fordist production of identical units to flexible creation of specialized and changeable outputs. In social-spatial terms, the old concentrations of blue-collar labor decline with headquarters and financial center agglomerations the main source of urban viability. Remaining heavy mass manufacture moves to stand-alone greenfield sites at peripheral locations. These changes eliminate the privileged working class, substituting a bifurcated labor force of the technically proficient at the top and a poorly paid service proletariat at the bottom. The middle shrinks. Driven by the need to compete in a world economy, all places must adapt, and more or less in the same way. As Roger Keil observes, the integrated global economy "comes down like rain" on all places (personal conversation September 1989; see also Keil 1988).

But just as the production, space, and labor configurations of mass manufacturing in fact differed around the world (compare the social and spatial histories of industrial Sweden, Japan, and the United States), the specifics of restructuring appear varied in their social, economic, and spatial dimensions and could become more varied still. There have been and will likely continue to be different species of capitalism with distinct local consequences.

The bifurcation of labor, for example, is not an inevitable outcome of a change in what people make or where and how they make it. The income or dignity of a job has never been intrinsic to the task performed, but a matter of institutional definition (see Reskin and Hartmann 1986). Early twentieth-century industrial jobs became high-paying in the United States because workers forced wage concessions from management, not because of the skill level suddenly discovered. In the same way, emerging service jobs like day care can be, as Myles (1988) points out, either well paid (based on the preciousness of early childhood or a putatively high skill required for so complex a task) or poorly paid (if conceived as involving little more than the exercise of ordinary and "natural" ability of women). Societies with similar industrial status thus differ in the proportion of their service sector that are good and well-rewarded versus bad and poorly paid (see Esping-Andersen 1985), in part as a result of the political struggles that structure labor and production.

Nations may devise welfare systems that are sufficiently broad and deep to protect workers from the vicissitudes of industrial change. Insulated from the anxieties of ill health and job insecurity, workers may become more innovative, cooperative, and productive (see Esping-Andersen 1985; also Kuttner 1984; Korpi 1985; Friedland and Sanders 1988), thus balancing out any efficiency costs exacted by social justice. Finally, although it may not work as a general solution, at least some localities (or countries) can move into a particular niche in the international system that spares any significant portion of its population the destiny of a poverty underclass (as in the case of Switzerland). Options exist for what restructuring can actually mean.

The U.S. Spatial-Political Context

The urban setting in the United States on which restructuring now falls was itself created through political manipulation, yielding spatial outcomes that now help shape the way larger economic forces affect lives. Originally, the United States industrialized through the expansion of central cities, continuously annexing surrounding hinterlands, thereby extending physical and social infrastructure to the growing productive apparatus. This was done as a series of willful political acts, framed by a specifically U.S. style of state and local governmental institutions. But through an analogous set of willful political acts, the growth of the American economy now occurs in a series of legally discrete but physically proximate jurisdictions instead of within great cities that expand to include whatever development takes place. Economic activity occurs in matrices of small-scale specialized locales.

The upshot is a new scattering of working-class enclaves across the landscape, mixed with all sorts of other units: cities of affluent residence, cities of nothing but industry; middle-class residential/mall towns, affluent residential/industrial cities, and a variety of other combinations. This new geography of production and residence in distinct and smaller-scale governmental units has important implications for how services and benefits are delivered to populations.

In a prior time, concentrations of workers in mass industries in a delimited number of jurisdictions provided workers with a basis for influence over the country's great cities, unionization of the work force, and strategic power in the American electoral system. True, the U.S. labor movement has always been relatively weak with no significant political party devoted to its interests. But workers had a sufficient degree of leverage to make the United States a sort of welfare state, albeit among the least socially advanced. The organized working class was able to influence production, local government, and the Democratic party through both local political power and direct party-union linkages at the national level. The result was the upgrading of industrial work of males to the "skilled" categories and the use of local government for ethnic career mobility in a range of fields. These arrangements were regionwide or nationwide, negotiated by industrial unions to apply across job categories and plant location.

Under the new order, the suburbanization of production allows a thousand urban flowers to bloom in their own uncoordinated way. Workers are concentrated in old central cities, usually smaller in population, area, and wealth production than their suburban belts. They are also scattered in specialized working-class residential suburbs that are fiscally almost as bad off as central cities (Logan and Schneider 1981). Working-class heroes may take over local governments, but the rewards are paltry: the wealth creation is no longer there and local options (fiscal and programmatic) have been sharply curtailed by suburban-dominated state and federal governments (Kantor 1988). Neither the unions nor the ghettos have sufficient power to propel either their agendas or the careers of their leaders at the federal level. In a complementary way, the movement of job creation into service sectors and smaller-scale productive units (the much-celebrated "small business entrepreneur") makes unionization more difficult.

The loss of strategic power for workers and related cutbacks in state spending lessen the resources for financing increments in production and social reproduction. This represents a reversal in American urban history. Vast public expenditures for urban infrastructure were provided by national, state, and city funding (railroads, canals, dams, harbors, waterworks, and, especially through the interstate highway program, roadways). Similar expansion occurred in provision of human services—at first professional fire and police protection and then mass schooling and other forms of welfare. Indeed the history of American urbanization can be conceived as a more or less continuous expansion of infrastructure and welfare services for city populations (Monkkonen 1988; Kantor 1988). But beginning with the last phase of the Carter administration and paralleled by developments at state and local levels, this has all changed.

The cutbacks mean, in particular, that problems emerging in the most recent period—like deinstitutionalization of the mentally ill (and the homelessness that partially stems from it) and the need for child care to serve working women—have been left for localities to solve on their own; even the AIDS epidemic is treated, in terms of prevention and care, as primarily a local matter.[4]

These cutbacks and withdrawal of federal responsibility do not stem from fiscal crises or international competitive pressures. The U.S. state continues to waste vast amounts even as it opts out of urban investment. The scheming deregulation of the savings and loans will alone cost as much (over $200 billion) as was saved by all the cutbacks in several of the largest federal welfare programs (housing, AFDC, and food stamps). Similarly, even a small proportion of the bloated defense budget would have had substantial impact if directed toward the poor. Bleeding the country through budgetary deficit is surely not an inevitable response to world restructuring but, according to Frances Fitzgerald's interpretations (1989) of the Reaganites' accumulating memoirs, results primarily from having an "amiable dunce" as President.[5] As these remembrances seem to make clear, neither the cutbacks nor the heavy national debt used to justify them were the result of clever plots (much less capitalist logics), but were a particular convergence of political ambitions, outworn ideologies, and psychological aberrations.[6]

While at the state and local levels the personages are less celebrated, the inaction has also represented only one among a number of options, particularly noticeable in the rich, developing areas of the country. Compare the emergence of New York City and surrounding regions at an earlier time in history with that of Los Angeles and the California region today. Although the hardships of the Northeast laboring class at the beginning of this century were extreme, their amelioration occurred through a combination of government activism at both local and federal levels. Localities were willing to tax themselves to support such services as neighborhood libraries, public hospitals, and free universities (all innovations of the day). As we look at the growing regions of the United States on the winning end of the restructuring process (particularly California), we can point to few analogous government initiatives and instead find cutbacks in the midst of sustained boom, with poverty, homelessness, and diminishing public goods.[7] There is thus a contrast, between eras and perhaps regions as well, in how localities deal with growth and wealth creation in their midst. Provision of public service, including social justice, is at least as much a function of political will as it is of aggregate material capacity.[8]

The Built Environment as Site of Struggle

Under the increasingly mean conditions of the last dozen years, the development of the built environment has become the point—increasingly the only point—where the public can generate resources to improve social, fiscal, and physical conditions. This fact combines with still another: the authentic deterioration of the natural environment and the decay of so much urban infrastructure after decades of mismanagement and deferred attention (including toxic residues from prior economic expansions). Citizens now experience the obvious need to prevent the environmental degradation and fiscal crises that have been associated with past patterns of runaway growth. This felt need is one of the lasting sensitivities from the social movements of the 1960s, sustained by the clarity of the consequences of ignoring it.

Thus there has been continuous expansion in the degree to which U.S. localities demand "linkages" and "exactions" from development (Deakin 1988). For some time, local governments have required contributions from developers to offset direct infrastructural costs associated with their projects (water, sewers, roads). These exactions have been broadened to include indirect effects, such as fees to offset traffic congestion generated at nonproximate sites. More ambitiously, localities are requiring developers to offset social costs by including day-care facilities in their office buildings, youth hostels at their luxury hotels, or low-income housing with their deluxe condos. Some governments require job training or stipulate that jobs must be offered to local residents in the completed facility (see Ehrlich and Dreier 1988; Shearer 1989).

The quality of urban existence and its differentiation from place to place, even within the same region of the same country, thus turn increasingly on the kinds of deals that local governments make with developers. Although current magnitudes of exaction are quite low, they are significant in their potential for reordering the provision of life benefits as they become more intensive and extensive in the future. I want to compare a number of places with which I have some familiarity to examine variations in local response. This will further an understanding of how localities may come to differ and also how local politics helps bring about those differences.

The California Cases

Despite the general economic travails of the United States, the southern California region booms along, not only in headquarters and service activities, but in manufacturing as well (Los Angeles is now the largest manufacturing center in the United States). Southern California grew in gross regional product by over 75 percent in the 1977–1987 period and is expected, both by the professional prognosticators and (if soaring real estate prices are any guide) by the speculators as well, to lead the country in economic growth in the future (Levy 1988; Soja 1987). It is also a region with an amalgam of governmental jurisdictions (cities and special districts) that run schools, colleges, transit systems, water supplies, sewer lines, mosquito abatement, as well as fire and police services. City and county governments have direct control over land use, but some of the special districts, especially water and sewers, also have the capacity to regulate land use. This system of governmental diversity, created in the first place to facilitate development (Hoch 1984) remains the institutional matrix through which growth still occurs.

Besides the general cutbacks common to the rest of the United States, California jurisdictions are now also confronted with the effects of two ballot initiatives that limit the capacity of localities and the state to pay the costs of infrastructure. Proposition 13 sharply limits property tax rates and Proposition 4 requires localities to return to taxpayers any revenues above a given maximum they nevertheless manage to generate. Several jurisdictions have already bumped against their Proposition 4 spending limits.

As with the federal cutbacks, the California tax and spending initiatives were also gratuitous in the sense that nothing required them. Proposition 13 was fueled by rising property taxes, which were due to skyrocketing property values (see Lo 1984). In other words, the cutbacks blamed on Proposition 13 (including draconian budget decreases for public hospitals, paramedics, coastal protection, and a proliferation of user fees for services formerly free) were due to wealth creation, rather than wealth erosion.[9] There were other ways to deal with home equities rising faster than their inhabitants' income. Government could have deferred tax payment (at death or sale of property) or shifted toward income of sales taxes as revenue sources (these alternatives failed to become public issues). Proposition 4 came at a time of especially thriving economic developments in California. Again, these propositions, as well as the fiscal conservatism of the current governor, do not seem rooted in any logics of the world economy.

But the consequence of these state measures, combined with federal policies, reinforces the exaction process as the feasible mechanism for amelioration. As tax options and other regulatory functions have been preempted by higher governmental units, land use controls have, almost alone, been left in local hands. This is a residue, in large part, of developers' fierce allegiance to local autonomy—the basis, after all, of their traditional means of making fortunes out of place. Now it is becoming a more mixed blessing as it is used to exact the funds for physical and social infrastructure, especially needed to support the costs of growth.[10]

The exaction process is enhanced through growth limitation policies. Controls have been enacted in hundreds of U.S. towns and cities with strong and broad-based voter support.[11] To overcome such restrictions, developers propose superior projects or accede to exaction demands. Even if growth controls fail to limit aggregate development—which indeed appears to be the case (Logan and Zhou 1989)—they enhance the projects that are built. While often explicitly oriented toward limiting the amount of development, the primary thrust of growth control has probably been to alter the ratio of public to private benefits from the projects that are built.

To understand the mechanisms through which places respond differently to the development process, Kee Warner and I are comparing three southern California localities—Santa Barbara, Santa Monica, and Riverside. Although substantially participating in the economic boom and consequent population pressures, these areas differ in the strategies of their local governments and the types of benefits exacted. These variations stem from contrasts in the social, economic, and ecological structures as well as in their indigenous politics. After briefly describing each one, I offer some preliminary judgments on how their differences are yielding distinctive development outcomes.

SANTA BARBARA. Long regarded a bastion of environmentalist sentiment, Santa Barbara contains affluent subcommunities whose residents have played a conspicuous role in land use policies.[12] Despite its notoriety as a center of inherited blueblood wealth, the Santa Barbara economy is based in agriculture, tourism, retirement, and a growing strip of high-technology research and manufacture (sometimes dubbed "Silicon Beach"). One-fourth of the core city population is Mexican-American; median family income in the city is below the overall state level.

Santa Barbara is one of the country's "autonomous" middle-size urban areas (Appelbaum et al. 1976), with its central city located more than twenty-five miles from its closest urban neighbor. It plausibly has the capacity to determine its own future without significant spillover problems arising from interlocal commutes or other neighborhood effects from adjoining zones. The city council, the county board of supervisors, and the most important water district board have majorities elected on growth control platforms. Growth and related environmental issues completely dominate local elections.

SANTA MONICA. An incorporated city located on the western edge of the Los Angeles metropolitan area, Santa Monica is fully integrated, economically and socially, into the larger metropolis. In recent years, it has experienced growing popularity as a site for residence and office development. Unlike Santa Barbara, Santa Monica's options are strongly influenced by its location in the midst of a larger metropolis. Any efforts at land use regulation can be confounded by larger area dynamics. Development restrictions aimed at easing traffic congestion, for example, will come to little if most traffic is nonlocally generated.

Also unlike Santa Barbara, Santa Monica's politics have been influenced by social welfare issues. Reformers have a leftist cast and have created low-cost housing programs that are on the cutting edge of the country's reform movement.[13] In Santa Monica there seems to be more of a tendency to accept growth, particularly industrial and commercial development, as a mechanism to fund social programs. For the past decade, Santa Monica has been heavily influenced by a successful rent-control movement. The Santa Monicans for Renters' Rights organization controls the elected rent control board and sympathetic candidates have now regained control of the city council. Environmentalism has also been a prominent election issue over the reform period, but secondary to rent control.

RIVERSIDE. Based on conventional indicators, the sprawling suburban belt made up of the city of Riverside and nearby towns is the least fertile ground for growth-control measures.[14] With an economy based in agriculture and manufacture, its large working-class population does not, at least according to certain strains of conventional wisdom, bode well for strong environmentalist organization.[15] Compared to the other two areas, Riverside has a less-developed grassroots politics, whether on behalf of environmental goals or social benefits. Increasingly integrated into the Los Angeles region, the Inland Empire (of which Riverside is a part) has gained large residential developments whose occupants commute to Los Angeles and Orange counties. Its population has increased rapidly, with a 6 percent annual growth rate in recent years.

The region's governments have been dominated by pro-growth coalitions, but in 1979, the city of Riverside (the most environmentalist jurisdiction in the area) established a greenbelt area with a minimum five-acre lot size and restricted hillside development. A 1987 initiative has banned any exemptions from the greenbelt law. In 1989, a countywide growth-control initiative made it to the ballot but failed by a substantial margin at the polls (environmentalists were outspent $1.7 million to $30,000).

Taken together, these three sites provide something of a cross section of the types of growth dynamics operating not only in the southern California region but many portions of the United States experiencing development pressures. We have, in Santa Barbara, a relatively autonomous place with a strong environmentalist tradition and much experience in policy development and implementation; in Santa Monica, a radically progressive city that is constrained by the larger metropolis in which it is embedded; and, in Riverside, a heavily working-class region that, as it is being called upon to play a changing and highly problematic role in the metropolis, is experiencing signs of rebellion against growth as usual.

Although all these places have some form of growth control in place, the precise nature of policy execution will determine the type of bargains with development that are made. These bargains will then cause some places to end up better off than others (in tax revenues, for example, or pollution levels, or public welfare) as new dynamics modify the mechanisms through which places are stratified. Besides limitations imposed by their incomes, people's futures will be determined by the kind of place they happen to end up in, a kind of "place luck" based on the inertia of birth location, family moves, and site of first job.[16]

In Santa Barbara, given the presence of strong environmentalist politics but only weak interest in social welfare, permission to develop seems to be exchanged for environmental exactions, particularly those that enhance beauty and lifestyle benefits. Despite local assumptions—by both developers and environmentalists— that no-growth policies are in effect, most forms of growth have not been stopped. Instead, the control doctrines are used to make exceptions for projects that meet criteria which, compared to other places, offset problems created for the physical environment.

Given the presence of a strong left in Santa Monica, growth pressures are likely being transmuted into high exactions to support social services and low-income housing. As in Santa Barbara, growth has been robust (far more robust in terms of absolute square footage). A strong coalition of progressive movements tracks each project and the dissemination of exaction moneys.

In Riverside the relatively weak mobilization on behalf of either environmental or welfare goals means that growth seems to proceed with low levels of exactions compared to the other two locations, although with high levels compared to the past. But besides their lower levels, a main difference appears to be the use to which the exactions are put: Riverside communities concentrate on site-related infrastructure that directly facilitates growth (such as sewer and road improvements) compared to social welfare or esthetic benefits. Growth is exploited to support still more growth. And given the commute crisis (substantial numbers of workers have four-hour round trips), any project that brings jobs is especially welcomed.

The outcome in each place thus represents a confluence of ecological, historic, and local economic circumstances, but tied to real choices that localities have to make through the political process. None of them is using up all available slack. Santa Barbara probably has the legal power to ban all growth but does not, even though surveys indicate that this is citizens' preferred option and fiscal analyses have shown it to be the most economical course. Santa Barbara could also go much further in using growth permissions to generate still higher levels of environmental protections or to demand benefits for the poor. Riverside's communities have options as well, although not the same list. They could insist, for example, that locals be employed in the approved industrial projects, to avoid the possibility that the new industrial plants will merely attract still more migrants who will bankrupt the public service with new service demands. Santa Monica's leaders have an analogous series of options.

In general, local politicians have enormous running room in their development policies. While the courts have ruled that exactions must plausibly be connected to costs imposed by the project (known as the "nexus" text), few cities have even come close to reaching their legal limits in terms of degrees of exactions or the types of uses to which they can be put.[17] Nor have exactions evidently become sufficiently burdensome to actually discourage developers in a given place. Boston, for example, one of the most demanding of localities, has exactions (special assessments beyond normal permit and development fees) estimated at only about 1 percent of developers' costs (Ehrlich and Dreier 1988).[18]

Attempts by citizens' groups to affect development represent an authentic grassroots effort to gain control over urban futures, albeit with uneven results. In a very imperfect system, exactions are one of the few viable mechanisms to generate social benefits from production. In a time when labor and ethnic movements are relatively quiescent, these growth-control efforts are the salient force outside established authority affecting community decisions in a socially responsible, however flawed, direction. It is a very imperfect way of providing for life, one way to pay for the social costs of capital investment.

There are real differences in the consequences of tapping wealth through local exactions compared to general taxation or industrial union negotiations. The evolving system is, in effect, one of "spot" taxation, which delivers idiosyncratic benefits across towns and cities, and even variation from parcel to parcel. Further, the degree and quality of the exaction is not subject to procedures analogous to uniform tax codes or labor contract precedents. Current laws and policies permit extreme variability in both process and substance. One locality can exact funds for still more growth in-

frastructure, another for child care, another for low-income housing, still another for public art. And this can change from project to
project and over time. Procedures can vary from comprehensive
point system and downzoning programs, or can be based on more
ad hoc, piecemeal negotiations with developers. In other words,
the distribution of fiscal costs and life opportunities is tied to local
political response to the development option. A new mode of
stratifying places is thus born, and the social safety net previously
established by federal or state standards (and union contracts)
becomes less significant compared to the vicissitudes of local
development.[19]

The mode of accommodating restructuring in the United States
is thus the breaking of the connection between national citizenship and access to life resources. A great metropolis can simultaneously be the location of great wealth creation, sophisticated
culture, and innovation as well as low-paid workers living in
service-poor municipalities. These and related developments, like
Proposition 13 and growth control, were not cooked up by some
conspiracy of power elites to serve the logics of capital.[20] Of
course, an all-out war by corporate elites against this system of
providing benefits would likely have precluded them. But unlike,
say, a threat of domestic communism, such crucial interests were
not at stake. Even with the current level of exactions (more than
the past, but not too much), the arrangement can be accommo-
dated. The profit system moves along satisfactorily.

Exacting benefits from the development process is a flawed
mechanism to compensate for the lack of responsible policies at
state and national levels. But it is certainly superior to the kind of
immiseration that would occur if growth machines maintained
their complete hegemony, providing no offsets whatever for development damage. But there are other ways of dealing with economic change at the level of people's lives, both more and less
democratic, and I now turn to other countries for instances.

The Deals Abroad

Borrowing from the work of other contributors to
this volume, as well as some of my recent research with Serena

Vicari on Italy (Molotch and Vicari 1988; Vicari and Molotch, forthcoming), I will sketch out what appear to be some alternatives.

The Italian situation is very different from the United States. Bargaining does go on in Italy between developers and local governments and the results do indeed inject a degree of "place luck" into the Italian system that parallels the emerging U.S. situation. The Italians are no less concerned with international competition and face a similar postmodernization of production. The difference is that Italian development does not occur in fragmented, autonomous jurisdictions and local citizens are not as heavily dependent on development deals for social benefits. Over 90 percent of local revenues are transfers from the central state (Martinotti, n.d., 1981). National laws and party policies provide social entitlements as well as housing tenure and local physical infrastructure. Rent controls and tenant stability are set by national legislation. There has been no rollback either at national or local levels in any way parallel to the events in the United States (or Britain). Homelessness is rare. Government protects housing tenure as well as other aspects of daily life from idiosyncratic local policies. Citizenship entitlements, in other words, adhere to national, rather than local, residence. This is the primary consequence of left parties (integrated at local and national levels) coming to power in Italy and will likely remain in place as long as the left is in power. The "red junta" governments of Bologna and other cities really did carry out significant redistributive policies as well as power decentralization to the neighborhood level (Martinotti, n.d.). Although these levels of left reform were disappointing to those who hoped for more radical change, the power of the left, in the context of a strong party system, gives Italian restructuring a more benign cast than in the United States.

Under the aegis of Thatcherism, the British government uses international competition as grounds for undermining virtually all protections, whether for declining industries, cities, or citizens. Privatization of government services extends to urban space as localities compete for investors both in terms of production and marketing of the built environment.

As Parkinson and Judd document (1988; see also Parkinson

chapter, this volume) the Thatcher strategy is at once one of centralization and decentralization. The government centralizes by eliminating the power or even existence of local governments, thereby obliterating units that, like the Greater London Council, have been a base for Labour politicians' counterinitiatives. At the same time, power has devolved into the hands of private firms, which now carry the initiative for local development while having a direct influence on the centralized policies through which their local operations function.

Although without the home rule land use controls found in the United States, the British system moves toward the U.S. model—not a coincidence given the current Conservative party's reigning infatuation with things American. Based on their study of restructuring in the town of Swindon, Bassett and Harloe (forthcoming) write that "the dangers are that a new growth coalition may come increasingly to resemble those which exist in the United States, an alliance of some local politicians, the middle class and business, pursuing their own sectional interests with little concern to link economic growth to redistributive social policies." I would be interested to know whether the British localities, so weakened by the Thatcher reforms, are in a position to demand progressive exactions from developers (or what benefits are derived from the public-private partnerships now in vogue). Is this one potential benefit of development (now occurring in some instances in the United States) present in the United Kingdom, or is the very worst of the growth machine system being replicated, without the recent U.S. salutary modifications?

In Japan, to hop across the biosphere, a highly centralized system of government-corporate domination meets up with the new phenomenon of restructuring. Japanese firms now go offshore in Southeast Asia to find lower-wage labor and to the United States to avoid import restrictions. There is thus a "hollowing out" of heavy manufacture from the Japanese economy (Fujita and Hill 1989) parallel to the decline of the Rustbelts in North America and Europe, with the same home shift toward services and the financial sector. But the Japanese system is distinctive, in the salience of its diversified conglomerate firms through which production, reproduction, government, and party are heavily managed. For that portion of the work force employed in these firms, there is income security, recreational opportunity, and housing. Because of these firms' diversity (some are already major factors in both manufacture and services), it is possible that workers will be shifted from one role to another as the Japanese economy reorients.

In spatial terms, the difficulty would be to transform industrial cities, like Toyota City, from a manufacturing center to a place suited to service agglomerations. Hill (1989) appears skeptical of this possibility. My point is that this is something to watch for as the Japanese system of corporate paternalism meets the challenge of restructuring. If the Japanese were to allow places and people to fend for themselves (even those in the protected bosoms of the conglomerates), the underlying cultural legitimacy of the productive apparatus would be put at risk in a way that does not apply in the United States or the United Kingdom.

The French variant described by Preteceille (1988; this volume) reveals the political struggle to manipulate the legal and fiduciary status of locality as a way of determining the distribution of benefits across classes and locations. Even as they participate in economic restructuring, the left and right modify (or even reverse) their positions on governmental structure because of its implications for social benefits. The left initiated government decentralization, but it was the rightist parties that later defended it when they won power in local elections. Now the fragmentation of power, including local fiscal inequalities that have come with it (but that were not inevitable) are a problem for the left. This appears to be, as in the United Kingdom, a basis for establishing a U.S.-style growth-machine system in France. But the seesaw of left-right control characteristic of recent France allows for no such easy conclusion.

The left may truly rise again in France, and the newly created local autonomy may turn—even without the intervention of the national authority—into a system of exaction demands that could, as in the emerging U.S. case, pull social benefits (albeit unevenly across places) from capital. Rejoined with the French tradition of centralism, the exaction pattern could depart from the U.S. system, establishing national standards and benefit sharing across places. In short, although the left now joins the right in its new-found respect for business needs, the country's policies do not otherwise indicate an inevitable shift toward a Thatcherite or Reaganite embrace of locality competition or national welfare meanness.

Conclusion: Deals Vary, Deals Change

Major economic change tends to break apart the social contracts previously established among productive segments. It takes time for grievances to accumulate and find modes of effective expression. Capital moves faster than culture and more rapidly than the victims of change can organize for reform. Without being too sanguine about the probabilities of effective response, it is plausible to think of a kind of cultural lag in which the less powerful need more time to organize than the high velocity of capital needs to make their troubles. In the United States, without a strong left tradition, reform is always ad hoc and operates through social movements rather than party (Flacks 1988). As change upsets former arrangements for exacting social justice, there is no ongoing system to make certain that the new economic order is socially continuous with the old. Hence (optimistically) rather moderate development exactions are coming as a first remedial solution. In societies like Italy, where the left remains in power, the parties guide and monitor restructuring such that its social consequences are kept under control.

The question ushered in by restructuring is whether nations and localities respond effectively and how quickly they do so. The politics of places, as embedded in their specific histories, remains a key factor in urban change, because it is both a useful explanatory device and a plausible arena for intervention.

NOTES

Acknowledgments: I am grateful to Nancy Kleniewski and the editors of this volume for helpful suggestions on an earlier draft.

1. A large critical literature (for some of the classics, see Theodorson 1961) documented so many exceptions that the paradigm eventually had to collapse. Especially noteworthy was that whereas European countries were dominated by a single great city (which virtually monopolized finan-

cial, political, and cultural power), the United States represented a pattern of greater dispersion. Similarly, within the United States, the southwestern "system of cities" (with Los Angeles as exemplar) never fit the model.

2. The parallel is with status attainment studies, which, after exhaustive searches for the factors affecting social mobility, finally conclude that a large portion of the variance is due to luck (or luck and pluck). See, for example, Jencks et al. 1979.

3. The descriptive substance of the globalization process seems quite similar in both the neo-Marxist and ecological presentations.

4. It is as though we were as ignorant of cross-jurisdictional infection as the authorities who dealt with bubonic plague.

5. The dunce characterization is attributed to Clark Clifford.

6. Given the real problems, as well as the imagined ones, making something as complex as restructuring work in a given place is no easy trick (see Mayer 1988).

7. Similarly, Manhattan's wealth boom of the 1980s, accompanied by the kind of density intensification that makes possible new economies of scale in service provision, has yet to induce a serious proposal for proportionate infrastructure improvement, such as a civilized means of garbage collection.

8. Every society must determine how its surplus will be exacted and distributed; some poor societies have been highly egalitarian (see Keyfitz 1965; Sahlins 1972).

9. Rising real estate value represents more than just "paper wealth" for owning residents. They are accumulating an estate for their heirs, some of whom will live in cheaper housing markets. Alternatively, they can generate cash through refinancing, using the proceeds for other investments or for immediate consumption, albeit possibly lowering the value of their estate at death.

10. Growth interests now assault local control through the courts as well as legislative efforts to promote their version of regional planning. But home rule, in part because of the legal and cultural precedents that growth elites helped establish, remains difficult to overcome.

11. Localities are voting for growth control even when, as is typical, developers outspend their opponents by as much as six to one (Glickfeld, Graymer and Morrison 1987; DeLeon and Powell 1988). These victories imply that the growth control/exaction system has a strong base which, unusual for electoral issues, can survive the campaign onslaughts of big-money interests.

12. For example, Santa Barbara was the first city in the United States to form an architectural board of review (in 1925).

13. For a general description of Santa Monica as one of the country's handful of progressive cities, see Clavel 1986.

14. The Riverside site includes only the northwestern portion of Riverside County.

15. See, for example, Sills 1975; Deacon and Shapiro 1975; Dowall 1981. For an alternative, see the literature survey of Van Liere and Dunlap 1980. Although most studies indicate substantial working-class support for development control, working-class people tend, in this realm as in others, to be difficult to organize into effective units (for evidence, see Logan and Molotch 1987: 134–42).

16. Contrary to public-choice theorists' notions of how people end up in given locales (see Tiebout 1956), it is usually due either to forced choice or dumb happenstance and not their "tastes" or skills at picking a winning spot.

17. Even with relatively high exactions and fees, it is still unlikely that localities are recouping the costs of development—even in the most advanced cities, at least according to preliminary results of our studies.

18. The Boston figure is low compared to estimates made for other places. Comparisons are difficult to make because of the variation among places in what is counted as an exaction and what is a matter of "normal" fee structures (costs of building permits, sewer and water costs, etc.). Total fees for single-family residential construction in southern California cities have been estimated at 7.7 percent of total developer costs (Snyder and Stegman 1986).

19. On stratification of place, see Logan 1978; Logan and Schneider 1981.

20. Corporate interests did not lead the fight for Propositions 13 and 4; indeed, some segments opposed it, although not with great vigor (see Lo 1984).

REFERENCES

Appelbaum, Richard, et al. 1976. *The Effects of Urban Growth.* New York: Praeger.

Bassett, Keith, and Michael Harloe. Forthcoming. "Swindon: The Rise and Decline of a Growth Coalition." In *Localities, Policies and Politics*, ed. M. Harloe, C. Pickvance, and J. Urry. London: Unwin Hyman.

Clavel, Pierre. 1986. *The Progressive City: Planning and Participation 1969–1984.* New Brunswick, N.J.: Rutgers University Press.

Deacon, Robert, and Perry Schapiro. 1975. "Private Preference for Collective Goods Revealed Through Voting on Referenda." *American Economic Review* 65:943–955.

Deakin, Elizabeth. 1988. "The Politics of Exactions." In *Private Supply of Public Services: Evaluation of Real Estate Exactions, Linkage and Alternative Land Policies*, ed. Rachelle Alterman. New York: New York University Press.

DeLeon, Richard E., and Sandra S. Powell. 1988. "Growth Control and Electoral Politics in San Francisco: The Victory of Proposition M in 1986," working Paper no. 3. San Francisco: Public Research Institute, San Francisco State University.

Dowall, David. 1981. "An Examination of Population Growth-Managing Communities." *Policy Studies Journal* 9:414–27.

Ehrlich, Bruce, and Peter Dreier. 1988. "Downtown Development and Urban Reform: The Politics of Boston's Linkage Policy." Boston Redevelopment Authority.

Esping-Andersen, G. 1985. *Politics Against Markets: The Social Democratic Road to Power.* Princeton: Princeton University Press.

Fitzgerald, Frances. 1989. "Memoirs of the Reagan Era." *The New Yorker,* January 16, pp. 71–94.

Flacks, Richard. 1988. *Making History.* New York: Columbia University Press.

Friedland, Roger, and Jimmy Sanders. 1988. "The Public Economy and Economic Growth in Western Market Economies." *American Sociological Review* 50:421–37.

Fujita, Kuniko, and Richard Child Hill. 1989. "Global Production and Regional 'Hollowing Out' in Japan." In *Comparative Urban and Community Research,* vol. 2, ed. Michael Smith. New Brunswick, N.J.: Transaction Books.

Glickfeld, Madelyn, LeRoy Graymer, and Kerry Morrison. 1987. "Trends in Local Growth Control Ballot Measures in California." *Journal of Environmental Law* 6:111–58.

Hill, Richard Child. 1989. "Comparing Transnational Production Systems: The Case of the Automobile Industry in the United States and Japan." *International Journal of Urban and Regional Research* 13(3): 462–80.

Hoch, Charles. 1984. "City Limits: Municipal Boundary Formation and Class Segregation." In *Marxism and the Metropolis,* 2d ed., ed. William K. Tabb and Larry Sawers. New York: Oxford University Press.

Jencks, Christopher, et al. 1979. *Who Gets Ahead? The Determinants of Economic Success in America.* New York: Basic Books.

Kantor, Paul, with Stephen David. 1988. *The Dependent City: The Changing Political Economy or Urban America.* Glenview, Ill.: Scott, Foresman.

Keil, Roger. "The Political Dimension of Urban Restructuring: Los Angeles." 1988. Paper presented at the Annual Meeting of the Association of American Geographers, Phoenix, Arizona, April.

Keyfitz, Nathan. 1965. "Political-Economic Aspects of Urbanization in South and Southeast Asia." In *The Study of Urbanization,* ed. Philip Hauser and Leo F. Schnore. New York: Wiley.

Korpi, Walter. 1985. "Economic Growth and the Welfare State: Leaky

Bucket or Irrigation System?" *European Sociological Review* 1(2):97–118.

Kuttner, Robert. 1984. *The Economic Illusion: False Choices Between Prosperity and Social Justice*. Boston: Houghton Mifflin.

Levy, Steven. 1988. "California Economic Growth: Regional Update and Projections." Palo Alto: Center for Continuing Study of the California Economy.

Lo, Clarence Y. H. 1984. "Mobilizing the Tax Revolt: The Emergent Alliance Between Homeowners and Local Elites." In *Research in Social Movements, Conflict, and Change*, vol. 6, ed. Richard Ratcliff. Greenwich, Conn.: JAI Press.

Logan, John. 1978. "Growth, Politics, and the Stratification of Places." *American Journal of Sociology* 84(2):404–15.

Logan, John R., and Harvey Molotch. 1987. *Urban Fortunes: The Political Economy of Place*. Berkeley and Los Angeles: University of California Press.

Logan, John, and Mark Schneider. 1981. "The Stratification of Metropolitan Suburbs, 1960–1970." *American Sociological Review* 46(2): 175–86.

Logan, John, and Min Zhou. 1989. "Do Suburban Growth Controls Control Growth?" *American Sociological Review* 54(3):461–71.

Martinotti, Guido. n.d. "From Dualism to Center-Periphery: The Changing Urban Structure of Postwar Italian Society." Unpublished paper, Department of Sociology, University of Milan.

———. 1981. "The Illusive Autonomy: Central Control and Decentralization in the Italian Local Financial System." In *The Local Fiscal Crisis in Western Europe: Myths and Realities*, ed. L. J. Sharpe. London: ECPR.

Mayer, Margit. 1988. "The Changing Conditions for Local Politics in the Transition to Post-Fordism." Paper prepared for the International Conference on Regulation Theory, Barcelona, June.

Molotch, Harvey, and Serena Vicari. 1988. "Three Ways to Build: The Development Process in the United States, Japan and Italy." *Urban Affairs Quarterly* 24(2):188–214.

Monkkonen, Eric. 1988. *America Becomes Urban: The Development of U.S. Cities and Towns, 1780–1980*. Berkeley and Los Angeles: University of California Press.

Myles, John. 1990. "States, Labor Markets, and Life Cycles," in *Beyond the Marketplace: Rethinking Economy and Society*, ed. Roger Friedland and A. F. Robertson. New York: Aldine de Gruyter.

Parkinson, Michael, and Dennis Judd. 1988. "Urban Revitalization in America and the UK—The Politics of Uneven Development." In *Regenerating the Cities: The UK crisis and the US experience*, ed. Michael Parkinson, Bernard Foley, and Dennis Judd. Manchester: Manchester University Press.

Peterson, Paul. 1981. *City Limits*. Chicago: University of Chicago Press.

Preteceille, Edmond. 1988. "From Centralisation to Decentralisation: Social Restructuring and French Local Government." Paper presented at meetings of International Sociological Association (RC21) Conference on Trends and Challenges of Urban Restructuring, Rio de Janeiro, September.

Reskin, Barbara, and Heidi Hartmann, eds. 1986. *Women's Work, Men's Work: Sex Segregation on the Job*. Washington, D.C.: National Academy Press.

Sahlins, Marshall. 1972. *Stone Age Economics*. Chicago: Aldine-Atherton.

Sassen, Saskia. 1988. *The Mobility of Labor and Capital*. Cambridge: Cambridge University Press.

Shearer, Derek. 1989. "In Search of Equal Partnerships: The Prospects for Progressive Urban Policy in the 1990's." In *Unequal Partnerships*, ed. Gregory Squires. New Brunswick, N.J.: Rutgers University Press.

Sills, David L. 1975. "The Environmental Movement and Its Critics." *Human Ecology* 3(1):1–41.

Snyder, Thomas, and Michael Stegman. 1986. *Paying for Growth: Using Development Fees to Finance Infrastructure*. Washington, D.C.: Urban Land Institute.

Soja, Edward. 1987. "LA's the Place: Economic Restructuring and the Internationalization of the Los Angeles Region." In *The Capitalist City: Global Restructuring and Community Politics*, ed. Michael Peter Smith and Joe R. Feagin. Oxford: Basil Blackwell.

Theodorson, George. 1961. *Studies in Human Ecology*. New York: Harper & Row.

Van Liere, Kent D., and Riley Dunlap. 1980. "The Social Bases of Environmental Concern: A Review of Hypotheses, Explanations, and Empirical Evidence." *Public Opinion Quarterly* 44(2):181–97.

Vicari, Serena, and Harvey Molotch. Forthcoming. "Building Milan: Alternative Machines of Growth." *International Journal of Urban and Regional Research*.

CHAPTER 8

Space for Progressive Local Policy: Examples from the United States and the United Kingdom

Pierre Clavel and Nancy Kleniewski

The main question posed by this volume is, given restructuring, what can localities do? In this chapter we argue that the space for local response is greater, not smaller, in the 1980s than in previous postwar decades, present evidence of the increased variety of local policy response in the United States and England, and conclude with a set of observations on the future policy implications of this new variation.

The Expansion of Space
for Local Policy Initiatives

Both business elites and government officials are responding to changes in global economic patterns, albeit in some-

199

what different ways. The response to restructuring forces has taken several different forms. Finance has concentrated and has pulled out of manufacturing, going instead into services and real estate development. The pattern of response is varied by sector and locality.[1] Ann Markusen (1988) has suggested a typology of "bidding down, bailing out, and building on the basics" which captures this diversity. A common response by local elites is simply to bail out of manufacturing altogether, shifting capital (via local development policy and through private-sector financial institutions) to office construction and inner-city gentrification projects. In a few cases, there has been a bidding-down approach designed to maintain manufacturing—at least for a time—by cutting labor, taxes, and other costs. Markusen's own work and the policy of the late Mayor Harold Washington in Chicago were an example of the building-on-the-basics approach: finding niches where manufacturing can prosper and helping support it through modernization (Markusen 1988, 173–84).

In both the United States and England, the political response to economic restructuring has been an increased polarization between right and left. With the decline of the established manufacturing firms, the liberal policy consensus based on Keynesian, demand-driven accumulation fragmented. The previous corporate-labor-government–led policy came under attack from both right and left (but more particularly from the right). The elections of Thatcher in 1979 and Reagan in 1980 helped to increase public support for an individualistic, profit-oriented classical capitalism. Both administrations used economic restructuring as a justification for the meaner welfare states, the upwardly redistributive tax reforms, and the increased military spending they have favored— all in the name of "increasing competitiveness" or "balancing the budget."

An apparent orthodoxy for local economic development, leading to what we call mainstream policy, exists in the United States today. It holds that localities are locked in a bidding war, attempting to attract hypermobile capital by providing as many preconditions as possible for maximum profits. Beneath the surface, however, there exists more variation in policy direction than there has been in the past thirty years. First, in several places local labor and community groups have mounted significant responses to the economic problems caused by restructuring, resulting in a growing body of thought challenging the dominant view. The political left has become increasingly articulate about local economic development issues, perhaps emboldened by the willingness of churches and elected officials to support community-based initiatives to step into the void that private capital has created.

Second, the business elite has become increasingly fragmented. Fragmentation, disintegration, and reformulation of relationships among firms, industrial sectors, and segments of the labor force have been part of the restructuring process. Firm decomposition, changes in corporate financing, and new ways of exploiting various segments of the labor force have undercut many of the previous era's business arrangements. There is a legitimate concern (for example, see chapter by Edmond Preteceille in this volume) that these changes have had a negative effect on labor. This flux, however, has also provided space for innovation that may allow labor and community groups to minimize their losses or even make gains. On the one hand, the loss of the large-scale, union-wage manufacturing jobs, where it has occurred, has been traumatic. On the other hand, retrenchment of the larger firms has produced economic innovation and has generated new jobs in smaller firms, reducing the degree of domination of local economies by small numbers of giant companies.

Recent decades in Britain have likewise seen a disaggregation of local policy approaches. In the late 1960s there was general discontent with the operation of the central bureaucracy and much casting about for ways to reorganize policy. Most dramatic were the national movements in Scotland and Wales, calling for drastic devolution of government functions. These movements, with wide electoral backing, were made more urgent by the background of violence in Northern Ireland. More generally, throughout Britain, discussions of regionalization of many government functions also led to the creation of economic planning boards and councils that helped stimulate a degree of independent administrative work. Another development was the 1972 Local Government Reorganization Act, which created six new metropolitan counties in addition to the previously established Greater London Council.

All this set the stage for the emergence in the late 1970s and early 1980s of dramatically new policy directions in local economics as radical Labour Councils gained majorities in places like London, Sheffield, Leeds, and the West Midlands. The local structures had been established, administrative capacity had been developed, and they were ready to be used when new political leadership took over. As Thatcherism began to dominate the economic stage at the national level, Labour leadership found the localities the main stage from which to operate.

Despite the conservative nature of economic policy at the national level, conditions remain fluid at the local level in both the United Kingdom and the United States. Both right and left have undertaken experimental programs aimed at rebuilding local economies from very different starting points. In England, the Conservative-backed development programs, which are anti-planning and market-oriented, are focused on the private sector and aimed at attracting new investment; while the Labour initiatives, which are pro-planning and production-oriented, are focused on the public sector and aimed at strengthening current industry (Benington 1986, 8). In the United States, there have been a dozen or more communities in which left-leaning groups have dominated or heavily influenced local government and have self-consciously set out a progressive local economic development agenda. These progressive cities have been guided by the aggressive use of public planning to shape the nature of the local economy and a commitment to democratic participation in local decision making by previously disenfranchised groups (Clavel 1986).

National turmoil has thus provided a certain "relative autonomy of the state" at the local level, and has given openings for nonelites such as labor and community groups to enter the policy debate. The current situation encourages local variation and experiment of both the mainstream (pro-business) and progressive (pro-labor and community) varieties.

Variation in Local Policy Response

Variation in local economic policy occurs on two major dimensions that tend to define community response to restructuring:

1. The extent of local and popular social control over restructuring.[2] Liberal and corporatist policies have entailed a minimum of control, preferring to leave control to the market or to business elites. An emerging form of progressive city government has questioned the market and opted either for its regulation or its replacement by public (or mixed) enterprises. (See Clavel 1986.)

2. The extent of acquiescence to the shift out of manufacturing into services. Places vary in the degree to which they wish to or can intervene in the speed of this sectoral shift. It can at least be an orderly retreat, with consolidation in some sectors. This issue also evokes the usefulness of social control: the more sophisticated and equitable the social control, the more likely a long-run adjustment that minimizes human and other resource waste.

These two issues are key dimensions of local variation around which we can organize our evidence and case studies. We have constructed Table 8-1 to illustrate types of variation in local policy response. Although the categories of response are ideal types rather than an exhaustive list of all actual responses, the table helps to differentiate responses along the dimensions we have described and to begin the process of building a taxonomy of cases of actual local policy responses.

Mainstream Manufacturing Policy

The normal course of action for local economic development agencies today, at least in the United States and Britain, is accommodating the community to the needs of business in order to attract or retain jobs for residents. Mainstream approaches to the manufacturing sector typically encourage workers and community residents to bid down the costs of industry in their area. Under the rubric of "creating a good business climate," local government attempts to provide the preconditions for higher profits by discouraging unionization, cutting wages, reducing unemployment benefits, lowering taxes, and giving incentives such as tax breaks, free land, and subsidized financing to manufacturers who will locate or expand in the area. Incentives such as tax abatements within enterprise zones and financing through industrial revenue bonds are so widely used that they are now expected by

TABLE 8-1. Directions in Local Economic Development Policy

Economic sectoral emphasis	Degree of social control	
	High (progressive)	Low (mainstream)
Manufacturing	Building on the basics (Community-labor coalitions)	Bidding down (Enterprise zones) (Industrial revenue bonds)
Services	Redistribution of service growth (Linkage)	Bowing out (Convention centers) (Downtown tax abatements)

many industrial companies (Wolman 1988). Thus, the return to classical accumulation is being carried out with the aid and blessing of federal, state, and many local governments.

Enterprise zones were first proposed by Peter Hall (1977) as a way to redevelop deteriorated central city areas in Britain. The idea was to reduce government regulation and taxation to stimulate new firm development and job creation. Enterprise zones quickly became a centerpiece of the Thatcher government's urban policy, and by 1983 twenty-four zones had been established. They provided a ten-year exemption from local property taxes, exemption from the land development tax, accelerated depreciation on land and buildings, and expedited government attention for planning permissions.

Controversy has raged over the zones. The effects seem to be mixed and difficult to disentangle from other policy effects. One assessment suggests that what success the zones have had has resulted as much from previous and ongoing local government industrial-attraction policies as from the zones themselves. Another problem has been a muddling of the original thrust, which was for "relief" from government regulation, to intense government involvement and assistance (Barnes and Preston 1985). Nonetheless, the enterprise zone was imported to the United States where it became the main urban policy initiative of the Reagan administration. (See, for example, Butler 1980, and critiques by Goldsmith 1982, and Wilder and Rubin 1988.) Although not adopted as federal policy by Congress, the enterprise-zone principle has been embraced by more than thirty states, chiefly operating as a targeted tax-abatement policy.

Although enterprise zones are geographically targeted to specific neighborhoods within inner cities, nongeographically specific subsidies for manufacturing, which cities began to use in the 1950s, have been intensified in the 1980s. One of the more extreme examples of the length to which local governments in the United States have gone to provide public subsidies for manufacturing was the 1980 agreement between General Motors (GM) and the city of Detroit for a new Cadillac plant (Jones and Bachelor 1984; Fasenfest 1986). The city provided local property tax abatements, property acquisition through eminent domain, aid in administering the project, aid in acquiring financing through the federal government, and tax increment financing to repay loans from the federal government (Jones and Bachelor 1984, 253–54). The project gained notoriety unparalleled in recent years because of the section of the agreement on land acquisition. Local officials acceded to GM's demands for space far in excess of that actually needed to build the plant, resulting in the destruction of a neighborhood of some 1,500 homes and 144 businesses—all paid for by public funds. More than one commentator at the time called GM's demands "corporate blackmail" because of the company's refusal to back down from its rigid position, in effect giving the city an "all-or-nothing" ultimatum.

An exacerbated case is that of the dependent manufacturing area in which a significant or even a majority proportion of employment is controlled by absentee owners. David Perry and his associates describe this case for Buffalo, based on a survey of firms in western New York's Erie and Niagara counties. They suggest that outside-owned firms are relatively more likely to divest, to have local plant-level issues decided in faraway headquarters locations, to substitute central for local purchasing, and to have fewer intralocal linkages. In such cases, plant-closing decisions are often made for reasons having little to do with the profitability of local plants. Absentee ownership also tends to avoid involvement in communities' political and economic issues. The result is severe difficulties in aggregating political authority within such a region and an inability to respond to opportunities for collective action on economic development problems (Perry et al., n.d.).

Mainstream Shift to Services

When mainstream policy is not designed to make manufacturing competitive, it is often aimed at bailing out of manufacturing altogether. Many city governments' main economic development goal is to facilitate the conversion from their manufacturing-based economies to business and financial service-based economies, fueling booms in downtown real estate development. Local governments have implemented policies such as giving tax abatements for hotel construction, helping arrange financing for private office buildings, facilitating retail expansion, and directing public investment to the communities' amenity infrastructures—their parks, museums, sports complexes, convention centers, waterfronts, and other leisure areas.

The headlong rush of city governments to fund the construction of convention centers is one manifestation of mainstream service-sector policy. The impetus for building a new convention center in Philadelphia, for example, arose in 1982 from downtown hotels, restaurants, and real estate interests, and The Reading (Railroad) Company offered to develop the new convention center on the site of its former train shed. The estimated cost was over $450 million for startup plus a yearly operating subsidy of $1 million, all to come from public funds (Byrnes 1984). Once the proposal was on the table, it proved extremely difficult to counter. Not only the downtown businesses and building trades unions but also the mayor, nearly the entire city council, and the quasipublic development agency were arrayed squarely behind the center. They viewed it as an easy way of getting new dollars pumped into the economy of Philadelphia. Opponents produced data showing that the center would not provide as many jobs as claimed and that the employment that would be created would be mostly minimum-wage, dead-end positions in low-level services. They argued that, rather than centralizing more economic development projects in the already booming downtown, an effort should be made to provide jobs for the displaced industrial workers in other areas of the city. The opposition succeeded in getting the construction delayed, having alternative sites considered, gaining agreements for hiring minority workers, and getting the state to share funding with the city. It was not successful, however, at changing the scope of the debate to question the necessity of the public investment in the center (Breslow 1987).

The Detroit and Philadelphia cases help illuminate the role of the public sector within mainstream economic development policy. First, in these public-private partnerships, the public partners increasingly are expected to provide the capital investment while the private partners make the profit. In Detroit, GM obtained more than $200,000 in "up-front" public funds and the city's commitment to forego at least $5 million per year in property taxes over a thirty-year period (Jones and Bachelor 1984). In the case of the Philadelphia project, the public sector has committed itself to invest $450 million (including both state and local funds) with only a dim faith that the public coffers might see some return on that investment over the next thirty years.

Second, the role of the local government within mainstream policy is to respond to initiatives proposed by the private sector rather than studying the local situation and proposing its own programs (that is, planning). This puts public officials in the position of upholding the corporations' criteria rather than formulating their own criteria for the success of economic development projects. It also encourages acceptance of simplistic policy orientations based on superficial or self-interested assessments of current economic trends ("becoming more wage competitive in manufacturing" or "building up the service sector") rather than a serious analysis of those trends and a search for new ideas of working with and around economic changes.

Third, mainstream policy assumes that all local economic development is driven by the companies' economic imperatives, and that the private sector is the best judge of what its own bottom line is. Jones and Bachelor (1984) argue that Detroit's total capitulation to General Motors was largely due to the asymmetry of information between the corporation and the city government, which permitted GM to keep the city ignorant of the real costs and subsidy needs for the project. The city accepted the company's definition that it should be in control of its financial information, despite the real possibility that the company was extracting from the city a subsidy in excess of what it actually needed to make the project viable. In the case of the Philadelphia convention center, the city accepted the highest of three projections of economic benefits, based on a study commissioned by the downtown development interests, despite obvious methodological errors pointed out by the city's own staff (Breslow 1987).

Although it currently dominates popular thinking about local economic development, mainstream policy has some inherent problems that make it inefficient, ineffective, and inequitable. One problem is the lack of performance criteria for companies receiving the incentives. In the case of Detroit, the city had no requirement that GM would actually build the Cadillac plant or put it into production, and negotiated no payback for the land in terms of jobs or taxes generated (Fasenfest 1986, 114). A second problem is that enterprise zones and other tax abatements do not turn out to be key factors in attracting new investment to communities. A growing body of empirical evidence shows that firms' locational decisions are relatively unaffected by tax differentials (Doeringer, Terkla, and Topakian 1988; Wilder and Rubin 1988; Wolman 1988; Legislative Tax Study Commission 1984). A third problem is that indiscriminate use of subsidies can exacerbate the very employment problems the programs are supposedly designed to solve. Squires (1984), for example, shows that industrial revenue bond financing does not necessarily add to manufacturing jobs and can have the effect of hastening rather than managing the deindustrialization of communities.

Each specific policy we have described as mainstream could be transformed into progressive policy. By requiring a *quid pro quo* in exchange for subsidies, by having the city administration plan and take the initiative in the kinds of projects to be undertaken, and by targeting subsidies to mitigate rather than exacerbate the negative impacts of overall economic trends, cities can push economic policy *within a capitalist framework* in a progressive direction. Moving beyond capitalism, as some cities are attempting to do, requires opening up the economy to public, cooperative, and mixed enterprises as well as strictly private-for-profit companies.

Progressive Policies—The Service Sector

The kinds of policies that we are calling progressive are primarily oriented toward labor and community groups rather than the corporate sector. They are based on a different set of assumptions about the relationship between capital and communities than those underpinning mainstream policies and represent a countervailing ideology. Instead of acting as uncritical agents of private growth, local governments are expected to harness, shape, and encourage the private sector in the pursuit of social goals defined by the community as a whole. They may nurture alternative forms of production and investment, such as public companies, cooperatives, and worker-managed enterprises, as well as maintaining the traditionally liberal emphasis on redistributive public services.

Progressive policies have taken many specific forms in different areas, depending on the economic and political circumstances in different communities. The economic context and history of a given community may produce conditions blocking growth in one economic sector while permitting it in another. Thus, officials must make strategic decisions about which industries have potential for growth and transformation. Politics, too, complicates the possibilities for progressive policies. The constellation of political groupings in each area forms political arenas that are more or less open to discussions of progressive alternatives to mainstream policy. We will discuss several cases of progressive policies, attempting to isolate important economic or political characteristics of the communities in which the policies were proposed or instituted.

One promising direction for progressive local policy in the United States has been in the area of harnessing and redistributing gains from the growth of the service economy. Cities using this approach have most frequently been tertiary cities such as San Francisco and Boston—communities dominated by tertiary-sector activities, such as business services. One way of redistributing growth in this sector is through linkage programs. These programs permit developers to build high-profit projects only on the condition that they build accompanying low-profit projects (low-income housing, day-care centers, and the like) or contribute to funding them. In their classic form, linkage policies are adopted partially because of pressures arising from the negative consequences of uncontrolled downtown development. (See Harvey Molotch's chapter in this volume, and Keating 1986.)

Boston's linkage program, for example, was partly the result of a negative reaction to growth. In Boston, as in many postindustrial central cities in the 1970s, the urban working class was rapidly being displaced by the expansion of the central business district and by gentrification from upper-income professional workers. Urban renewal programs and a severe land shortage provided a framework within which gentrification caused rapidly rising housing prices. In 1983, after gaining the support of neighborhood groups, a linkage proposal passed on a nonbinding referendum in Boston. State Representative Mel King and City Councilmember (later mayor) Ray Flynn were the public officials most closely associated with the linkage proposal, which resulted in a new city ordinance under Mayor White, later strengthened by the Flynn administration. The initial provision of the linkage policy was a fee of $5 per square foot, to be paid to a fund for low-income housing; the formula was later changed to refine the length of the payment period and to include a $1 assessment for job training (Ehrlich and Dreier 1988).[3]

Although it is most commonly found in tertiary-dominated cities, tertiary-sector strategy has sometimes been pursued by cities with slowly growing (or declining) mixed service and manufacturing economies. Hartford and Chicago implemented programs that were variations on the classic linkage policy. In both communities, large segments of manufacturing were in decline, but certain sectors of the service economy were growing rapidly, thus producing real estate booms in highly localized areas. The progressive thrust of the policy was to redistribute some of that economic activity to those who would not otherwise benefit from it.

Hartford, Connecticut, made one of the earliest efforts to capture and use its service-sector growth for the community. In the early 1970s, the populist city council majority leader, Nick Carbone, put through legislation allowing the city to ask for concessions in return for granting permission to develop a downtown civic center. In exchange for a public bond issue, rezoning, tax abatements, and redevelopment agreements, the developer agreed to hire a certain number of city residents and unemployed members of minority groups. After the civic center project's success, the city council refined its list of tradeoffs for tax and regulatory advantages to developers to include hiring guarantees for minority and resident construction personnel, hiring agreements to cover the life of the project, a city share of the income from the project, a city share of capital gains upon refinancing, and city shares for secondary development in the neighborhood of the project (Carbone 1982). Rather than a public-private partnership where the city's role is simply to aid private profit, the Hartford plan was a prototype of the public enterprise, with social goals and public profit.

Some observers have argued that linkage can be successful only in high-profit, high-demand downtowns, especially those that have instituted some form of growth controls. However, at the time that Hartford instituted its policy, the city had not yet undergone the office construction boom of the 1980s, and Hartford real estate was not in great demand. The city administration thus could not use permission to develop as its sole incentive; it also provided financing aid and a tax reduction. What makes Hartford an interesting case is that, even in the face of relatively low demand for land, the city was able to obtain exactions from developers in return for city participation. This indicates that slowly growing cities can use linkage policies if the city's role is properly defined.

There are other ways of harnessing service-sector growth and using it for progressive purposes. Burlington, Vermont, in 1986 passed a "boom-pie ordinance," which set up a program to enforce female and minority hiring on city-funded or -controlled construction projects and simultaneously established a support program to recruit, train, and organize prospective female workers. By 1988 the city had moved some sixty women through training programs and into construction jobs. In addition, the city developed a land trust to hold down speculative increases in land values and rents, lobbied the state for tax reform that would favor low-income residents, used tax revenues for an innovative youth program, and established a revolving loan fund for small and worker-owned businesses.

Like Burlington, Berkeley has put a major emphasis on making good jobs accessible to populations traditionally deprived of them. The city founded an Office of Economic Development in 1985 and established the First Source hiring program for private employers. Under this program, the city requests that companies give first preference to interviewing Berkeley residents who are part of the program. The program screens women, members of minority groups, people with handicaps, and other economically disadvantaged people and refers them to the employers. Companies that participate in the First Source hiring program are given preferential treatment when requesting city loans, access to city-owned property, and other economic assistance (Mayer 1989).

These case studies provide us with some evidence that the direction of economic policy is driven by more than economics—that, indeed, the battle over the control of local economies is largely political. Despite the disparate economic conditions in the United States cities that implemented progressive service-sector policies, there was an underlying political similarity: the existence of populist movements that took over local government through city council majorities, control of the mayor's office, or both. In Berkeley, Citizens' Action, a progressive coalition on the city council, worked with Mayor Gus Newport to put its policies into place. In Hartford, the leader was Councilmember Nick Carbone, a populist with strong community ties. In Burlington, it was Mayor Bernie Sanders, an independent socialist who ran on a platform of honesty, efficiency, and redistributive policies. In Boston it was also the mayor, Ray Flynn, closely allied with the neighborhood movement. The good news about this is that local economic policymakers have more flexibility than is commonly acknowledged; the bad news is that progressive electoral coalitions are often unstable.

Progressive Policies—The Manufacturing Sector

The manufacturing sector is marked by contradictory trends. As capital becomes more mobile, as mechanization continues, and as the service sector grows, a smaller proportion of the work force will be employed in manufacturing. At the same time, many new manufacturing jobs are being created, especially but not exclusively in the high-technology industries. As Castells (1985) has shown, the decline and growth of manufacturing jobs have exacerbated the regional pattern of boom and recession. The question for progressive policymakers is not how to stop these trends but how to respond to them. Progressive industrial policy has often followed Markusen's "building on the basics" strategy, using existing infrastructure and skilled labor but reorganizing them with new investors, new markets, and new products.

In the United States, there have been only a few comprehensive programs of this type. An early proposal was the plan for rebuilding Detroit's industrial base. In 1981, two economic analysts, Dan Luria and Jack Russell, published *Rational Reindustrialization: An Economic Development Agenda for Detroit.* They proposed that Detroit put its resources behind a scheme to save jobs in the manufacturing sector by diversifying into products other than autos in the "metal-bending" trades that already proliferated in the city. They identified energy-producing equipment as the industry with the most potential for Detroit, given the skills of residents, potential for job generation, relationship of the industry to the business cycle, potential profitability, and several other criteria. Thus, they laid out a plan for redirecting a good deal of the declining auto industry to the production of three types of energy-producing hardware: deep oil- and gas-drilling equipment, mine-mouth gasifiers, and electricity cogenerators. They proposed that the transition be funded and directed by the local government through a series of publicly controlled enterprises.

The essence of the Rational Reindustrialization plan was a strategic retreat from automobiles into related manufacturing as an alternative to either staying in the automotive sector through wage-cutting strategies or building up the low-wage service sector. After a substantial effort to gain support for the scheme, however, Luria and Russell had to admit failure. Neither industry leaders, the United Auto Workers Union, nor city officials were willing to shift away from an auto-related industrial strategy. As a result the city continued to rely on mainstream policy, providing incentives for General Motors to build its Cadillac plant (without any exactions) and constructing the downtown Renaissance Center to attract tourism and move into the service economy.

Another attempt at rebuilding manufacturing with cooperation of business, labor, and the community was the creation of the

Pittsburgh area's Steel Valley Authority. The idea first came into being in Youngstown, Ohio, where three major steel plants closed in the late 1970s. Labor and community leadership attempted to buy and reopen one of the plants but were thwarted by an inability to raise the necessary capital for plant modernization. When similar steel closures occurred in Pittsburgh and nearby Monongahela Valley communities, the organization evolved into the Tri-State Conference on Steel, led by community, labor, and church groups.

Tri-State's idea was that a Steel Valley Authority, similar to the Tennessee Valley Authority, be created with the power of eminent domain to take over steel plants threatened with being shut down. New ownership and management would then be arranged, probably through some form of employee stock ownership program. The authority was legally established and has been joined by several communities in Pennsylvania, including the city of Pittsburgh. Thus far, the major focus of its work has been the attempt to raise funds for feasibility studies on reopening closed production facilities. The effort has been vigorously opposed by the steel companies, which want to keep the closed facilities out of production. Whether the authority will be politically successful and whether changes in the steel industry will make reopening the plants profitable are still open questions (Deitch and Erikson 1986; Stoudt 1986).

While Rational Reindustrialization and Tri-State have provided some ideas and partial solutions, there have been a few more complete success stories in the search for progressive policies toward manufacturing. One of the most important programs affecting the structure of manufacturing production in the United States was begun in Chicago under the administration of Mayor Harold Washington. His mayoralty, from 1983 until his death in 1987, is justly noted for its role in enfranchising the city's black population and for his progress in reforming Chicago's notorious political machine, but some of his most remarkable policy innovations were in local economics. Under the Washington administration, Chicago was able to involve more than one hundred neighborhood organizations in economic development, create an industrial antidisplacement strategy, and exert pressure to restructure basic industry in the face of pressure to disinvest.

The Chicago strategy was rooted in neighborhood populism, a longstanding tradition in Chicago left politics. Harold Washington's appointee as Commissioner of Economic Development, Robert Mier, had been head of University of Illinois's Center for Urban Economic Development and was in close touch with the neighborhood movement in Chicago. Mier was instrumental in developing Chicago's strategic plan, known as "Chicago Works Together," which set out the city's economic development goals: job opportunities, balanced growth (in different economic sectors and geographical areas), neighborhood development, and public participation (Mier, Moe, and Sherr 1986, 301). He also helped expand the city's aid and technical assistance to neighborhood groups.

An early initiative that rose from Mier's ties to the neighborhood movement was the Westside Jobs Network, a city-funded group of labor, community, and university participants organized to gather information about potential plant closings. This network was instrumental in the Playskool case, where Hasbro-Bradley planned to shut down a plant that had been partially funded through city-sponsored revenue bonds. Because of information gathered by the network, the city of Chicago was able to move immediately to bring suit against the company. This program's success was qualified, since it was solely a defensive campaign, able to mitigate the worst effects of the shutdown but not able to prevent it or to create more jobs. But the symbolic effect of the suit set the tone for several subsequent actions.

The city addressed the problem of deindustrialization in a proactive way by initiating a collaborative task force to analyze the steel industry and make recommendations for policy in light of industry changes. The Task Force on Steel and Southeast Chicago was made up of representatives from business, labor, universities, and city government. It produced a set of wide-ranging proposals for the future of the steel industry in South Chicago, collectively called "Building on the Basics." Task force recommendations included retaining existing steel-making and steel-using facilities through increased public investment in research and modernization; creating an advanced-technology program for Chicago-area basic industries through the cooperation of state governments, universities, and industry; instituting training programs for new and displaced workers; finding ways to cut energy costs for manufacturing; and planning for the orderly development of real estate in the South Chicago area. The overall thrust of the program was to adapt to industry changes in ways that would retain and build on the industrial and human capabilities already present in the South Chicago area (Mayor's Task Force, n.d.; Markusen 1988).

Another significant industrial initiative supported by Chicago's Economic Development Department was a program to counteract industrial displacement. Residential and commercial development was forcing up rents and threatening manufacturing operations in the Goose Island–Clybourn corridor north and west of the downtown area; this in turn was threatening the city's job base and the stability of the residential neighborhoods that had coexisted with the industrial firms. The city worked with a coalition of local community and industry groups, surveying the needs of businesses to allow them to remain or expand in their current locations. Ultimately, the administration backed a change in the zoning law to create planned manufacturing districts and to protect these areas from encroachment by nonmanufacturing land uses (Giloth and Mier 1989).

While Chicago's industrial strategy stressed efficient use of manufacturing infrastructure, the approach of officials in Jamestown, New York, was to increase the efficiency of plant organization. William F. Whyte and his associates (1983) have described how, in the early 1970s, Jamestown faced the dual problem of plant closings and the inability to attract new manufacturing concerns. Business owners said the city had a "bad labor climate," by which they meant a highly unionized work force prone to strikes. In 1972, representatives of industry, labor, and city government under Mayor Stan Lundine established the Jamestown Area Labor-Management Committee (JALMC), co-chaired by a business and a labor delegate. They concentrated on four items: business-labor relations, worker training and development, local economic development, and productivity. The JALMC succeeded in establishing dozens of plant-level committees, which analyzed productivity by examining problems that hampered the work process. They negotiated productivity agreements between workers and plant management and subsequently prevented a number of plants from leaving the area.

In an analysis that was unusual at the time but is widely accepted today, the committee argued that productivity was not merely a question of making workers work harder but of the proper organization of the plant and personnel. The furniture industry, Jamestown's mainstay, had a shortage of skilled workers severe enough that even the slightest absenteeism could threaten the output of entire lines of products. The labor-management committee brought together the United Furniture Workers Union of America, the Jamestown Manufacturers' Association, and Jamestown Community College to design a program for worker training. Skilled furniture workers and college professors together designed successful training courses for young people who otherwise would not have entered the industry (Whyte et al. 1983).

Overall, JALMC's innovations were to introduce a nontraditional perspective on labor-management relations and to reinforce factory-level negotiations with the areawide committee. The traditional approach to labor relations had always been to negotiate a narrow range of issues: wages, benefits, and a few other items within a framework of conflict between labor and management. Organization of factory production had traditionally been considered a management prerogative. The Jamestown approach instead focused on reorganizing work for the benefit of both workers and management.[4]

Local governments in England have been bolder and more systematic than their American counterparts in creating strategic plans for manufacturing. Beginning in the 1970s, community development projects were established in twelve local areas to examine the relationship between deindustrialization and local government policy. These projects "challenged local governments' preoccupation with problems of welfare distribution, and began to focus attention on local industry and the economy" (Benington 1986, 10). The experiments in "local socialism" (Boddy and Fudge 1984) established in the early 1980s by left-Labour councils were specifically designed to stretch the limits of public intervention in the economy. The Greater London Council (GLC), for example, developed comprehensive plans for finance, labor, and industry;

its industrial strategy aimed at nothing short of "reclaiming production" for workers and the community. The GLC's chief economic agency, the Greater London Enterprise Board (GLEB), was set up to invest in selected enterprises with the goal of reconstructing London's deteriorating industries, technologies, work spaces, and work force (London Industrial Strategy, n.d.).

Compared with mainstream British policy, GLEB's explicit principles of operation were to exert greater social control over companies, to give priority to new forms of ownership, to work closely with unions, and to encourage the production of socially useful products. In addition to investing directly in companies (it claims to have saved or created 2,000 jobs in its initial year), GLEB instituted an early-warning system to prepare for possible plant closings, set up technology networks linking polytechnic schools with community groups to develop new products, and renovated industrial buildings to provide work spaces for small businesses and to slow real estate speculation (GLEB, n.d.).

The London Industrial Strategy (LIS) was hampered by both a scarcity of models to follow and a shortage of personnel competent to conduct industrial policy. LIS's economic planners implemented a sophisticated, sector-by-sector program for the local economy, but their actions often had mixed results. For example, GLEB's initiative to aid small firms that supplied parts to automakers was praised for creating jobs and increasing social control over production while it was criticized for increasing polarization between workers in the core auto companies and those in the peripheral shops (Eisenschitz and North 1986).

In Sheffield, as in London, a left–Labour-controlled council instituted a progressive manufacturing program. The local economy, heavily dependent on steel and related engineering activity, had lost tens of thousands of jobs in the 1970s and early 1980s. This economic devastation provided a backdrop against which the development policies of the Thatcher government were judged to be detrimental to the local area. Although Sheffield had been a Labour bastion for some fifty years, a shakeup in the local party occurred in 1980 as a result of discontent over the direction of local economic conditions, bringing a new, more radical leadership to the fore (Kraushaar 1988).

Under this leadership, Sheffield city council created a Department of Employment, which analyzed the local economy and determined the areas in which the city could have an impact. One asset it discovered was that the city was the largest employer in the region, a position that gave it substantial potential to influence the local economy. The city used its position to set the area standards, pressuring private companies through contract compliance, health and safety regulations, and mandatory training programs. The Department of Employment also identified needs not being met by the private sector and established municipal enterprises to provide for them. Two of these were a lift maintenance firm to service elevators in publicly owned buildings and a trade waste collection service to dispose of industrial refuse. The department also aggressively encouraged the development of new socially useful technologies; for example, it hired unemployed engineers to design dehumidifiers for local council flats and hearing aids for people with severe hearing losses. A final dimension of Sheffield's strategy was to foster the development of cooperatives and other alternative forms of businesses (Kraushaar 1988; Benington 1986).

Although the Labour councils' policies concentrated most overtly on economic processes, their programs included a number of social and political dimensions as well. They were predicated on the need for ongoing social audits—planning to assess the social impacts of investment decisions. They attempted to strengthen labor unions and community groups, linking them into larger, more diverse political networks. Their labor-force policy included acknowledgments of unrecognized work. And they sought to shift the balance of power between localities and corporations by mobilizing the local state as an economic actor (Benington 1986). This self-conscious linking of economic goals to the political and social dynamics of the community and the nation makes the British programs more sophisticated than the progressive programs we have seen in the United States to date.

Local councils' attempts to intervene in economic restructuring were not unproblematic on the left, however. A key question raised within the Labour party was whether local actions in support of labor should be attempting to eliminate private capital altogether or to manage its restructuring in more equitable ways.

The dominant view within the Labour party held that strengthening industry would strengthen labor; left critics, however, questioned the value of rationalizing capitalist industry rather than attempting to move more directly toward socialism (Eisenschitz and North 1986; Palmer 1986).

Labour's experiments in municipal socialism were ultimately undone, not through internal divisions so much as by the central government, through such regulations as imposing a ceiling on local taxes (rate capping) and preventing localities from putting noneconomic conditions on contracts. Ultimately, the national government abolished the metropolitan county councils, which had been in the forefront of economic intervention, although local governments (such as Sheffield) still have limited autonomy in local economic development policy. In the short run, given the likelihood of another Conservative electoral victory, the central government will probably continue to limit future experimentation by local authorities. Over the long run, however, as Britain's underlying economic problems continue, these models may provide the Labour party with the foundation of a new programmatic direction, one that attempts to shape the production process itself rather than simply defending against its abuses and redistributing its profits.

Three major differences stand out in comparing the United States with Britain, two making conditions in Britain more favorable for instituting progressive policies and one making them less favorable.[5] First, the economies of the industrial cities had sunk to lower levels over a longer period of time in England than in the United States. Such extreme devastation allowed policymakers to stretch the limits of acceptable economic intervention in a way that was rarely dreamt of in the United States. Second, the English officials had the benefit of greater ideological and theoretical space in which to maneuver. They used their close ties with the Conference of Socialist Economists not only to develop new ideas for policy but also to obtain high-level staffers to work in their agencies, establishing and overseeing the local planning and enterprise boards. On the other hand, one area in which British municipalities lacked freedom relative to their American counterparts was that of administrative flexibility. Since resources and decision-making power are more centrally controlled in England than in the United States, the central government was able ultimately to abolish the British local agencies altogether. It is ironic, but consistent with our argument, that the failure of U.S. cities to employ policies as radical as those in England is largely self-imposed rather than a systemic constraint.[6]

Discussion and Implications

We have so far argued that local responses to economic restructuring in Britain and the United States have been more varied in the past decade than in previous postwar decades.[7] While we have not attempted an encyclopedic catalogue of all U.S. and British community policy, our illustrations have suggested the variety of current practice. The taxonomy suggested in Table 8-1 would have been gratuitous, even unthinkable, in the 1950s and even as late as the 1960s. At that time, although the massive shift to services was underway, manufacturing was still dominant, enjoying both business and labor support, and the progressive policy options that began to be explored in the 1970s were almost unknown.

The implication is that the space for local policy is greater than it was previously, and that local governments have more maneuvering space than is commonly assumed. Where does this increased space lead us? It could lead to additional research and to filling out our taxonomy, but that is a task for the future. It could also lead us to some more general theoretical possibilities, which we will present without exploring them fully.

Conditions Fostering Progressive Policy

What has happened to create the space for progressive policy? In the cases we have summarized, a few conditions have emerged as important in providing the political space for progressive policy options. First, in several of the progressive cases described above, analytical capacity in the public sector—and sometimes progressive watchdog organizations outside of government—was a precondition to informed action. In Chicago, the commissioning of an independent report on the prospects for steel manufacturing made possible recommendations for dealing creatively with steel industry retrenchment in southeast Chicago. A neighborhood-based survey of manufacturing industry north of the Loop made possible the city's industrial displacement strategy. In Britain, the Conference of Socialist Economists played an important role vis-à-vis the Labour-left councils, providing research, support, ideas, and staffers. A history of ten years of community development projects in English cities had provided additional research that laid the foundation for effective intervention in the local economy.

A related factor has been the development of nontraditional process capacities within and outside city governments. The cultures of both the corporation and the labor movement can present rigid barriers to innovation in industry. Tradition within both American and British society (to a larger extent than even other capitalist societies) prevents local government from overstepping very narrowly drawn boundaries in its relations with the private sector. Bringing outsiders such as academics and religious leaders into decisions formerly monopolized by business, labor, and elected officials may, as it did in Jamestown and Chicago, produce new perspectives and solutions. Because these outsiders are not tied to local vested interests, they are able to mediate among them. Because they are independent of the formal economic development agencies in the community, they are able to confront issues that are typically left unresolved.

The spread of progressive policy has been partly attributable to national and international networking. Gatherings in the United States organized by the Conference on Alternative State and Local Policy brought together activists and officials from many jurisdictions and stimulated exchange. Literally hundreds of people from different places met each other for the first time at these meetings and began relationships that have persisted to this day. Journals such as the conference's *Ways and Means* and the now-defunct *Working Papers for a New Society* have provided additional channels for contact. Since 1980, functionally specialized subgroups working on issues such as housing and economic development have proliferated. In England, the Conference of Socialist Economists, the smaller Conference of Socialist Planners, and the participants in the community development projects have been the major vehicles for dissemination of ideas, strategic thinking, and sharing of experiences among progressive policymakers.

Another important condition fostering progressive policy has been the development of strong community-based organizations of various types.[8] These were crucial in places like Boston and Chicago, forming a major part of the electoral mobilization that elected Flynn and Washington. Community groups' organizational capacities had grown slowly throughout the 1970s, often fueled by local social and economic problems: housing, jobs, women's and gay rights, and so on. Such groups have often faced a tradeoff between doing issue work full time and putting some effort into the electoral arena. Where local politics are unstable, particularly where the traditional machines are in decline, these organizations have been able to use the electoral route more effectively than in those areas where machine or pro-business forces remain politically entrenched. Mature community-based organizations have also, in some cases, proved to have unexpected administrative benefits for elected officials attempting to put new policy initiatives into place, since their research and advocacy experience may provide them with better issue resources than are available to a newly elected local government.

One of the characteristics of many of the progressive regimes has been the dramatic takeover of local government machinery accomplished by progressive coalitions. Officials have used drama as a political instrument to expand the space for local action. Ken Livingstone of the Greater London Council and Bernie Sanders of Burlington used the symbolic value of their socialist rhetoric to change political ground rules and redefine the proper nature of urban policy. Ray Flynn and Harold Washington used a more populist rhetoric with similar results: a public sense that "things would be different now." The drama of the political moment of election changed expectations of what was permissible on all sides and helped to mobilize new bases of support.

The recent election of Mayor Daley in Chicago, however, shows the fragility of progressive coalitions and clearly illustrates the political nature of the struggle between the growth machine and the grassroots. The younger Daley's electoral coalition, like his father's, was heavily dominated by developers and real estate interests, and it is no surprise that Daley's development philosophy is decidedly anti-manufacturing and pro-gentrification. While the Washington administration changed the rules of the local economic game from those favoring speculative real estate development to those favoring balanced economic growth, Daley is expected to turn the clock back to the pro-development era (Moberg 1989). The fact that alternative policies existed, however, has become part of the history and the public culture of the city, and as such will be difficult to undo completely.

Finally, once progressive coalitions are established, progressive policy can be fostered by the existence of a vocal left opposition within the local political spectrum. In Boston, for example, Mel King's campaign pushed the debate about economic policy to the left, and even though King lost the election, his candidacy helped to provide the political space for Flynn to implement a linkage policy. In Berkeley, Citizen Action has been pushed by the "more radical" left to pursue policies it otherwise might not have. Left oppositions, often tied to neighborhood or other interest groups, can also prevent the administrations from becoming preoccupied with internal questions and from becoming oligarchical. Where the progressive administrations have lasted for more than a few years (Berkeley, Burlington), tensions between the progressives and the left opposition have become a permanent feature of local political life.

Surprisingly, one factor that has *not* proved to be related to the development of progressive policy is economic decline per se. In some cities, like Sheffield and Hartford, the local economy was so devastated that mainstream policy was widely regarded as insufficient. Local elites associated with the declining industries lacked the political strength to push through a program more favorable to business, thus providing an opening for the development of progressive alternatives. In Detroit, however, the devastated manufacturing economy was not accompanied by a decline of the traditional power groups, and the administration continued to hew to the mainstream policy line. Rather than overall economic decline, many of the progressive cities (London, Boston, Burlington) have been characterized by the severe dislocations caused by economic transition: a mosaic of growth and decline among groups accustomed to stability.[9]

The Impact of Post-Fordism on Local Policy Options

Another theoretical implication of our discussion regards theoretical debates about post-Fordism. The lack of uniformity that we have documented in local economic development policy has resulted from different political responses to the uneven effects of global economic restructuring. This restructuring has been widely characterized as the transition from a Fordist to a post-Fordist system of accumulation, with an attendant breakup of vertically organized firms, reduction of standardized production of goods, changes in the composition of the work force and looser relations between workers and employers. The implications of this transition for economic policy are controversial, even among those who agree on the basic trends.

One aspect of the debates around these issues is the question raised by Aglietta (1976): how is the change to post-Fordism affecting the situation of the working class? To date, a great deal of the debate about the transition from a Fordist to a post-Fordist regime has addressed the question of whether the transition is good or bad for workers. Theorists such as Piore and Sabel (1984), for example, are optimistic, arguing that post-Fordism provides opportunities for a new prosperity, making the economies of the advanced industrial societies more competitive on the global scale. British economist Robin Murray is also, on balance, positive about the implications of post-Fordist production, arguing that it is less wasteful and less authoritarian than the Fordist system (Rowbotham 1989). These views have been challenged by theorists such as Jamie Gough (1986), who thinks that the new system of production is increasing unemployment by increasing the organic composition of capital, and by Swasti Mitter (Rowbotham 1989), who argues that the main impact of post-Fordism is the creation of a two-tiered labor force that has exacerbated divisions in the working class. Edmond Preteceille (in this volume) cautions that the smaller firms characteristic of the post-Fordist regime often exploit their workers more than do the waning giants. The implication of these debates is that workers and their political allies have a choice of either cooperating with or resisting the economic transition to post-Fordism.

This literature does not consider the possibility that workers do not have that option; that their actions will not be able to stem the decline of the vertical firms that formerly provided workers with stable employment and high benefit levels. What options do they have? Our cases suggest that labor and communities can shape the local response to the vacuum left by the decline of the large vertical firms of the Fordist era.[10] As we have pointed out, the progressives in both the United States and Britain have recognized that fact and are experimenting to find their niches in the post-Fordist system, not taking its impact for granted but attempting to shape it in a more pro-worker direction.

This is a *political* problem. Aglietta's argument (1976) is helpful in this respect. He showed that the Fordist system of large plants with stable, homogeneous work forces laid the conditions for the development of the large industrial trade unions. While this gave workers increased power over their economic conditions, it tended to separate the workplace from the residential community, thus separating the locus of workers' economic activity and struggles from the locus of their political activity and struggles. But an implication of the change to post-Fordism, with increasing numbers of small firms and a less stable and more heterogeneous, nonunion work force, is that the locus of economic and political struggles may become more entwined. The decline of political influence of the trade unions may be partly balanced by the rise of other community-based organizations.

One arena of increased opportunities for progressive policy and working-class efficacy in the post-Fordist era is collective consumption or community economics, as Castells (1977, 1983) has argued. Not only public service consumption but workers' interests as community residents have become central political questions (for example, rent control, the central issue in several progressive political campaigns). A second arena of struggle is the increasing politicization of economic issues. Since economic rights of workers are no longer secure through the process of bargaining with individual employers, more collective and more political forms of economic policy are being developed, dealing with workers' rights, legislated conditions of work, and so on. Current debates in the United States over minimum wage, child care, and a national health program signify a new round of legislative struggles (at the state and local as well as the national level) over the social wage.

Constraints on Progressive Policy

The final theoretical implication we wish to discuss is the right way of thinking about constraints on progressive policy. Although we have suggested that localities are freer than is usually thought, we still must grapple with the fact that there are real constraints on localities' actions in the economic development arena. Critics and skeptics from all political persuasions have emphasized—perhaps overemphasized—the limitations that progressive policymakers face. Nonetheless, this policy work continues, and it behooves us, the outside analysts, to try to differentiate between actual constraints and ideological mystifications. We have chosen three problems for brief examination.

The first is the problem of economic marginality. Among others, Michael Parkinson in this volume notes that the limited success of the local socialist regimes in England is partially attributable to the fact that their actions have been peripheral to market forces. This is partly true, but a marginal impact is not the same as no impact. As Adam Sharples points out, "Council interventions in the private sector will always be working on the margins with limited resources. The aim should be to turn this marginal impact to the best effect" (1986, 30). Sharples goes on to underscore the importance of analyzing the local economic situation to discover where public resources can have the most impact. Furthermore, as Blunkett and Green (1983) argue, although local projects cannot counteract global economic trends, they can provide incubators for qualitatively different kinds of enterprises characterized by new social relations of work and new relationships between the public and private sectors. At a minimum, programs such as linkage provide real products and services that would not be otherwise provided through the market. At a maximum, programs such as the Sheffield Department of Employment can foster the process of socially controlled conversion of industry.

The second oft-cited constraint is the problem of economic growth versus redistribution. Michael Parkinson argues that promoting the city as a place for investment merely moves existing jobs around rather than creating new employment. Our response is that this opposition between growth and redistribution is part of a traditional ideology which assumes that growth is the province of only the private sector and redistribution the role of only the public sector. In reality, however, both sectors can create growth *and* redistribute resources. The proponents of mainstream development policy have already undercut their own argument by giving public money to the private sector to "stimulate growth." The progressives are simply advocating the next steps: using public money to create publicly controlled growth (for example, in municipal enterprises) and exacting a redistributive program within the private sector (for example, changing corporate hiring and wage policies).

The third constraint on local policy is the tension between using local resources and attracting outside resources for development. Mainstream policymakers have tended to assume that capital is highly mobile, something existing "out there" that can be attracted to a locality only through offering economic incentives. Progressives have tended to emphasize the potential of using locally generated investment capital, to the extent that some writers (such as Goodman 1981) have constructed an entire program around the possibilities for regional self-sufficiency. Although the authors of this volume have argued that capital is not infinitely mobile, it is also true that local resources alone in most cases will not be sufficient to provide a local economic base. The successful local programs have tried to balance efforts at retaining existing investment capital (both locally based and outside), finding new or underutilized sources of local capital (such as public pension funds), and placing limits on new outside investment to prevent local dependency on absentee capital.

One inescapable conclusion of our review is that the economic issues that supposedly bind local governments are in large part symbols being manipulated by the economically powerful for their own interests. For example, if local socialism was an ineffective strategy for economic development, why was the Conservative government so intent on destroying it? Only if it *was* effective, and thus providing a counterexample to the model of economic recovery through unbridled capitalism, would it have to be abolished. For another example, pro-business forces claim that economic incentives to build the corporate bottom line are the only effective means of attracting new investment. These incentives, however, have been shown to play a very small role in businesses' *economic* calculations of location; instead, businesses increasingly consider them largely symbols of a pro-business attitude on the part of local government (Wolman 1988). We agree with Walton (1982) that pro-business local economic development policies have gained hegemony not because of their effectiveness but as a "marriage of convenience" between political officials being pressured to create jobs and corporations interested in maintaining the continued upward redistribution of income. The benefit of the experiments in local socialism in Britain and the progressive cities in the United States is that they provide the counterexamples necessary to galvanize political organizing around alternative programs.

Whether these progressive programs expand in the future will be a function of the political atmosphere as much as the demonstrated effectiveness of the policies themselves. Sheffield's John Benington notes with cautious optimism:

> At this stage direct involvement by local authorities in economic and employment matters is felt to be controversial and interventionist. However, there are many indications that (as with previous frontiers of radical local intervention, like public health last century) these pioneering initiatives will gradually be incorporated into the mainstream structures and procedures of local government. Notwithstanding these routinising tendencies, a core group of "new left" local authorities in this new field still see their work as the front-line of a fundamental battle of ideas about economic and industrial problems—a crucial opportunity to forge and test the components for a national alternative economic strategy (1986, 9).

Although we have argued that the space for local policy is greater than it was previously, and that local governments have more maneuvering space than is commonly assumed, such space is limited and will continue to be limited in new ways by the changing context. However, as Krumholz (1982) has argued, local officials and planners can learn to recognize and seize the opportunities that exist and can manipulate the local situation to create new opportunities for public intervention in the market. It is possible for local governments to respond to economic restructuring in different *political* ways—the "late capitalist" type of response lets corporations take the lead while the public role is reduced to ensuring continued corporate functioning. Such a response involves mystifying local economic problems as derived from global economic trends, thereby discouraging participation by labor and community groups. A progressive response is also possible—one in which local government plays an aggressive role in brokering between corporations and community, planning for economic and social needs, and developing mechanisms for meaningful participation of all interests.

NOTES

1. In the United States, the private elites are not currently united in their strategy, resulting in a brittle and unstable national economic situation. Ferguson and Rogers (1981) describe the conflict between Eastern and Western capital, for example: the tilt to the Sunbelt and Pacific Rim in the 1970s is shown to be both a deep schism within capital and a cause of the resurgence of the Republican party in the 1980s.

2. We are aware that conflating *local* and *popular* begins to combine two tendencies that have often been opposed or have been seen as opposed. For many socialists and liberals, *popular* is seen as allied with nonlocal, national, or international aggregations and coalitions. But we have aligned these two axes consciously. First, as Frug (1980) suggests and as many others have argued, the restriction of local power has been historically delegitimizing for popular control. Second, as we argue below, current restructuring in national and international economies seems to have opened the local arena for popular control rather than closed it. Our analytical scheme is designed to capture such developments as they occur empirically.

3. There are those who imply that linkage is a radical program and

others who attack it as not radical enough. We make neither point but simply argue that linkage is the kind of outcome that can occur when community groups put sufficient pressure on government to achieve public-private partnerships where the public has a significant impact on the compromises that result.

4. The question of plant organization also arises in proposals for dealing with the decomposition of the large, vertically integrated firm and the proliferation of smaller businesses. An important policy question is how to increase the number of new jobs with potential for promotion, security, and the other advantages of working in the larger firms. Piore and Sabel (1984) advocate networking small firms so they can coordinate operations through computer and transport links, arguing that this form of organization can provide increased employment, greater industrial flexibility, and increased community control over investment.

5. The insights in this section are derived from an unpublished manuscript by Clavel and Kraushaar (1989).

6. However, local power even in American cities is still limited; see Frug (1980) on the steady erosion of legal powers of municipalities in the United States.

7. Preteceille (1981) makes the same point for the local policy situation in France.

8. As Susan Fainstein notes in this volume, the absence of both the trade unions and strong community groups is a crucial factor in producing political regimes that support mainstream pro-development economic policies.

9. The other side of this finding is that economic growth per se is also without "automatic" consequences for policy direction. Although we have argued that rapid growth is not a necessary condition for instituting linkage, it is politically easier (as Harvey Molotch argues in this volume) to adopt linkage policies in areas suffering from the negative consequences of too-rapid growth.

10. Likewise (as Dan Marschall pointed out in a private communication), unions will be unable to maintain the traditional adversarial relationships they have had with management and will, in all likelihood, become more and more involved in the process of joint labor-management decision making that is currently so controversial within the labor movement.

REFERENCES

Aglietta, Michel. 1976. *A Theory of Capitalist Regulation: The U.S. Experience.* London: New Left Books.
Barnes, Ian, and Jill Preston. 1985. "The Scunthorpe Enterprise Zone: An Example of Muddled Intervention." *Public Administration* 63:171–81.

Benington, John. 1986. "Local Economic Strategies." *Local Economy* 1:7–24.

Blunkett, David, and Geoff Green. 1983. "Building from the Bottom: The Sheffield Experience." London: Fabian Society.

Boddy, Martin, and Colin Fudge, eds. 1984. *Local Socialism? Labour Councils and New Left Alternatives.* London: Macmillan.

Breslow, Marc. 1987. (Philadelphia City Council staff member.) Personal interview, July 29.

Butler, Stuart. 1980. "Urban Renewal: A Modest Proposal." *Policy Review* 13:95–107.

Byrnes, Gregory. 1984. "Convention Center's Price Going Up." *Philadelphia Inquirer* September 23, pp. K1, K14.

Carbone, Nicholas. 1982. "The City as Real Estate Investor." Lecture, Cornell University, May.

Castells, Manuel. 1977. *The Urban Question: A Marxist Approach.* Cambridge: MIT Press.

———. 1983. *The City and the Grassroots.* Berkeley and Los Angeles: University of California Press.

———. 1985. "High Technology, Economic Restructuring, and the Urban-Regional Process in the U.S." In *High Technology, Space and Society* ed. M. Castells. Beverly Hills, Calif.: Sage.

Clavel, Pierre. 1986. *The Progressive City.* New Brunswick, N.J.: Rutgers University Press.

Clavel, Pierre, and Robert Kraushaar. 1989. Unpublished manuscript.

Deitch, Cynthia, and R. Erikson. 1986. "Save Dorothy: A Political Response to Structural Change in the Steel Industry." In *Redundancy, Lay-Offs and Plant Closures: The Social Impact,* ed. R. Lee. London: Croom Helm.

Doeringer, P. B., D. G. Terkla, and G. C. Topakian. 1988. *Invisible Factors in Local Economic Development.* New York: Oxford University Press.

Ehrlich, Bruce, and Peter Dreier. 1988. "Linkage and the Politics of Urban Reform." Unpublished manuscript. Boston: Redevelopment Authority.

Eisenschitz, Aram, and David North. 1986. "The London Industrial Strategy: Socialist Transformation or Modernizing Capitalism?" *International Journal of Urban and Regional Research* 10:419–40.

Fasenfest, David. 1986. "Community Politics and Urban Redevelopment: Poletown, Detroit, and General Motors." *Urban Affairs Quarterly* 22:101–21.

Ferguson, Thomas, and Joel Rogers. 1981. "The Reagan Victory: Corporate Coalitions in the 1980 Campaign." In *The Hidden Election,* ed. T. Ferguson and J. Rogers. New York: Pantheon.

Frug, Gerald. 1980. "The City as a Legal Concept." *Harvard Law Review* 93(6):1057–154.

Giloth, Robert, and Robert Mier. 1989. "Social Change and Social Justice: Alternative Economic Development in Chicago." In *Economic Restructuring and Political Response,* ed. R. Beauregard. Beverly Hills, Calif.: Sage.

Goldsmith, William. 1982. "Enterprise Zones: If They Work, We're in Trouble." *International Journal of Urban and Regional Research* 6:435–42.

Goodman, Robert. 1981. *The Last Entrepreneurs.* Boston: South End Press.

Gough, Jamie. 1986. "Industrial Policy and Socialist Strategy: Restructuring and the Unity of the Working Class." *Capital and Class* 29:58–81.

Greater London Enterprise Board. n.d. "More Than Bricks and Mortar: Making Property Work for People." London: Greater London Enterprise Board.

Hall, Peter. 1977. "Green Fields and Grey Areas." Proceedings of the Royal Town Planning Institute Annual Conference, London.

Jones, Bryan, and Lynn Bachelor. 1984. "Policy Discretion and the Corporate Surplus." In *Urban Economic Development,* ed. R. Bingham and J. Blair. Beverly Hills, Calif.: Sage.

Keating, W. Dennis. 1986. "Linking Downtown Development to Broader Community Goals." *Journal of the American Planning Association* 52:133–41.

Kraushaar, Robert. 1988. "Cities in Cloudless Air: Progressive Planning in Sheffield, England." Paper presented at the Association of Collegiate Schools of Planning annual meeting, Buffalo.

Krumholz, Norman. 1982. "A Retrospective View of Equity Planning: Cleveland, 1969–1979." *Journal of the American Planning Association* (Spring): 163–74.

Legislative Tax Study Commission. 1984. "Interstate Business Locational Decisions and the Effect of the State's Tax Structure on After-Tax Rates of Return of Manufacturing Firms." Albany, N.Y.: Legislative Tax Study Commission.

London Industrial Strategy. n.d. "Introduction." London.

Luria, Dan, and Jack Russell. 1981. Rational Reindustrialization. Detroit: Widgetripper Press.

Markusen, Ann. 1988. "Planning for Industrial Decline: Lessons from Steel Communities." *Journal of Planning Education and Research* 7:173–84.

Mayer, Neil. 1989. "Berkeley's Progressive Strategy for Economic Development." *Planners Network* 75:3–4.

Mayor's Task Force on Steel and Southeast Chicago. n.d. "Building on the Basics: The Final Report of the Mayor's Task Force on Steel and Southeast Chicago." Chicago: Department of Economic Development.

Mier, Robert, K. J. Moe, and I. Sherr. 1986. "Strategic Planning and the

Pursuit of Reform, Economic Development, and Equity." *Journal of the American Planning Association* 52:299–309.

Moberg, David. 1989. "Daley on Development: Economic Policy, Like Father, Like Son?" *(Chicago) Reader*, February 24, pp. 8, 38.

Palmer, John. 1986. "Municipal Enterprise and Popular Planning." *New Left Review* 159:117–24.

Perry, David, with R. Kraushaar, J. Lines, and E. Parker. n.d. *Ending Regional Economic Dependency: Economic Policy for Distressed Regions.* Buffalo: SUNY Department of Environmental Design and Planning.

Piore, Michael, and Charles Sabel. 1984. *The Second Industrial Divide.* New York: Basic Books.

Preteceille, Edmond. 1981. "Left-wing Local Governments and Services Policy in France." *International Journal of Urban and Regional Research* 5:411–20.

Rowbotham, Sheila. 1989. "A Step Ahead: Combining Economic Strategy with Vision." Interlink (February–March): 11–14.

Sharples, Adam. 1986. "The New Local Economics." *Local Economy* 1:25–33.

Squires, Gregory. 1984. "Industrial Revenue Bonds and the Deindustrialization of America." *Urbanism Past and Present* 9:1–9.

Stoudt, Mike. 1986. "Reindustrialization from Below: The Steel Valley Authority." *Labor Research Review* (5):19–33.

Walton, John. 1982. "Cities and Jobs and Politics." *Urban Affairs Quarterly* 18:5–18.

Whyte, William F., et al. 1983. *Worker Participation and Ownership.* Ithaca: New York State School of Industrial and Labor Relations Press.

Wilder, Margaret, and Barry Rubin. 1988. "Targeted Redevelopment through Enterprise Zones." *Journal of Urban Affairs* 10:1–17.

Wolman, Harold. 1988. "Local Economic Development Policy: What Explains the Divergence Between Policy Analysis and Political Behavior?" *Journal of Urban Affairs* 10:19–28.

PART IV

Reflections

CHAPTER 9

Beyond the City Limits:
A Commentary

Saskia Sassen

The central question in organizing this volume is whether differences in national political systems and in national-local relations explain the diversity of forms assumed by economic restructuring and local responses to it. At least three general conclusions can be drawn from these essays. First, notwithstanding the diversity of forms that economic restructuring has assumed in specific localities and the diversity of policy responses, these chapters mostly show that larger translocal economic forces have far more weight than local policies in shaping urban economies. The cases examined here are by no means simple, self-evident instances of this proposition. Fainstein asks what conditions made possible a convergence in urban policies between two such different cities as New York and London. She finds that in both, urban politics have become centered on economic development and withdrawn from broader public welfare objectives. Central to the main explanation for this convergence are the impact and the constraints of economic restructuring. Hill, in examining production systems in the auto industry in the United States and Japan, finds that national and international interests of capital are a major factor in shaping outcomes for the two key locations of this industry—Detroit and Toyota City. Finally, Preteceille shows that finance and other aspects of economic restructuring came to dominate the agenda of the socialist government in France and found their way to many localities, bringing back private enterprise after the nationalizations of the earlier years.

Second, these essays show that national policies are more influential in shaping cities than local policies. This is evident in Hill's discussion of the Japanese auto industry and in Parkinson's examination of the United Kingdom. Parkinson notes that the central state has taken away power from the boroughs in London and put a large number of administrative entities in charge of areas the boroughs used to control. Among the measures implemented to curtail the power of boroughs are rate capping (limiting revenues available for spending), compulsory letting (requiring private contractors to bid for public services), and selling public housing to private buyers and voluntary associations. The new administrative units, on the other hand, have considerable power to implement agendas aimed at economic growth and efficiency as defined by dominant business interests. This is also, to some extent, evident in France, where Preteceille shows how changes in the national agenda of the socialist government toward finance and privatization influenced many local municipalities. It is clearly evident in the United States, where the reduction of funding to localities has had significant impacts on local governments. At the same time these papers show that national policies have not escaped the influence and constraints of economic restructuring and global forces that are part of it.

Third, a few of the chapters show that under certain conditions local governments or local initiatives can resist the tendencies of economic restructuring and of national political objectives. These specific conditions include the citizens' coalitions fighting the "growth machines" described by Molotch, the municipalities run by leftist governments in France described by Preteceille, and several cities in the United States and the United Kingdom, described by Clavel and Kleniewski, that resisted the overall tendencies of economic restructuring by implementing progressive or mainstream agendas for economic growth.

In showing the limitations cities confront in addressing or responding to major economic forces and national politics, the collection accomplishes two important objectives. It establishes—with considerable authority, given all the authors' long-term work on the subject and the diversity of cities and countries covered—a current picture in which (a) economic forces carry much greater weight than local politics in determining the shape of local development; (b) because of differences in national political systems, economic restructuring can assume different forms in different countries; and (c) the natural tendency of these economic forces, if left alone, is to override local concerns and undermine the socioeconomic conditions of significant sectors of the population. Second, these chapters have thus cleared the shelf and provided a beginning for an inquiry into what spheres of local development can be objectively and ideologically relocalized. The globalization of the economy and its detrimental effects on local politics increasingly rob localities even of the notion that local politics matter. The chapters by Molotch, Preteceille, and Clavel and Kleniewski raise these issues.

At a time when major economic forces are mostly beyond a city's control and politics are national, how can we relocalize the question of politics and economics? How can we specify spheres of action in a city that, while dominated by translocal economic forces, could be recovered for local action and control? And how can we reestablish the importance for a locality of economic activities—notably, industrial services and various types of manufacturing—that under the current, partly ideological, dominance of global finance and information industries appear as insignificant and unimportant, even though they are central to the economic well-being of many localities?

Two central questions come out of the deciphering of economic and political process contained in this collection: one concerns the relationship between economic restructuring and political restructuring; the other, political restructuring and its meaning for local action. The specific form that political restructuring has assumed is the withdrawal of the central state from local government activity. Practically speaking, this has often meant the withdrawal of federal resources and hence the lifting of multiple regulations imposed on their disbursement. This process has different starting points and combinations in different countries with diverse national regimes. In the United Kingdom the growing power of the central state under Thatcher is in good part a response to the dominance, at the local level, of labor governments intent on public housing, public welfare, and manufacturing-based economic development. In the United States, the overall effect is in many ways similar, in that localities have lost federal resources for public expenditures and for economic agendas that respond to the interests of workers and the poor. Notwithstanding a very different national government, localities in France have also wound up with less central government participation, beginning with the local movements for autonomy in the 1970s and further implemented by the French socialist government in the 1980s. In most cases this has meant that local governments have become more subject to pressure by the dominant business sectors and their call for a better business climate, thus pressure to facilitate economic restructuring.

When we juxtapose the concept of a global economy with that of local politics we will tend to make politics exogenous to economics. But we cannot simply oppose politics to economics since transformations in political structures are part of the overall process of economic restructuring. The fact that in the United States, the United Kingdom, and France most localities have followed accommodation rather than confrontation is not simply an indication of servility, lack of information, and lack of political will on the part of local governments. It is that local governments to some extent may share in the benefits that restructuring has brought about for certain sectors—and clearly not all—of capital. Restructuring means that the conditions for profitable operation and participation in the system have changed. New York City's government gained a massive increase in tax revenues from its support in the 1980s of real estate developers and leading financial and service industries. The fact that this strategy generated severe social and budgetary costs for many sectors of the population and of the government bureaucracy was overshadowed by the billions that came in as taxes (Sassen 1990). This points to the contradictory interests in much economic growth and in many government policies.

Savitch shows the influence of national politics on market

forces. In both Paris and London there is now a multiplicity of political units that can participate in the market. In Paris they receive considerable revenues from the central state and can actually shape market forces to some extent. In London, on the other hand, resources have been withdrawn from the boroughs and more power given to local development corporations; hence borough governments are caught in the market with many far more aggressive competitors. The national state emerges as a key element in either facilitating or deterring the interests of leading business sectors. But the state itself has withdrawn, though in variable degree, from key areas of production and social reproduction and allowed the market to expand in both. This is a central component of the overall process referred to as economic restructuring.

The whole notion of the crisis of the Fordist regime entails a transformation in the role played by the state in the process of accommodating to conflicting interests and in the employment relation. The broader institutional framework linking key sectors of business and labor, anchored in the centrality of mass production for mass consumption, created very specific regulatory and public welfare obligations for the state. The decline of this arrangement and its consequences also entailed the decline of a set of specific functions of the state. To the point here is Preteceille's observation that changes in state structures and urban policies are a tentative response to the hegemony crisis that accompanies the economic crisis.

It can be argued that political restructuring has created a void at the local level, and that this void could entail, in principle, a greater space for local government, as Clavel and Kleniewski argue. The political question is whether this represents a loss of local autonomy or a gain. It can leave municipalities more exposed to business pressures, the prevalent case in the United States and the United Kingdom. It is in this void that business coalitions can gain renewed weight in pushing local governments to implement policies that facilitate or carry out various aspects of economic restructuring. Or it can be seen as increasing the autonomy of localities, as suggested by cities with leftist or progressive governments or citizens' coalitions.

It is in this void created by the withdrawal of central government resources to localities that the question of politics assumes

new meaning. The examination of localities that have implemented pro-business policies and those that have resisted indicates to what extent economic restructuring and the translocal
processes that make it up are the dominant force. It also demonstrates that it takes determined political resistance and implementation of alternative policies to avoid the consequences of
restructuring. The editors posit that the variety of political responses we can find today in the United States, the United Kingdom, and France indicates that there is a realm for local urban
politics and that economic restructuring or the market logic can
go only so far. Yet the fact that there is great variety in the local
expression of economic restructuring and in local political responses and initiatives does not necessarily refute the proposition
that economic restructuring is the dominant force in shaping local
development. That variety describes a range of possibilities, not
necessarily a systemic property. As the editors themselves say,
economic restructuring works through a concrete set of social and
political relations; it does not exist outside the concrete context in
which it is embedded. Insofar as economic restructuring is embedded, one would expect such variety. The variety of local forms
of restructuring and policies can be seen as revealing little more
than the concrete characteristics of each locality. It is unsatisfac-
tory to derive the weight of politics from the fact of diversity in
local policies. And yet, the cases of France's leftist-dominated
municipalities, Clavel's progressive cities, and Molotch's anti-
growth coalitions indicate that through policies an arena for local
action can be recovered. These cases indicate that this is so even if
economic restructuring is the dominant force. The detailed deciphering of political and economic processes in these chapters
goes beyond their individual contribution and lays out elements
for the work of recovering an arena for local political action precisely because it documents in great detail the power of economic
restructuring and of the national state.

REFERENCES

Sassen, Saskia. 1990. *The Global City: New York, London, Tokyo.* Princeton, N.J.: Princeton University Press.

CHAPTER 10

Theoretical Methods in Comparative Urban Politics

John Walton

This volume provides both a signal and exemplar of changes currently taking place in urban social science. As the editors argue in their introduction, urban studies have reached an impasse—a theoretical deadlock between approaches that explain urban development, distributional patterns, and ecological form as the result of either market mechanisms or structures embedded in the political economy. The tendency in each case is to deduce an explanation of urban events from the respective models of market competition or structural constraint and contradiction. As several authors in this collection note, the analytical style of both market competition and political economy is to "read off" interpretations of empirical events from a theoretical logic; to sustain the case by illustrating (not testing) the plausible fit between theoretical assumptions, selected empirical events, and proffered normative judgments. Ironically, both theories are economically determined—mirror images that stress, respectively, the inexorable force of market competition with its generally agreeable results or the irresistible contradictions of capitalism, which generate mostly losing struggles over inequality. The authors represented in this collection propose to find a way out of the impasse. Their aim is to rekindle urban studies by shifting simultaneously its analytical style from deducing theoretical uniformity to explaining empirical variation and its interpretive emphasis from economics to politics.

In this conclusion, I shall attempt to frame the diverse contributions: to identify their common purpose, evaluate its successful realization, and indicate the directions in which it may fruitfully lead. The editors have stated the aims of this enterprise in what I judge to be three well-taken points.

> 1. Neo-conservative market-oriented analyses (for example those by Peterson, Kasarda) and, with greater emphasis here, neo-Marxist political economy (for example Bluestone and Harrison, Castells, Harvey) have produced erroneous theoretical accounts of urban change. Their common errors include: the reification of markets or structures, a failure to recognize or explain variation in the patterns of urban policy and performance, and a neglect of agency.
>
> 2. By focusing on the political process it is possible, on one hand, to incorporate the urban effects of markets and economic structures and, on the other hand, to demonstrate how these forces are politically mediated to produce a variety of policy and practical outcomes.
>
> 3. Theoretical generalization will proceed from an accumulation of comparative studies that allows for the identification of essential causes of urban change across cases and behind the welter of case-specific factors.

These are, as I say, sensible points and together they provide the foundation for a fresh start.

The Premises Elaborated

In the first place, the problems of urban theory deserve a little more elaboration. I am dubious about the symmetries drawn between the theories of the market and political economy, although I would not dispute the explanatory limitations of each. The editors give more space to criticizing the second approach, which is fine if that is meant to suggest that political economy is the more challenging of current explanatory models. It must be stressed, however, that these two approaches have never been direct competitors in any temporal or theoretical sense, despite some recent reinterpretations that would make them so (Gans 1985). Within urban sociology, for example, the market model of ecological dominance and succession was moribund and generally supplanted by studies of community power and social organization (Gans 1962; Suttles 1968) long before political economy enjoyed its meteoric rise in the 1970s in response to other developments including the "urban crisis" and a short-term radicalization of the discipline. Indeed, political economy theorists like Harvey (1973) and Castells (1977) argued with relish that their approaches faithfully incorporated the reliable empirical detail of work on land use and urban ecology, but went on to supersede it in general interpretations.

Market theories, moreover, talked past the issue of political determination without really engaging the process, while structuralist approaches at least attempted to link economic exigencies with political action through the vaunted subject of social movements—which, to be sure, typically owed their existence to contradictions between the decisive economic demands of capitalist accumulation and secondary political responses. That said, however, political economy has continued to strive for a more integral or relatively autonomous treatment of class struggles and political movements, notably, for example, in the recent work of David Harvey (1985), which moves some distance from the contradictions of capitalism in order to explain the politics and symbolism of the Paris commune. If, debatably, political economy viewed urban politics in a refracted structural light, it is nevertheless true that it privileged the study of social movements and endeavored to relate them to broader structural trends in a manner that is still instructive.

Concerning the editors' second premise, it seems to me important that we not conflate ontology and social science theory. That is, although one may argue forcibly that markets and politics are ontologically inseparable, different surfaces of the same social whole, it is equally true that social science theory must privilege some features of that whole as the causes or explanatory terms of other features. This is in the nature of theory, the unavoidably artificial assumptions and parsimony that we impose on the world for the purpose of identifying hypothesized regularities. The theoretical question, therefore, is not whether, say, economy and polity are separable, but how effective is one theory that posits a separation in contrast to another theory that develops, as it must, a conceptual integration of these two considerations in order to explain something else. Concretely, do market models explain urban policy, urban socioeconomic organization, or, indeed, whatever they purport to explain, and if not exactly where do they fail? Alternatively, exactly how does a theory of politically determined markets integrate these two factors and how much more does it explain? These are precisely the questions that David Harvey labored over in his book *Social Justice and the City* (1973), which did so much to revolutionize urban social science just over fifteen years ago. These are problems of theory construction and research, not of ontology. If Harvey's theoretical formulation, or any one of a variety of others, does not yield satisfactory explanations, then we need to develop one that does.

The separation of markets and politics may be, indeed has been, addressed in many ways. One avenue that pertains to this collection is concerned less with the editors' reasonable assertion that "markets are always embedded in particular social and political relations" than with the conditions under which a change in their interrelationship is urged ideologically and institutionally. That is, under what conditions is greater political regulation of the economy successfully advocated, such as in the Progressive and New Deal eras in the United States following economic and political crises, and when are political restraints on the market dismantled, as in Britain's current experience with privatization? This involves a comparative and historical approach to the theoretical question. In that connection, it is worth noting that major social theories of industrial capitalism observe an increasing institutional separation of economic control and political or class conflict (Dahrendorf 1959; Giddens 1973), although they offer different characterizations and explanations of the phenomenon, ranging from shifting authority relations to economistic cooptation of the working classes.

The classic work on this subject, of course, is Karl Polanyi's *The Great Transformation* (1944), which argues that the rise of capitalism was precisely a process of eliminating feudal constraints on the self-regulating market accomplished by modern state systems. "A self-regulating market demands nothing less than the institutional separation of society into an economic and political sphere [yet, paradoxically] to allow the market mechanism to be the sole director of the fate of human beings and their natural environment, indeed, even of the amount and use of purchasing power, would result in the demolition of society" (pp. 71–73). The self-regulating market, therefore, is a "crude fiction" and a "frail" institution, which generates enormous wealth just as it erodes the social foundations on which it rests and sets up countermovements to redress the destruction. Polanyi continues: "Social history in the nineteenth century was thus the result of a double movement: the extension of the market organization in respect to genuine commodities [i.e., raw materials, manufacturers] was accompanied by its restriction in respect to fictitious ones [i.e., land, labor, money]. While on the one hand markets spread all over the face of the globe and the amount of goods involved grew to unbelievable proportions, on the other hand a network of measures and policies was integrated into powerful institutions designed to check the action of the market" (p. 76). Polanyi's analysis indicates not only the conditions under which market movement and political countermovement check one another, but also how the system can collapse, as it did in the European interwar crisis leading to fascism.

For present purposes, the lesson to be drawn from Polanyi and other social theorists is that the scope of markets and their political regulation is less an axiomatic question than a problem of comparative theory and research. If cities are presently the objects of a new movement of market deregulation, what brought this on? Where is it taking place? What are its effects? Where are the countermoves? Or is collapse a possibility? And what kind of theory do we need to encompass these developments? So stated, the problem is consistent with the aims of this collection, but also, I hope, more clearly focused and heuristically linked to a theoretical tradition.

The third and final point concerns the comparative method, a research strategy understood by the contributors to this volume in the rudimentary sense of crossnational comparisons of two or more cities. None of the authors deals explicitly with the logic of comparison—the sense in which a given set of cities provides an appropriate comparison for the purpose of establishing a particular kind of conclusion. Conversely, no one seems to recognize that there are different comparative strategies appropriate to logically distinct general arguments. Instead, the chapters display a variety of unstructured, even opportunistic, comparisons that say little about similarities and differences between the cities compared or the extent to which the chosen set may "control" for diverse potential causes of a pattern of results—whether, for example, a nonstrategic comparison of New York and London is capable of reaching any general conclusion about their similarities (Fainstein) and differences (Savitch) or whether the cities are constituted so differently and the causes of their political action so divergent that no unifying conclusion may be drawn from the set. For example, Fainstein and Savitch employ, respectively, the contrasting comparative logics that Przeworski and Teune (1970) call "most different and most similar systems," but without explicitly recognizing or capitalizing on their special advantages and limitations.

A number of other writers have addressed these problems with the aim of characterizing different comparative strategies and the defensible logic of each (Armer and Grimshaw 1973; Smelser 1976; Skocpol 1984; Ragin 1987). Charles Tilly's lucid treatment observes that the choice of a particular comparative strategy should depend on "the relationship between observation and theory," the kind of generalization that the observed comparisons are intended to support. He goes on to show that there are at least four strategies distinguished by the theoretical purpose of the comparison: (1) individualizing comparisons, which "contrast specific instances of a given phenomenon as a means of grasping the peculiarities of each case"; (2) universalizing comparisons, which aim "to establish that every instance of a phenomenon follows essentially the same rule"; (3) variation-finding comparisons, which identify "a principle of variation in the character of intensity of a phenomenon by examining systematic differences among instances"; and (4) encompassing comparisons, which place "different instances at various locations within the same system, on the way to explaining their characteristics as a function of their varying relationships to the system as a whole" (Tilly 1984, 82–83).

In light of Tilly's analysis, it is clear that the editors of this collection favor the variation-finding strategy. In their words, "our main theme is variety—variety in urban policy, in urban form, and in urban outcomes. We explore this variety through comparative case studies. By highlighting differences, the comparative method makes contingent the conditions that appeared necessary in a single case." In fact, however, the individual chapters pursue different strategies that span Tilly's categories and jointly yield a limited consensus of theoretical purpose. In varying degrees of explicitness, Clavel and Kleniewski, Molotch, and Savitch are concerned with variation finding: each attempts to identify the factors that explain why some cities are capable of "progressive" or effective policymaking in the face of economic restructuring while other cities are not. The Parkinson and Preteceille comparisons are mainly individualizing: they probe the British and French cases, respectively, in an effort to identify key particularities that distinguish those cases from others. Hill's approach is encompassing: auto-industry cities in the United States and Japan are differently located in one global economic system and their development and decline lie in their relationship to that system, especially as it evolves over time. Fainstein provides a universalizing comparison: New York and London converge on a common form of market restructuring owing to a similar set of causes, including conservative political regimes and postindustrial social relations that override national differences of institutional structure.

Comparison and Interpretation

Based on these three points, which are really elaborations of the unifying argument developed by the editors, I want to reconsider the combined results of the chapters. My discussion will apply the three elaborated points in reverse order. That is, first I shall ask whether the results of separate chapters can be codified in a format that finds regular variations in urban policy, despite the different comparative strategies employed in each one. Second, I shall connect those results with broader theories about politics and markets. Finally, I shall discuss briefly an indicated direction for the analysis and interpretation of political action.

The preceding chapters endeavor to explain somewhat different outcomes of global and national processes of urban restructuring (neatly defined in Fainstein's chapter). A central concern is the conditions that produce varied urban political responses to growth, uneven development, or the unrestrained exploitation of urban land and markets for private accumulation on an expanded scale. The range of variation in urban responses designed to cope with or adapt to this new regime of restructuring growth runs from the more effective, progressive cities and policies, which aggressively defend local interests, to the more compliant cities and policies, which take what they can get from uneven growth or find themselves unable to muster coordinated political action on the issue. Authors vary in their treatments of restructuring and political response. Hill interprets restructuring as the localized fallout of globally organized industrial production, while Molotch understands it as willful action by local operators of growth machines. Other chapters come somewhere between these positions (if this is a linear dimension at all) with emphases on the state and varied forms of capital. Similarly, if Clavel and Kleniewski claim that there are real progressive-city winners in the restructuring wars, other authors see little more than varied forms of defeat—cities making the best of a bad bargain (Molotch) or routed by financial capital, conservative states, and privatization ideologies (Parkinson, Fainstein).

Recognizing these different conceptions of what is to be explained and where the most appropriate explanation lies, I shall propose nevertheless that the results of the separate chapters are susceptible to a synthesis. To the extent that editors and authors have a mutual aim, it is to explain the variation in more and less effective urban policies for engaging the forces of restructuring—

let us say, progressive versus compliant responses. As Tilly shows, there are other valid forms of comparison, but this one unites editorial intent and the largest single group of authors. Collectively, the chapters suggest conditions that are either conducive to effective action (positive correlates of a progressive response) or undermine and defeat it (negative correlates of a progressive response). That is, by restating as principles of variation the (universalizing or encompassing) arguments of some authors, we can combine their conclusions with others. The following synthesis, therefore, is a set of hypotheses about progressive urban responses to economic restructuring.

POSITIVE CORRELATES.   Cities that have effectively developed policies aimed at averting local economic decline or defended themselves against uneven development are characterized by (1) a historical tradition of popular action, experience, and memory whether in the form of populism, labor militance, civic action, or environmentalism (see Clavel and Kleniewski, Molotch); (2) a current and extensive network of community-based organizations that participate in politics and provide, among other things, a left opposition (see Clavel and Kleniewski, Molotch); (3) regional autonomy in the sense of geographical independence, decentralization, and intergovernmental cooperation (see Molotch, Savitch).

NEGATIVE CORRELATES.   Cities that have failed to develop progressive responses to economic restructuring are characterized by (1) polarized social classes and a large working class threatened by unemployment (see Fainstein, Molotch); (2) extensive integration with a larger metropolitan area or national and global systems of investment, marketing, and production (see Molotch, Hill, Fainstein, Savitch); (3) domination by conservative parties, political centralization, and economic ideologies (see Fainstein, Parkinson).

NONCORRELATES.   Urban political responses are unaffected by (1) economic decline per se (Clavel and Kleniewski) and (2) dissimilar institutional or governmental structures (Fainstein).

This summary may appear slim, even unsurprising. We cannot even be sure it is true. Yet it does provide a grounded set of hypotheses and, I shall suggest, some theoretical leads. It is worth knowing that researchers working independently and in different cities of advanced industrial societies nevertheless converge on some regularities. At least it is a start; at most it is a rough map pointing to where the answer lies.

The most engaging feature of the summary is the general contrast between the conditions conducive to progressive urban politics and those that frustrate local action—conditions that, taken together, stand for a historical tradition of popular action and autonomy sustained in contemporary organizations versus conditions that indicate the incorporation of cities into broader economic and political regimes where local interests are usurped. If economic circumstances per se, and perhaps governmental forms, do not figure in the explanation, then the results may point to some deeper political tradition of local control or self-determination fashioned historically to confront state and economic forces that intrude on urban interests. Seen in this light, the issue is one of explaining why some cities are capable of resisting broader forces of domination—how they mount policy initiatives for local control of the depredations stemming from incorporation into market relations extended at the behest of the state. Preteceille's chapter captures this idea by recasting the question of economic restructuring in the relations of political power:

> More than any direct response to economic changes, and not underestimating their considerable pressure and . . . internationally homogenizing character, changes in state structures and urban policies are closely related to the tentative answers to the hegemony crisis that goes with the economic crisis. And these answers are always specified by the nationally and historically variable capacity of political forces to express all diverging or different social interests, to crystalize those divergences or differences in demands, projects and alternative or conflicting policies at the local and national level.

The key issue is domination or resistance, "answers to the hegemony crisis," and the directions cities take in response to the issue are determined by their historically fashioned political capacities.

With this lead in mind, let us step back for a moment from the enveloping particulars of economic restructuring (growth, privatization, flexible accumulation, tertiarization, internationalization of capital) and ask, When does the current question of urban domination by restructuring arise? What are the origins of the "hegemony crisis?" Oddly, the authors in this collection give little attention to the question of crisis origins, although several agree that urban responses to the problem are essentially historical resultants. In fact, of course, the contemporary question of economic restructuring arises in the early 1970s under specific conditions: a long postwar era of international market and welfare state expansion, a global monetary crisis and economic recession (in 1973 and again in 1979–1981), and a conservative political resurgence following on the first two developments (Reaganism, Thatcherism, and their crossnational equivalents). The "hegemony crisis," therefore, comprises a set of political and economic struggles over whether and how restructuring can adapt to these changes, in all their social class and redistributional implications. And where does that leave us? I suggest that it neatly brings us back to Polanyi's problem—namely the exigencies of market extension and the political movements and countermovements that determine the effects of the process.

The fit between Polanyi's historical analysis and the preceding chapters, which converge on an explanation of progressive urban policy, lies in the significance of the latter as a countermovement to politically restructured markets. The summary of positive and negative correlates of these countermovements points suggestively to the idea that urban policy responses arise from the *intersection* of market restructuring and local capacity for political action. As the comparative case studies illustrate, cities from the desultory California coast to European world capitals are the objects of growth machines and restructuring regimes. Where a tradition of popular action perseveres in broadly mobilized community organizations, countermovements may restrain the maldistributive effects of unfettered growth. Yet where the forces of economic incorporation and conservative ideology are strongest, countermovements either do not arise or, as in London, go down to defeat in their efforts to control market restructuring. In general, therefore, an explanation for the varied urban political responses to restructuring may lie in the configuration of market pressures and local capacities for action.

What do we know about the problem formulated in this way? A good deal, I suspect, assuming we know where to look for separate pieces of the answer and how to put them together. We need to know, first, what the nature, strength, and scope of restructuring forces have been, particularly since 1970, and how they affect different cities. What is the nature of the assault on Santa Barbara and London and how much does it affect the city's capacity to respond? The question relates to my earlier defense of political economy because the strengths of that approach lie precisely in the examination of economic constraints and contradictions surrounding recent urban development (namely, studies of the fiscal crisis, Harvey's changing circuits of capital accumulation, the mobility of capital and labor, deindustrialization and service expansion, and the like).

Second, we need to know about the capacity for local political action, particularly as it engages the economic and ideological mechanisms of market reorganization. If, arguably, this has been the failure of political economy, it is the strong point of a rich literature on collective action (for example, Tilly 1978) and urban social history (Stedman-Jones 1971; Katznelson 1985). Connecting this work to contemporary urban questions may require something of a theoretical stretch, which is a good thing because that is exactly the kind of reasoning urged in the original meaning of "middle range" theory (Merton 1957). Insightfully developing the same idea, Stinchcombe (1978) argues that the most profound explanatory theories are built from thoroughly understood cases and "analogies" between the casual texture of actions of people in structurally similar situations. Here I have in mind the firm parallels between modern political responses to urban restructuring and nineteenth-century labor (counter) movements in the face of industrial reorganization.

Aminzade, for example, examines French industrial protest by posing the same theoretical question as the editors of this collection put to urban political action (1984, 437). In order to explain the variation in action across cities, Aminzade hypothesizes,

"Temporal and spatial differences in the incidence, form, targets, and contents of industrial protest are explained in terms of the way in which divergent local patterns of capitalist industrialization intersected with national-level political changes to alter workers interests/grievances and capacities" (1984, 437). Proletarianization, in ways analogous to restructuring, spread unevenly across industries in French cities, generating protest grievances where it was strongest, but the form and scale of ensuing action depended on the interplay of motive and the organizational capacity of workers shaped by "the persistence of preexisting traditional communities, labor market vulnerability, and the changing political opportunity structure" (p. 437). If an analogy were drawn between Aminzade's causes of industrial protest and the previous correlates of progressive urban policy, an enriched theory would suggest that varied collective actions are explained by an interaction of the scope and timing of market reorganization and the history and organizational resources of local communities. Pressing the analogy further, key to the local capacity for action is in a cross-class alliance of community organizations that is able to restrain the ambitions of capital in some strategic fashion.

The point here is not that nineteenth-century labor and twentieth-century urban political action are the same substantive problem. Rather, it is that they raise sufficiently similar theoretical questions to suggest that a contemporary explanation built on the casual analogy may take us a long way toward more robust theories of urban politics. The parallels drawn with Aminzade's study of industrial action in French cities is apposite, but alone merely suggestive. The argument deserves further development, focused particularly on the role of culture and consciousness. Fruitful analogies lie in Foster's comparative study of class politics in Lancashine industrial towns (1974) and in the intriguing differences between urban rebellion in Paris (Harvey 1985) and London's indemnified class politics (Stedman-Jones 1971) in response to similar restructuring regimes in the late nineteenth century.

Max Weber once remarked that "the materialist interpretation of history is no cab to be taken at will" (1958, 125). The same can be said about the comparative method. If we set out in that vehicle, comparing cities along the way, then we must stay on board for the journey's end of comparing theoretical explanations.

REFERENCES

Aminzade, Ronald. 1984. "Capitalist Industrialization and Patterns of Industrial Protest: A Comparative Study of Nineteenth-Century France." *American Sociological Review* 49:437–53.

Armer, Michael, and Allen Grimshaw. 1973. *Comparative Social Research: Problems and Strategies.* New York: Wiley.

Castells, Manuel. 1977. *The Urban Question: A Marxist Approach.* Cambridge: Mass.: MIT Press.

Dahrendorf, Ralf. 1959. *Class and Class Conflict in Industrial Society.* Stanford, Calif.: Stanford University Press.

Foster, John. 1974. *Class Struggle and the Industrial Revolution: Early Industrial Capitalism in Three English Towns.* New York: St. Martin's.

Gans, Herbert. 1962. *The Urban Villagers: Group and Class in the Life of Italian-Americans.* New York: Free Press.

———. (1985). "American Urban Theories and Urban Areas: Some Observations on Contemporary Ecological and Marxist Paradigms." In *Cities in Recession: Critical Responses to the Urban Policies of the New Right,* ed. Ivan Szelenyi. London: Sage Publications.

Giddens, Anthony. 1973. *The Class Structure of the Advanced Societies.* New York: Barnes and Noble.

Harvey, David. 1973. *Social Justice and the City.* Baltimore: Johns Hopkins University Press.

———. 1985. *Consciousness and the Urban Experience.* Baltimore: Johns Hopkins University Press.

Katznelson, Ira. 1985. "Working Class Formation and the State: Nineteenth-Century England in American Perspective." In *Bringing the State Back In,* ed. Peter B. Evans, Dietrich Rueschmeyer, and Theda Skocpol. Cambridge, Mass.: Cambridge University Press.

Merton, Robert. 1957. *Social Theory and Social Structure.* Glencoe, Ill.: Free Press.

Polanyi, Karl. 1944. *The Great Transformation: The Political and Economic Origins of Our Time.* Boston: Beacon Press.

Przeworski, Adam, and Henry Teune. 1970. *The Logic of Comparative Social Inquiry.* New York: Wiley.

Ragin, Charles. 1987. *The Comparative Method: Moving Beyond Qualitative and Quantitative Strategies.* Berkeley and Los Angeles: University of California Press.

Skocpol, Theda. 1984. *Vision and Method in Historical Sociology.* Cambridge, Mass.: Cambridge University Press.

Smelser, Neil. 1976. *Comparative Methods in the Social Sciences.* Englewood Cliffs, N.J.: Prentice Hall.

Stinchcombe, Arthur L. 1978. *Theoretical Methods in Social History.* New York: Academic Press.

Stedman-Jones, Gareth. 1971. *Outcast London: A Study in the Relationship Between Classes in Victorian Society.* London: Oxford University Press.

Suttles, Gerald. 1968. *The Social Order of the Slums: Ethnicity and Territory in the Inner City.* Chicago: University of Chicago Press.

Tilly, Charles. 1978. *From Mobilization to Revolution.* Reading, Mass.: Addison-Wesley.

———. (1984). *Big Structures, Large Processes, and Huge Comparisons.* New York: Russell Sage.

Weber, Max. 1958. *From Max Weber: Essays in Sociology,* trans. Hans Gerth and C. Wright Mills. New York: Oxford University Press.

ABOUT THE CONTRIBUTORS

PIERRE CLAVEL is Professor of City and Regional Planning at Cornell University. His most recent book is *The Progressive City* (Rutgers University Press, 1986), a study of populist and radical politics and planning in Hartford, Cleveland, Berkeley, Santa Monica, and Burlington. He is co-editor of a forthcoming set of essays on local economic policy and neighborhood response in Chicago under the late Mayor Harold Washington, and a founder of the Harold Washington Neighborhood and Economic Development Papers, an archive at the Chicago Historical Society.

SUSAN S. FAINSTEIN is Professor of Urban Planning and Policy Development at Rutgers University. She is the author of numerous books and articles on urban political economy and urban redevelopment, including *Restructuring the City* (Longman, rev. ed., 1986). She is currently working on a book comparing New York and London.

RICHARD CHILD HILL is Professor of Sociology and Urban Affairs at Michigan State University. He is a co-author of *Restructuring the City* (Longman, rev. ed., 1986) and *Detroit: Race and Uneven Development* (Temple University Press, 1987). He is currently at work on a comparative study of industrial and urban restructuring in the United States and Japan.

NANCY KLENIEWSKI is Associate Professor of Sociology and Director of Urban Studies at the State University of New York, College at Geneseo. She writes frequently on urban problems and policy for both professional journals and nonacademic publications. She is co-author of a forthcoming book on social inequality in Philadelphia and is currently working on a text in urban sociology.

261

JOHN R. LOGAN is Professor and Chair of the Department of Sociology, State University of New York at Albany. He is the co-author, with Harvey Molotch, of *Urban Fortunes: The Political Economy of Place* (University of California Press, 1987). His current research includes studies of growth politics in suburban regions, national urban policy, ethnic suburbanization, and support systems for older persons.

HARVEY MOLOTCH is Professor of Sociology at University of California, Santa Barbara, where he conducts research on communication and urban studies. His book co-authored with John R. Logan, *Urban Fortunes* (University of California Press, 1987), won the Robert Park Award and the Distinguished Scholarly Contribution Award from the American Sociological Association.

MICHAEL PARKINSON is Director of the Centre for Urban Studies, University of Liverpool. He is currently conducting research into urban regeneration in North America and Europe financed by the Leverhulme Trust. He is the author of *Liverpool on the Brink* (Policy Journals, 1985) and editor of *Reshaping Local Government* (Policy Journals and Transaction Books, 1987), *Regenerating the Cities: The UK Crisis and the American Experience* (Scott Foresman, 1989), and *Leadership and Urban Regeneration* (Sage, 1990).

EDMOND PRETECEILLE is director of research at CNRS, Centre de Sociologie Urbaine, Paris. He has published on urban policies and collective consumption, from *La Production des Grands Ensembles* (1973) to *Capitalism, Consumption and Needs* (Blackwell, 1985) and *Ségrégation Urbaine* (Editions Anthropos, 1986). His present research is focused on the reactions of local policies to economic restructuring and social polarization of the cities.

SASKIA SASSEN is Professor and Chair of Urban Planning at Columbia University. She is the author of *The Global City: New York London Tokyo* (Princeton University Press, 1990) and *The Mobility of Labor and Capital: A Study in International Investment and Labor Flow* (Cambridge University Press, 1988).

H. V. SAVITCH is Professor at the School of Urban Policy, College of Urban and Public Affairs, University of Louisville. He has written for a number of professional journals and has authored *Urban Policy and the Exterior City* (Pergamon, 1979), *Post Industrial Cities* (Princeton University Press, 1988), and is co-editor of a forthcoming volume entitled *Big City Politics Compared* (Sage). Professor Savitch served as consultant for David Dinkins, who is presently Mayor of the City of New York.

TODD SWANSTROM is Associate Professor of Political Science at the State University of New York at Albany. His book, *The Crisis of Growth Politics: Cleveland, Kucinich, and The Challenge of Urban Populism* (Temple University Press, 1985), won the Best Book in Urban Politics Award in 1988 from the American Political Science Association. Currently, he is co-authoring a text on urban politics with Dennis Judd and doing research on homelessness and neighborhood change.

JOHN WALTON holds a joint appointment in the Departments of Sociology and Anthropology at the University of California, Davis. He has served the international Sociological Association as an officer of its Research Council and Research Committee on Urban and Regional Development. His books include *Elites and Economic Development* (Institute of Latin American Studies, 1977), *Labor, Class, and the International System* (Academic Press, 1981, co-authored), and *Reluctant Rebels: Comparative Studies of Revolution and Underdevelopment* (Columbia University Press, 1984), which won honorable mention for the 1984 C. Wright Mills Award. Since 1984, he has occasionally served as a special news correspondent, reporting on the civil war in El Salvador, the debt crisis, and price riots in the Third World.

SUBJECT INDEX

Auburn Hills (Michigan), technical park, 76–78

Beame, Abe (New York mayor), 156
Boston: linkage policies, 209–10, 224; school compact, 105
British Urban Development (BUD), 106
Burlington (Vermont), linkage policies, 211

California, and rent control in Santa Monica, 185
California, urban restructuring outcomes, 182–84; in Berkeley, 211–12; environmental and social degradation, 189; in Riverside, 185–88; in Santa Barbara, 184–86; in Santa Monica, 185–87; use and need of linkage policies, 183–84, 187–89
California, urban tax authority centralized, public services decentralized, 183–84
Capital, global: destroys urban economies, 19–20; divides local elites, 55n6; emergence, 8; globalization of, 150–54; power and effect summarized, 228–29, 238–39; and world-class cities, 152. See also Growth control; Ideology and urban policy; Production systems; Urban economic policies

Capitalism, unitary theory of, 5–6, 13
Centralization, political. See Decentralization; all Government entries
Chicago, economic policy, 200, 214–16, 223–24
Chirac, Jacques (Paris mayor), 40, 156, 160
Cities, world class. See Urban hierarchy
Community: building coalitions, 223–24, 226–27; and environmental protection, 181–82; and environment in California, 182–86; and environment in London, 136, 161–62; and environment in New York, 156; mobilization vs. deindustrialization, 39–41, 46–48, 55n10; often divided, 43–44, 55n6, 240. See also Decentralization; Deindustrialization; Environmental concerns; Housing, public; Linkage policies; Urban economic policies
Community Development Block Grants (U.S.), 131
Conference of Socialist Economists (Great Britain), 220–22
Conference of Socialist Planners (Great Britain), 223
Consumption norms, 34–35
Cooperatives, urban: in England, 98; in France, 46–48, 55n10. See also Deindustrialization
Core and periphery, 8. See also Capital, global

264

AUTHOR INDEX

271